Peter

Apostle for the Whole Church

Studies on Personalities of the New Testament

D. Moody Smith, *General Editor*

Peter

Apostle for the Whole Church

by Pheme Perkins

University of South Carolina Press

Copyright © 1994 University of South Carolina

Published in Columbia, South Carolina, by the
University of South Carolina Press

Manufactured in the United States of America

Library of Congress Cataloging-in-Publication Data

Perkins, Pheme.
    Peter : apostle for the whole church / Pheme Perkins.
      p. cm.
    Includes bibliographical references and index.
    ISBN 0–87249–974–X (alk. paper)
    1. Peter, the Apostle, Saint. 2. Church history—Primitive and
early church, ca. 30–600.   I. Title.
    BS2515.P47   1994
    225.9′2—dc20
    [B]   93–5983
                                            CIP

Contents

INTRODUCTION

First Among the Disciples   1
The Apostle in a Divided Christianity   3
Peter in a Changing Church: Roman Catholicism   6
Peter as an Ecclesial Centrist   9

CHAPTER 1 • A LIFE OF PETER

Familiar Stories   18
Asking Historical Questions   21
Peter in the Gospels   26
Peter in Acts   33
Archaeology and the Quest for Peter   38
The Name ''Peter''   39
Excursus: Peter and Rome in Eusebius   41

CHAPTER 2 • PETER IN NEW TESTAMENT NARRATIVES:
            MARK AND MATTHEW

Peter as a Narrative Character   52
Peter in the Gospel of Mark   57
Peter in the Gospel of Matthew   66

CHAPTER 3 • PETER IN NEW TESTAMENT NARRATIVES:
            LUKE AND JOHN

Peter Among the Apostles   81
Peter in the Gospel of Luke   84
Peter in the Acts of the Apostles   88
Peter in the Gospel of John   95
Excursus: Peter and the Twelve   101

CHAPTER 4 • PETER IN THE NEW TESTAMENT EPISTLES

In the Shadow of Paul   109
Peter in Paul's Epistles: Fellow Apostle or Opponent?   111
Excursus: The Jerusalem Council   118
1 Peter: The Apostle as Fellow Elder   120
2 Peter: Guardian of the True Faith   122

CHAPTER 5 • PETER, WITNESS AND MARTYR

Completing the Story   131
Expanding on Gospel Traditions   132
Early Testimony Concerning Peter's Martyrdom   138
Excursus: Nero, the Fire, and the Christians   139
The Apocryphal *Acts of Peter*   140

CHAPTER 6 • PETER AND AUTHENTIC TRADITION

Peter's Teaching as True Tradition   151
Peter Opposes the Heretic, Simon Magus   152
Peter as Spokesperson for Conventional Christianity   156
Peter as a Gnostic Apostle   159

CHAPTER 7 • PETER, BISHOP OF ROME

From Martyr to Bishop   168
Founding Martyr of the Roman Church   169
Succession Lists and Petrine Authority   171
Peter and Episcopal Authority   173
Excursus: Interpreting Matthew 16:17–19   176

CONCLUSION • PETER FOR THE WHOLE CHURCH?   183

SELECTED BIBLIOGRAPHY   187

INDEX OF SUBJECTS AND MODERN AUTHORS   199

INDEX OF SCRIPTURE REFERENCES   205

Peter

Apostle for the
Whole Church

Introduction

FIRST AMONG THE DISCIPLES

Most people who are asked to name the followers of Jesus of Nazareth will respond, "Peter and Paul." Many also know that Peter had been a fisherman, and Paul a tentmaker. They also know that Peter was a leader of Jesus' circle of disciples and that Paul was a missionary. However, many Christians assume that Paul had known Jesus personally. They are surprised by the conflicts between Peter and Paul referred to in Paul's account of the Jerusalem Council and the incident at Antioch (Gal. 2:1–14). Since Roman Catholics are taught that Peter's position among the disciples provided the basis for the ongoing authority of the bishop of Rome,[1] they are surprised to find that Peter appears to have become subordinate to James, the brother of the Lord, in Jerusalem (Gal. 2:9; Acts 15:1–21).

Even those who do not believe that the bishop of Rome continues to exercise a pastoral office which Jesus gave to Peter are uncomfortable with the possibility of serious differences among the earliest Christian leaders. Two centuries of historical-critical study of early Christian writings have taught scholars to doubt constructions of an ideal, harmonious period of origins followed by decline. But the debates which rage over whether or not we can draw any historically reliable picture of either Jesus' teaching or his intentions for the movement that took shape around him[2] place an increased emphasis on the role of the disciples of Jesus in the founding of Christianity. If the earliest disciples of Jesus were at odds with one another, how can Christianity claim any relationship to its historical founder?

For many Christians, the most troubling aspect of this question lies

---

Unless otherwise indicated, scripture quotations are from the New Revised Standard Version of the Bible, copyright 1989 by the Division of Christian Education of the National Council of the Churches of Christ in the USA.

1

in the disputes between Peter and Paul. Paul himself did not know Jesus. Nor does he make extensive use of traditions about Jesus in his letters. The Pauline emphasis on the crucified and risen Christ as the focus of Christian life requires only minimal information about the teacher from Nazareth (e.g., Gal. 4:4–7). For some intellectuals, the historical question is irrelevant in the twentieth century. Christianity, like other religious expressions of profound human truths, should be seen for the great artistic achievement that it is. The British novelist and philosopher Iris Murdoch speaks of the Gospel writers and St. Paul as "five artists of genius" who were responsible for the emergence of Christianity.[3] Of course, Christianity's artistic and moral power does not stop with the canonical texts but continues to be embodied in the great aesthetic works of the tradition.

Understood from an aesthetic viewpoint, divergence and even clashes of perspective enhance the fascination, the beauty, and even the credibility of an artistic vision. Such visions are not trivial. Unlike "objective facts," they have the power to move the human heart and mind beyond the narrow limits of a particular personal or even social experience. Theologians, like Paul Tillich, who are attentive to the symbolic formation of human life, insist that even history requires imaginative participation on the part of the historian. Tillich writes: "Without a union of the nature of the historian with that of his object no significant history is possible. But *with* this union the same period and the same historical figure have received many different historically significant interpretations on the basis of the same verified material. . . . The historian's task is to 'make alive' what has 'passed away.' "[4] It is easy to see that the historian of early Christianity must reconstruct the past in order to make it live. We are faced with gaps in our experience at every turn.

In a sermon on Matthew's account of the calling of Peter, Andrew, James, and John (Matt. 4:18–22) I heard recently, the preacher suddenly stopped to remark that it seemed too harsh for them all to just abandon their friends, boats, and family; and then he concluded, "Well, it probably didn't happen exactly like that." What he did not note is that other Gospel writers did not imagine it happening just like that either. Luke and John have quite different stories. In Luke's case, Jesus has already preached in the synagogue and gone from there to cure Peter's mother-in-law (4:16–39). The summons to discipleship is mediated through a miraculous catch of fish after the disciples have labored all night without catching anything (5:1–11). In John's version,

Peter's brother Andrew is identified as one of two disciples of John the Baptist, who become followers of Jesus (John 1:35–40). Andrew goes and gets his brother, Simon Peter (1:41–42). In the Johannine case, Peter is not even the first disciple to follow Jesus. Since John's Gospel bases its truth on the testimony of a mysterious figure called the "Beloved Disciple" (John 21:24), who appears in the Passion and Resurrection accounts as the one closest to Jesus, interpreters have seen his footprint here. The "other disciple" with Andrew represents the Beloved Disciple in this view.[5] Though Peter may have been the most prominent of Jesus' Galilean disciples—a fact which John does not deny —he is not the "first" in establishing its vision of Jesus.

Indirectly, this Johannine alteration conveys an important truth about Peter: he is associated with the foundations of the Christian witness about Jesus. Two examples from Paul's letters indicate that this role is not merely an imaginative creation of the evangelists. Paul reports that three years after his conversion, he went to Jerusalem and spent two weeks with Peter (Gal. 1:18). In a creedal formula that he uses to affirm the centrality of Resurrection belief, Paul tells the Corinthians that he is passing on what he had been given (1 Cor. 15:3–5). This formula speaks of Peter as the first witness to the Resurrection. 1 Corinthians 15:3–5 may well be part of the tradition which Paul received during that visit to Jerusalem. However, as we shall see when we discuss the treatment of Peter in the Gospels and in the Pauline letters, we have no reason to assume that Peter's testimony grounds a single, univocal vision of Jesus.

THE APOSTLE IN A DIVIDED CHRISTIANITY

The New Testament evidence itself suggests that the figure of Peter played very different roles for diverse communities. Peter as he was known or remembered in the Pauline and Johannine traditions is very different from Peter in the synoptic Gospels and Acts. One of the difficult judgments that the student of early Christianity must make is whether to maximize the differences or to create a harmonizing account of the divergent views. The choice is not merely a matter of individual preference. Any particular interpreter's ecclesial commitments often shape what is perceived as an adequate representation of early Christian reality.

Since the Reformation, Catholics have emphasized the Petrine foundation of papal authority in Matthew 16:17–20. The definitions of papal authority promulgated at Vatican I in *Pastor Aeternus* understand Jesus' words to Peter in John 1:42, Matthew 16:15–20, and John 21:15–16 as the historical transmission of a ruling power much as the Roman emperor might designate a successor.[6] On the Protestant side, ecclesial authority requires that individuals be called through the Spirit. Peter's call cannot be inherited by others.

Hans von Campenhausen insists that the true Christian concept of authority is discovered by Paul. Authority as a gift of the Spirit rests in the apostolate to which God has called the apostle. It is not transmitted by communities or individuals.[7] Whatever the apostle demands of his communities in calling them to remain faithful to the Gospel, he must obtain by persuasion. The reality of Christian freedom makes it impossible for the true apostle to compel the obedience of others.[8]

Emphasis on the sharp dichotomy between Petrine and Pauline Christianity was a staple element in much Protestant church history during the nineteenth century. The founder of the Tübingen school, Ferdinand Christian Baur, saw a dialectic struggle between the legalistic, Jewish Christians led by Peter and the law-free Pauline Christians. As the divisive struggles with Gnosticism made evident the dangers of freedom without structure, the Pauline message of freedom in the Spirit had to be tempered with law. Writings from the Pauline school like Acts and the Pastoral Epistles created an eirenic synthesis of the two positions.[9] Once Baur had focused scholarly attention on the necessity of reading the New Testament texts themselves as the product of divergent and conflicting theological views, scholars could no longer assume that all the pieces of the New Testament belonged to the same jigsaw puzzle. Baur's original proposal of two opposed forms of Christianity does not accommodate all of the diverse strands of evidence in the New Testament.[10] However, the diversity in early Christianity might be evaluated by measuring other traditions in terms of their relationship to a normative vision which is alleged to express true insight into the Gospel. Von Campenhausen's study of spiritual power and authority in the early church treats the Pauline understanding of ecclesiastical authority as focusing principle.

Two twentieth-century developments have made the Petrine texts and the issue of diverse visions of Christianity more than a mere historical exercise. Roman Catholic scholars became major contributors to exegesis in the mid-twentieth century. The importance of the Peter in that tradition makes it difficult to marginalize the apostle or the Petrine Epistles as failed Paulinism. And the growing ecumenical movement has given renewed importance to the evidence for substantive diversity in New Testament Christianity. Rather than assume that ecumenical unity will produce a generic Christianity, New Testament diversity provides the opening for many types of Christianity.

Oscar Cullmann's book *Peter: Disciple—Apostle—Martyr* sparked extensive discussion of the Petrine evidence and its ecumenical implications.[11] Cullmann sought to advance ecumenical understanding by treating the New Testament material as evidence for a synthetic, eirenic account of Peter's significance in early Christianity. He grants that the earthly Jesus had given Peter a prominent place among his disciples and that Peter played a crucial role in the establishment and leadership of the earliest communities. However, that leadership was not exercised as a form of "primacy." When Peter left Jerusalem for missionary activity after his release from prison (Acts 12:17), James became the leader of the Jerusalem community. Nor could Peter's authority be transferred to a subsequent generation or to a particular regional church. The division of missionary activity between Peter and Paul is an example of a peaceful and necessary division in Christianity. Both unity and commitment to a joint effort were maintained through the collection for the poor.[12]

Cullmann clearly framed his discussion so that historical and exegetical analysis might provide the foundation for a theological convergence between Protestant and Roman Catholic viewpoints. Even though individual scholars will interpret the story being told in the New Testament texts differently, Cullmann's challenge to develop an ecumenical theology remains. Can the first-century diversity in early Christianity provide a normative model for understanding the unity and diversity of Christian churches in the twentieth century? Specifically, ecumenical theology seeks an understanding that would foster a form of common communion while retaining the distinctive characteristics of the various denominations.

The figure of Peter need not be the rallying point for the primacy of one communion over the others. Precisely because there is not an exclusively Petrine tradition in the New Testament, the apostle might serve as a unifying figure for diverse forms of Christianity. James D. G. Dunn suggests, for example, that Peter is the true centrist in the New Testament tradition. Traditions associated with James, Paul, and John are determined by individual particularities which make them inappropriate as the focus for the unity of the whole Christian community.[13]

Ecumenical discussion of historical and exegetical issues has been central to academic dialogues between communions. The most important study of Peter was produced by a Lutheran-Roman Catholic group in 1973.[14] That work, *Peter in the New Testament,* adopts the methodology of historical criticism to analyze the texts in the New Testament which deal with Peter. Its authors argue that even though we cannot assume that the New Testament provides any more direct access to the historical Peter than it does to the historical Jesus, the question is not what would have been videotaped in Palestine during the earthly ministry of Jesus. Rather, the question to be answered concerns the role that Peter played in first-century Christianity. This role will more accurately be determined by our asking how Peter was perceived by early Christians than by our ability to establish historical facts.[15] The authors of the study do presume that analysis makes it possible to provide a line of development through the New Testament material on Peter that results in a coherent set of images. They also assume that the conflicts depicted in the New Testament do not refer to a Christianity that was fundamentally broken from the beginning.[16] Both assumptions may be correct, but they are not directly "given" by the New Testament evidence. Rather, a heuristic principle that early Christianity possessed an underlying unity which can be described in terms of the history of the development of traditions guides the reading of the texts.

PETER IN A CHANGING CHURCH: ROMAN CATHOLICISM

Though the recently published catechism of the Roman Catholic church uses the Petrine texts to bolster its understanding of the supremacy of the bishop of Rome over the other bishops who constitute the successors to the apostles, it affirms the shift in emphasis at Vatican II. The second Vatican council shifted attention away from using the Petrine texts as evidence for papal jurisdiction and infallibility to understanding Peter as the head of the apostolic college.[17] In his relationship to the larger group of apostles, Peter is the foundation for the unity of the church. Roman Catholic exegetes and theologians now regularly emphasize Peter's relationship to the other disciples of Jesus. The evidence that Peter was a prominent figure in that group both before and after the Resurrection of Jesus is highlighted by Roman Catholic scholars.[18] Though Peter may not have exercised the juridical or teaching functions characteristic of later popes, his role in guiding the group of disciples provides the basis for legitimating later develop-ments.

Other Roman Catholic theologians have sought to use the New Testament evidence as the basis for rethinking the relationship between the Church and its founder. The Dutch Dominican Edward Schille-beeckx seeks to reform ecclesiology by insisting that the church recover its origins in the eschatological community of those who came to believe in the renewed presence of God through Jesus. Such an ecclesiology serves to emphasize the mission of the Christian church as witness to the world along the lines dictated by Vatican II.[19]

Schillebeeckx conceives his reconstruction of early Christian com-munity as one pole of a theological apologetic. Its task is to make credible in the late twentieth century the claim that universal salvation is mediated through Jesus. Unless Schillebeeckx can advance some historical claims about Jesus' consciousness of God, Jesus' way of being human with the sinner and the marginal, and the continuity of that project in the early Christian community, the argument will fail to address the unconverted. Schillebeeckx insists upon the perilous con-nection between faith and history as the only way to assure that Christianity is not merely an ideology.[20] He comments:

> The only way, therefore, in which the affirmation of Christian belief can be shown to have credibility is twofold: (a) on the one hand by means of the historical study of Jesus' baptism, his words and actions, life and death and of finding out what they may possibly signify, and (b) on the other hand by showing how the Christian claim to universal-ity is substantiated in the true humanness of "being human" as that confronts us in Jesus of Nazareth. . . . What is ultimately at issue is the intrinsic relationship between Jesus of Nazareth and the kingdom of God and the final good and happiness of human beings.[21]

For Schillebeeckx, the Resurrection affirms Jesus' inseparable link with God. It demonstrates God's fidelity to Jesus and establishes the fact that God's offer of salvation is extended to humanity even after the rejection of that offer evident in the crucifixion.[22]

Without this certainty that the offer of salvation which God extended in the ministry of Jesus had survived the cross, the disciples would not have been able to preach salvation in Jesus' name. Schillebeeckx places particular emphasis on the conversion of Peter. His experience links the ministry of the historical Jesus to the emerging church. Though Schillebeeckx discusses the appearance of Jesus to women disciples at the tomb and the stories of Paul's conversion, these episodes are not invested with the ecclesial significance of the appearance to Peter.[23] Peter is the first to see the risen Lord, to convert and return to following the Lord, and to reassemble the circle of disciples. As a result, he is the "rock" or foundation of the church.[24] Thus the traditional interpretations of Matthew 16:18 which focused on Peter's authority to interpret the teaching of Jesus or to exercise juridical authority fail to grasp the origin of this saying. According to the conversion model of the disciples' Resurrection experience, Peter's place as "rock" should be understood as equivalent to Luke 22:31–32; after a period of Satanic testing, Peter will turn to strengthen his fellow disciples. This understanding of Matthew 16:18 was advanced by Rudolf Bultmann as evidence that the saying goes back to a primitive, Aramaic stratum of the tradition. It was omitted from Mark's treatment of Peter because the Hellenistic, Pauline Christianity from which Mark comes was opposed to the legalist Jewish Christianity represented by Peter.[25] Bultmann's use of the dichotomy of legalist Jewish Christianity over against a Pauline Christianity of freedom in the Spirit supports his insistence that the pericope points to doctrinal or disciplinary authority. In his view, the Jewish Christian community required such authority precisely because it understood itself to be the eschatological community of the just.[26]

The advantage to Schillebeeckx's emphasis on the post-Resurrection experience of the disciples as one of conversion and discovering again a salvation which they had experienced in the presence of the historical Jesus is that it avoids legalist assumptions about the early Jewish Christians. However, this model locates Resurrection faith in the subjective experience of Jesus' disciples. It does not convey any "new" revelation about Jesus or about God's plan of salvation. Schillebeeckx suggests that the real meaning of "seeing" the risen Lord is found in the disciples' recognition that their sin of cowardice, flight, and denial was forgiven. Though he admits that this experience required the shared experiences of the apostles gathered as a group, Schillebeeckx focuses his account of the actual "event" on Peter. He concludes that the various New Testament references to the priority of Peter are based on the fact that he was the first to "see" this truth and gathered the others.[27]

Indeed, Schillebeeckx's account places even more importance on

Peter's experience than the more traditional juridical or disciplinary interpretations. Peter gathered the other distraught disciples and revived their experience of the presence of the living Jesus. Without Peter, no Christianity. Does the credibility of the Christian witness rest upon the conversion and testimony of Peter? The view that to some degree at least it does is certainly congenial to Roman Catholics. However, Paul's statements about his call and mission to the Gentiles in Galatians 1:11–24 assert that he received the apostolic call to evangelize from the risen Lord without human mediation. He did not journey to Jerusalem to meet with Peter until three years after that experience. Further, James, the brother of the Lord, did not belong to the group of disciples during Jesus' lifetime. He too received a call from the risen Lord according to 1 Corinthians 15:7. Whatever role Peter may have played in gathering the community of disciples after Easter, he did not succeed Jesus by receiving his master's spiritual authority as Elisha did Elijah's, for example. Through the Spirit, the risen Lord called others to be apostles and to guide the ongoing mission of the church. The stories of Paul's conversion and of Peter's initial mission to the Gentiles in Acts 9–11 make this point in narrative form. Nor can we assume that those called to engage in mission and church founding shared a single understanding of their task or message. The dispute between Peter and Paul at Antioch, over fourteen years after Paul's initial visit with Peter (Gal. 2:11–14) poses a challenge to anyone who imagines the earliest community as a harmonious, Spirit-guided movement.

PETER AS AN ECCLESIAL CENTRIST

Rather than identify Peter with one pole of early Christianity that was in tension with the Pauline churches, some exegetes have focused attention on the separation between Peter and James. When the conflict between Peter and Paul which is mentioned in Galatians 2:11–14 occurred, Peter's association with gentile Christians in the Antioch community offended "certain persons from James" (v. 12). Raymond Brown and John Meier suggest that Peter took a centrist position in the disputes over Jewish and gentile Christianity.[28] They argue that Paul probably lost the argument over whether or not Jewish Christians should be required to share a common meal with the Gentiles. Peter and Barnabas agreed to the demands of those from Jerusalem that they separate from the Gentiles in order to prevent immediate schism in the early Church. The gentile Christians at Antioch later accepted the rules in the decree of Acts 15:20–29 so that a single fellowship meal could be celebrated by Jewish and gentile Christians.[29]

This reconstruction concedes Cullmann's point, made over two decades earlier, that the Antioch episode demonstrates that Peter was not the "patriarch" or "pope" with sovereignty over the other apostles. Peter was forced by those from Jerusalem to change his own practice. However, Peter does not side with Jewish Christian anti-Paulinists. If his own strategic response to the dilemma permitted the adaptation of rules that permitted gentile Christians to join with their Jewish Christian counterparts, then Peter, not Paul, played the more significant role in resolving the crisis. Meier suggests that the prominence attributed to Peter in Matthew's Gospel might stem from the solution to the Jew/Gentile clash that he mediated in the Antioch church.[30]

The Antioch incident also provides a glimpse of the role Peter may have played as a missionary among Jewish and even gentile Christians. In both Galatians 2:7–9 and 1 Corinthians 9:5, Paul's wording suggests that by the late 40s or early 50s A.D., Peter was no longer resident in Jerusalem—as he seems to have been when Paul made his first visit there (Gal. 1:18). However, Peter had come to a community which had already been established by others and was even able to support missionaries of its own—as in the case of Barnabas and Paul. If Peter's ties with Antioch are based on an association with that community for some period of time during which he was instrumental in resolving a major crisis, then theologians might argue that Peter exercised some authority in other churches. As we shall see, there is no surviving evidence about how Peter came to be in Rome. We know from Paul's letter to the Romans that a diverse community of Jewish and gentile house churches had come into existence there before either Paul or Peter arrived in the city. Tensions appear to have existed between gentile Christians and their Jewish Christian brothers and sisters (Rom. 11:13–36, 14:1–15:13). Though we have no early, reliable evidence for Peter's activity in Rome, the hypothesis that Peter was an ecclesial centrist suggests that he could have played a significant role in building bridges between the divided house churches in Rome as well.

These examples show that Roman Catholic exegetes view the origins of Christianity from a Petrine perspective.[31] A lecture delivered at the Gregorian University in Rome by the Lutheran exegete Eduard Lohse turns the question around. What did Paul think of Peter as an apostle?[32]

The lack of any reference to Peter in Romans indicates that up to the time at which Paul wrote to the church there, Peter had not come to Rome. Nor is there any reason to detect veiled references to Peter behind other Pauline texts such as the reference to Christ as the church's foundation in 1 Corinthians 3:10–11 or the dispute with the so-called "super-apostles" in 2 Corinthians 10–13.[33] Consequently, the relevant evidence for Paul's view of Peter is limited to the specific references to Peter in 1 Corinthians and Galatians. The creedal formula which Paul inherited and passed on to his churches included Cephas as the first witness to the Resurrection (1 Cor. 15:5). In 1 Corinthians 15:3–11, Paul's primary concern is the chain of witnesses which begins with Peter and concludes with his own vision of the Lord. Paul establishes his own apostleship on the same basis as that of Peter and the Twelve.[34]

Because Paul's apostleship stands on the same footing as that of the other apostles, he could claim the same right to support as Peter and the others (1 Cor. 9:5, 14). For Paul, all apostles preach the gospel of the Lord. The temporal priority of Peter's call does not establish a hierarchical order among those who are called to apostleship. Lohse even suggests that alone Paul's doctrine of salvation through faith prohibits distinctions of temporal calling just as much as it does distinctions between the Jews, who had first heard God's word, and the Gentiles.[35] Paul's account of his call and relationships with the Jerusalem community in Galatians makes the same point. Both serve a common gospel. Neither the account of Paul's visits to Peter in Jerusalem nor the critique of Corinthian partisanship (1 Cor. 1:12) attacks Peter or others associated with him. Therefore, Lohse concludes, there is no evidence from Paul's side for a rift between the two.[36]

In order to maintain this interpretation, Lohse must advance an even more eirenic reading of Galatians 2:11–14 than that propounded by Brown and Meier. Lohse rejects the commonly held view that Paul left Antioch as a result of this controversy; instead, he takes Paul's programmatic statement about his missionary efforts in Romans 15:20 as the reason for Paul's departure from the established community in Antioch. Lohse insists that Paul's arguments demonstrate a desire to engage in a continuing dialogue with Peter.[37] The conclusion Lohse draws for ecumenical theology rejects the view that divergent forms of Christianity are authorized by the differing forms of theological expression and practice which appear in the New Testament. Such a "divided church'' approach to the New Testament undercuts the real unity which Paul consistently sought to attain. Christians ought to recognize the unity which exists in their common baptism and common confession that Jesus Christ is the one foundation of the church.[38]

Even today, one's ecclesial commitments are deeply invested in one's understanding of Peter. Lohse is surely right to remind all sides that Jesus Christ is the true cornerstone of the Christian community (e.g., 1 Pet. 2:4–5). The questions about the nature of early Christianity which have been raised by New Testament scholars in the past century are neither trivial nor easily resolved. While there is good reason to move away from the old dualism of a Spirit-guided Pauline Christianity over against the legalistic Jewish Christianity of Peter that continues to crop up in the literature, the real problem of unity and diversity has not been resolved. As ecumenical discussions between Christians and Jews continue to make us aware of the false characterizations of Judaism rampant in much scholarship, the earliest accounts of Christian Jewish practice take on new importance. This dialogue has practical as well as theological consequences. Many of us now deal with interfaith Jewish and Christian families at the parish level on a routine basis. Most clergy are as ill prepared for those situations as they were for dealing with Protestant and Catholic families a quarter of a century ago. Although the heat of the argument in Galatians led Paul to describe Peter's practice as ''hypocritical,'' Peter was able to live both as an observant Jew among Jews and as a Gentile among Gentiles. This ability to straddle the heritage of both communities undoubtedly contributed to the significance of Peter for the Christians to whom Matthew addressed his Gospel. Matthew himself envisaged Christian scribes who would be able to ''bring out of his storehouse both new things and old ones'' (Matt. 13:52).[39]

Peter also captures the Christian imagination because he is the most prominent of Jesus' disciples. Though none of the writings attributed to him come from the apostle himself, the portraits of Peter drawn in the Gospels and Acts define what it means to be a follower of Jesus just as strikingly as the letters of Paul do. For many Christians at the parish level, Paul's complex arguments and often polemical tone make him a very distant figure. On the other hand, the stories about Peter in the Gospels present a character whose weaknesses and strengths seem more accessible to the average Christian. Instead of thinking of Peter and Paul as the legitimate founders of different ways of being within the Christian church, many parishioners like to think of them as representatives of different styles of faith. Paul's faith was born of an intense intellectual involvement with his Jewish religious tradition. Initially, he had persecuted the new Christian movement until his experience of the risen Lord persuaded Paul that God's promise of salvation was being fulfilled in Christ. Peter's faith, on the other hand, grew out of the experiences he had with Jesus, himself. Unlike Paul, a Pharisee from the Greek-speaking diaspora, Peter shared the world of the Galilean peasants and craftsmen with Jesus. Like Jesus, he had grown up in the Judaism of the Galilean synagogues and had probably participated in annual pilgrimages to Jerusalem. When Peter encountered the risen Lord, he met a friend, and a hope that had appeared dashed was reborn.

Just as Schillebeeckx presents Peter as the bridge between the group of disciples around the historical Jesus and the post-Easter church, so many Christians think of him as the bridge between their own uncertain faith and their community with Jesus. They are enchanted by Peter's boldness in charging ahead even when he later fails—as in his promise never to desert Jesus (e.g., Mark 14:27–31). They identify with Peter's ability to recognize that Jesus is truly God's anointed and yet with his inability to grasp the suffering that Jesus will undergo (e.g., Mark 8:27–33). They admire the transformation which makes this willing but awkwardly uncertain disciple the courageous spokesperson for the good news about Jesus in the opening chapters of Acts. And they certainly agree with the author of 2 Peter that there are many things in Paul's letters "hard to understand which the ignorant and unstable twist to their own destruction" (2 Pet. 3:16).

As we have seen, the image of Peter has played a crucial role in shaping Christian communities. We will begin with a survey of those details about the historical Peter that can be gleaned from the New Testament and other early traditions about the apostle. We recognize that the New Testament writers did not set out to provide biographical descriptions about the apostle. They use the figure of Peter as a disciple to explore what it means to believe in Jesus. Each Gospel writer has a unique perspective on the figure of Peter. The letters attributed to Peter in the New Testament use the image and authority of the apostle to address problems that arose among a later generation of Christians. The fact that letters were written in Peter's name was probably due to the growing importance of collections of Paul's letters in the early church. Our study of Peter will extend beyond the New Testament into writings from second- and third-century Christianity. The legends about Peter which developed in the early church show that the conflict between Peter and Paul was used to play out other disputes within the community. These legends also show us how the earliest Christians developed the hints about Peter's character and his fate contained in the New Testament into full-fledged stories about the apostle.

As we discover the rich diversity in these treatments of the apostle, we remember the dual tasks of historical study and theology. The historian's task, as Tillich so eloquently put it, is to "make alive" what has "passed away." The theologian's task is always finally apologetic. She or he must make Christian faith credible. Schillebeeckx has reminded us that credibility is not won by ignoring our history. Rather, we must recover from that history a credible, living memory to sustain the present and guide us into the future.

NOTES

1. The recently published catechism uses the Petrine texts of the New Testament to affirm the position of the pope as "pastor of the whole church" and leader of the college of bishops. It asserts that no ecumenical council can have any authority unless its conclusions are accepted by the successor of Peter. See secs. 880–84, *Catéchisme de l'église catholique* (Paris: Mame/Plon, 1992). Though this view of Roman primacy is official Roman Catholic teaching, its historical roots lie in the medieval extension of papal authority to cover sees outside Italy. The synod of Arras in 1025 repeated Isidore's view that the powers conferred on Peter had been granted to all the apostles. See Colin Morris, *The Papal Monarchy: The Western Church from 1050 to 1250* (Oxford: Clarendon Press, 1989), 32. The extension of papal authority in the mid-eleventh century served to reform the church (*The Papal Monarchy*, 98–101). In the thirteenth century, Innocent III took the doctrine beyond the boundaries of ecclesial affairs. He asserted that Christ had conveyed to Peter governance of the whole world (*The Papal Monarchy*, 431–32).

2. E.g., J. D. Crossan, *The Historical Jesus: The Life of a Mediterranean Jewish Peasant* (San Francisco: Harper Collins, 1991); and John P. Meier, *A Marginal Jew, Rethinking the Historical Jesus 1: The Roots of the Problem and the Person* (Garden City: Doubleday, 1991). Both scholars defend the possibility of reconstructing an account of the historical Jesus based on early Christian and contemporary Jewish materials; the resulting conclusions differ widely.

3. Iris Murdoch, *Metaphysics as a Guide to Morals* (New York: Viking Penguin, 1993), 82–83.

4. Paul Tillich, *Systematic Theology*. (New York: Harper and Row, 1951), 1:103–4.

5. While it is easy to see the literary appropriateness of this suggestion, the lack of any further clues makes the hypothesis difficult to defend. One may conclude that if the Beloved Disciple had been a Judean disciple of the Baptist, then it would not be surprising that he was not one of the twelve Galilean followers of Jesus. See George R. Beasley-Murray, *John*, WBC 36 (Waco, TX: Word Books, 1987), lxx–lxxiii.

6. See the sympathetic discussion of Roman primacy by an Anglican theologian, John de Satgé, in *Peter and the Single Church* (London: SPCK, 1981), 120–21.

7. Hans von Campenhausen, *Ecclesiastical Authority and Spiritual Power in the Church of the First Three Centuries*, trans. J. A. Baker (Stanford: Stanford University Press, 1969), 31–53.

8. Von Campenhausen, *Ecclesiastical Authority*, 47–48.

9. See the account of the development of Baur's thought in Werner Georg Kümmel, *The New Testament: The History of the Investigation of Its Problems*, trans. S. MacLean Gilmour and H. C. Kee (Nashville: Abingdon Press, 1972), 127–43. For a detailed critique of the continued influence of Baur's ideological dichotomies on the interpretation of the New Testament, see Craig C. Hill, *Hellenists and Hebrews: Reappraising Division within the Earliest Church* (Minneapolis: Fortress Press, 1992), 5–17. Hill observes that scholars have continued to read the Hellenists and Hebrews of Acts 6:1–8:4 as ideological camps with distinctive agendas. They have assumed that a radical rejection of the temple and Jewish cult by Stephen and other Hellenists led to persecution of Hellenist leaders, while James, Peter, and other Jewish Christians remained secure as members of a Jewish sect (*Hellenists and Hebrews*, 11–15). Some scholars have recognized that we lack secure evidence for this hypothesis. The terms "Hellenists" and "Hebrews" may not refer to a Jerusalem church divided on linguistic grounds between Aramaic and Greek speakers. Paul, for example, clearly speaks and writes in Greek but describes himself as "a Hebrew" (Phil. 3:5; 2 Cor. 11:22). The false apostles referred to in 2 Corinthians were clearly active in a Greek-speaking, gentile church.

10. See James D. G. Dunn, *Unity and Diversity in the New Testament: An Inquiry into the Character of Earliest Christianity* (Philadelphia: Westminster Press, 1977), 3–4.

11. Oscar Cullmann, *Peter: Disciple—Apostle—Martyr*, 2d ed., trans. Floyd V. Filson (London: SCM, 1962). See also the Roman Catholic analysis by Otto Karrer in *Peter and the Church: An Examination of Cullmann's Thesis*, QD 8, trans. Ronald Walls (New York: Herder and Herder, 1962). An Anglican, De Satgé treats Cullmann's detailed concern with

Matthew 16:17–20 and his argument for Petrine leadership, which cannot be transferred to successors in a geographical location, as the bridge between the older and the post-Vatican II ecumenical discussions. See *Peter and the Single Church*, 34–36.

12. Cullmann, *Peter*, 30–59.
13. Dunn, *Unity*, 385.
14. Raymond E. Brown, Karl P. Donfried, and John Reumann, eds., *Peter in the New Testament* (New York: Paulist Press, 1973).
15. R. E. Brown et al., eds., *Peter*, 7–20.
16. See the discussion of the presuppositions of *Peter in the New Testament* by De Satgé in *Peter and the Single Church*, 15–19.
17. *Lumen Gentium*, secs. 18–19. Though the council reaffirms the canons of Vatican I, it begins its consideration of apostolic ministry in the church with the commissioning of the Twelve.
18. See Rudolf Pesch, *Simon Petrus*, Geschichte und geschichtliche Bedeutung des ersten Jüngers Jesu Christi. Päpste und Papstum Bd. 15 (Stuttgart: Anton Hiersemann, 1980), 22–24.
19. See Edward Schillebeeckx, *Jesus: An Experiment in Christology*, trans. H. Hoskins (New York: Crossroad, 1979), 592–94. Schillebeeckx does not presume that the church today could simply recreate first-century models. Rather, by holding that eschatological community in memory, the church will find appropriate ways of affirming the radical identity with the outcast and poor which characterized the life of its founder. This new emphasis also shifts the focus of Christology from the divinity of Jesus to the special form of human transcendence that is expressed in the Christ (*Jesus*, 597–601).
20. "[F]aith utterances must have a basis in the history of Jesus; were the opposite the case, they would have a disjunctive, thus and ideological relation to the real state of affairs" (Schillebeeckx, *Jesus*, 604).
21. Schillebeeckx, *Jesus*, 605.
22. *Jesus*, 641.
23. For a general evaluation of Schillebeeckx's attempt to treat the Resurrection traditions as conversion experiences, see Reginald H. Fuller and Pheme Perkins, *Who Is This Christ? Gospel Christology and Contemporary Faith* (Philadelphia: Fortress Press, 1983), 28–38.
24. Schillebeeckx, *Jesus*, 389.
25. Rudolf Bultmann, *The History of the Synoptic Tradition*, 2d ed., trans. John Marsh (New York: Harper and Row, 1968), 138–40.
26. Bultmann, *History*, 140.
27. Schillebeeckx, *Jesus*, 391.
28. Raymond E. Brown and John P. Meier, *Antioch and Rome: New Testament Cradles of Catholic Christianity* (Ramsey, NJ: Paulist Press, 1983).
29. *Antioch and Rome*, 39–43.

30. *Antioch and Rome*, 41.
31. Not surprisingly, the discussion of the distinction between Petrine and Pauline Christianity by Franz Mussner in *Petrus und Paulus—Pole der Einheit*, QD 76 (Freiburg: Herder, 1976) begins with the Petrine material.
32. Eduard Lohse, "St. Peter's Apostleship in the Judgment of St. Paul, the Apostle to the Gentiles: An Exegetical Contribution to an Ecumenical Debate," *Gregorianum* 72 (1991): 419–35.
33. Lohse, "St. Peter's Apostleship," 421–23.
34. "St. Peter's Apostleship," 425.
35. "St. Peter's Apostleship," 426.
36. "St. Peter's Apostleship," 430f.
37. "St. Peter's Apostleship," 433–34.
38. "St. Peter's Apostleship," 435.
39. W. D. Davies and Dale C. Allison, *Commentary on Matthew VIII–XVIII*, vol. 2 of *The Gospel According to St. Matthew*, ICC (Edinburgh: T. and T. Clark, 1991), 444–47.

CHAPTER 1

A Life of Peter

FAMILIAR STORIES

Most Christians feel that they know a great deal about Peter because he appears in the Gospels more frequently than any of the other disciples of Jesus. Jesus summons Peter, his brother Andrew, and the sons of Zebedee, James and John, to be his first followers (Mark 1:16–20; Matt. 4:18–22; Luke 5:1–11 omits Andrew). John 1:40–42 presents Andrew as a follower of John the Baptist. Andrew is the one who calls his brother. Jesus heals Peter's mother-in-law (Mark 1:29–31; Matt. 8:14–15; Luke 4:38–39). Peter appears more perceptive than the other disciples in recognizing the identity of Jesus as God's agent of salvation (Mark 8:27–30; Matt. 16:13–20; Luke 9:18–22; and the variant tradition in John 6:66–71). Peter is included with the sons of Zebedee in a smaller circle of disciples who witness the healing of Jaïrus' daughter (Mark 5:37), the Transfiguration (Mark 9:2; Matt. 17:1; Luke 9:28), and Jesus' agonized prayer in the garden (Mark 14:33; Matt. 26:37). During the Last Supper, Peter boasts that though the other disciples might abandon Jesus, he will remain loyal even to death (Mark 14:29–31; Matt. 26:33–35; Luke 22:31–34; also John 13:36–38). While the other disciples flee when Jesus is arrested (Mark 14:50; Matt. 26:56), Peter follows the arresting party into the courtyard of the high priest's house, only to deny having anything to do with or any knowledge of Jesus (Mark 14:54, 66–72; Matt. 26:58, 69–75; Luke 22:54–62; John 18:15–27).

At least one version of the early tradition about the Resurrection affirms that the risen Jesus appears to Peter and then to the Eleven (1 Cor. 15:5, Luke 24:33–34). Since there is no explicit narrative account of an encounter between Peter and the risen Jesus in the New Testament, most Christians assimilate these references to the scenes in which Jesus appears to the disciples as a group (on a mountain in

Galilee, in Matthew 28:16–20; or at a meal in Jerusalem, in Luke 24:36–43 and John 20:19–23). However, Peter does not play a role in any of these episodes. John 21 contains a variant of the risen Jesus' encountering his disciples in Galilee, which does give special treatment to Peter. At Peter's instigation, a group of disciples have been fishing fruitlessly all night when Jesus appears on the shore at dawn. He instructs them to cast the nets on the other side of the boat, where the nets are then filled to near-breaking. As soon as Peter learns that Jesus is the mysterious stranger on the shore, he leaps into the water (John 21:1–14). Because this episode contains details that are similar to two episodes concerning Peter in the synoptic Gospels—Peter's call in Luke 5:1–11, and Peter's precipitous exit from the boat to walk on water in Matthew 14:28–33—scholars are not sure that these narratives reflect primitive tradition. Some exegetes give priority to the Resurrection setting as an appropriate moment for the commissioning of the apostle. John 21 continues with such a commissioning episode. While giving Peter the opportunity to retract his denial by professing love for the Lord three times, Jesus commands him to "feed my sheep" (John 21:15–17).

None of these episodes separates Peter from the other disciples. Schillebeeckx's insistence upon Peter's conversion at the Resurrection appearance, in fact, draws heavily on Luke's depiction of Paul's experience. The Gospel narratives all assume that the disciples gather together prior to their discovery that the Lord has been raised. We do not know if anyone assembles the scattered disciples. The traditions as we have them are divided between those which suggest that the disciples flee back to Galilee after the Crucifixion and see the Lord there, and those which have the group remain in Jerusalem. The Fourth Evangelist patches over the conflict between the two versions by having the return to Galilee follow a rather extended stay in Jerusalem. He marks the appearance by the sea as the third time the risen Jesus appears (John 21:14). However, the story itself shows no indications of being composed to follow upon earlier experiences of the risen Lord.

Because the Peter stories found in John 21 include a commission to care for Jesus' flock, many interpreters suggest that Peter's role in the early community was based upon a word of the risen Lord. The more famous commissioning of Peter in Matthew 16:18–19 might have been formulated on the basis of sayings of the risen Lord rather than an episode during the earthly ministry of Jesus.[1] However, Peter's position as a prominent member of the group of disciples appears in all the traditional material about him. Even if the focus on Peter has been sharpened by the role that he plays in the community after Easter, he is always spokesperson for and representative of the disciples as a group. Just as the saying about "binding and loosing" is applied to Peter here, and to the community as a whole later (Matt. 16:19, 18:18), so Jesus' words to Peter may have singled him out in a way that was representative of the disciples as a group.

When Paul visits Jerusalem a few years after Jesus' death, he comes to see Peter, an indication of Peter's stature in the community there (Gal. 1:19). Later, Peter is associated with John and James, the brother of the Lord, as leaders in the Jerusalem community (Gal. 2:6–10). Peter also traveled to preach the Gospel in other communities (with his wife, according to 1 Cor. 9:5). In Paul's brief references to Peter, one gets the impression that Peter's position in relationship to the Jerusalem community may have changed. Though Paul admits to having met James, his first visit is to Peter. By the second visit, for the so-called "Jerusalem council," Paul sets Peter's mission to the "circumcised" alongside his own to the Gentiles. The decision about the conditions for accepting Gentiles who remain uncircumcised requires the agreement of three apostles—Peter, James, and John. When the conflict between Peter and Paul breaks out at Antioch, Peter apparently changes his behavior to accommodate the objections of persons who have come from James. Therefore, Peter no longer appears to be a leader in the Jerusalem church.

The image of Peter in these references in the Pauline letters differs from that which many Christians have derived from Acts. Luke depicts Peter as the primary figure in the Jerusalem community from its earliest days. However, Peter disappears from the narrative without explanation after Luke's account of the Jerusalem council. When Paul returns to Jerusalem, James is in charge of the community there (Acts 21:18). Acts depicts Peter as one who exercises both juridical and teaching authority. He determines how Judas is to be replaced (Acts 1:15–26), preaches the new message in Jerusalem (2:14–36, 3:11–26), defends it before the authorities (4:8–12, 5:29–32), heals the sick (3:1–10, 5:15–16), exercises ecclesiastical discipline (5:1–11), and preaches the gospel to the Gentiles (10:1–11:18).

Just as Acts never tells the reader what the result of Paul's trial and imprisonment at Rome was, even though Luke must have known that Paul was eventually martyred, so Peter drops out of sight once Paul's independent mission to the Gentiles is launched. Though Peter's martyrdom is not described in the New Testament, John 21:18–19 presumes that the reader knows what happened to Peter. Since 1 Peter 5:13 asserts that the writer is in "Babylon" (= Rome), the tradition that Peter died in Rome is also attested in the New Testament.

This brief sketch of the New Testament evidence already indicates some of the problems involved as soon as we begin to read the stories about Peter carefully. The various traditions are not always in agreement, though in some cases it may be possible to construct an hypothesis about how two stories may have diverged from an earlier account. But, as in the case of the miraculous catch of fish, it is by no means evident whether the catch belongs to the call story or to the post-Resurrection commissioning. Furthermore, the apostle is not the central interest of any of the New Testament narratives. Peter appears in the New Testament only because of his relationship to Jesus. All of the evangelists have reworked inherited traditions about Peter.[2] Though Peter is consistently pictured as the spokesperson for the Twelve, he is usually not the center of any of the narratives in which he figures. His role is primarily functional. Peter provides a personality for the circle of disciples and guarantees the continuity of early Christian preaching from Jesus to the gentile mission.[3]

ASKING HISTORICAL QUESTIONS

Most Christians read the Gospels as though they were modern reports about contemporary events. If we say that each Gospel addresses a different situation from a unique point of view, the majority of people presume that the divergence is something like an account of recent events from different ideological perspectives. Since Peter figures so prominently in the Gospel picture of Jesus' disciples, many Christians assume that we can more easily understand Peter as a person through the Gospel stories. When our parish Bible-study group was going through the Markan account of Peter's denial of Jesus (Mark 14:54, 66–72), a general consensus emerged that here was someone the members of the group could relate to. They had not had the same response to the Lukan story of Peter's call associated with the miraculous catch and the summons to become a "fisher of human beings" (Luke 5:1–11). The first story, they felt, gave them a clue about a person. The second, only a legendary figure. After reflecting on the political setting of the arrest, trial, and execution of Jesus, one member of the group even gave all his friends blanket permission to run away from him or to deny knowing him if they were ever caught in such a situation. Not quite the lesson Mark intended Christians to take away from this episode!

This discussion shows that everyone brings some judgment to bear on the stories that he or she reads in the Bible. Since the nightly news makes us constantly aware of the dangers that people suffer under authoritarian or broken political regimes, we assume that only the most extraordinary individuals manage to take a public stand against military thugs. Most adults, at least, know themselves well enough to suspect that in Peter's shoes, they would also deny knowing someone who is clearly destined for public execution. The measuring stick which the study group used to discuss the story of Peter's denial was their own understanding of personal conduct in a situation of political violence. Accordingly, Luke's account of the call of Peter did not seem "true to life" to them. A sober-minded realist with experience of the marginal economy involved in occupations like fishing insisted that even granting such a sudden catch, who would walk away from all those fish? (As a child, I used to wonder who had to clean all those fish when the disciples left!) Like it or not, you've got to pay for your equipment and pay your hired hands. Besides, adult sons cannot just walk out on the old man in a family business.

The story about the call of Peter has two strikes against it for contemporary readers. The first confronts us whenever we read one of the so-called "nature miracles"—miraculous catches, calming storms, multiplying loaves and fishes, changing water into wine, walking on water. The world does not work that way. We all know amateur fishermen who constantly repeat the story of the big one they caught with the last catch of the day after hours out on the lake. But this story concerns professionals working with nets in waters that their ancestors had fished before them. It even involves several boats working in the same area of the lake. Luke's version of the story at least has enough realism to credit Peter with a thoroughly professional objection to the command to toss his net out again (Luke 5:5a). However, Peter's capitulation, "If you say so, I will let down the nets" (v. 5b), requires some additional understanding about Jesus. The second strike against the story lies in the pattern of social relationships that it depicts. Hardworking fishermen pressed by lack of fish would not drop everything to follow some obscure preacher even if he did show an ability to summon fish from nowhere.

We noted in the introduction that the Fourth Gospel associates a miraculous catch with an appearance of the risen Lord (John 21:1–14). Some scholars think that Luke 5:1–11 was based on a post-Resurrection appearance story. A post-Resurrection setting would explain why Peter refers to Jesus as "Lord" and is willing to obey his word. Those exegetes who emphasize the element of conversion in Peter's encounter with the risen Lord see his confession that he is a "sinner" as a reference to the earlier episode in which he denied Jesus. As we have seen, the Fourth Gospel has the risen Jesus rehabilitate Peter with a threefold profession of love (John 21:15–17). This explanation lessens some of the tensions that people feel when reading this story because the risen Jesus is clearly identified with God. A direct command from God could override the familial, economic, and social improbabilities more easily than the words of someone whom the disciples know only as a rather unusual human being.

The difficulty with this type of explanation is the lack of textual evidence that Luke thought this was a post-Resurrection tale. Modern scholars are often quick to spot post-Resurrection influences in all the nature miracle stories because that relieves the demand for a realistic account of "what happened" to give rise to such a story. The hypothesis that Resurrection stories were retrojected into narrative accounts of the life of Jesus has been formulated to deal with our contemporary sensibility. If the historian is to make the past "real" for the present, then the narrative of those past events that he or she reconstructs has to be "realistic," that is, it must admit of plausible events, motives, and actions in the world as we know it.

Since the problem of determining "what happened," or rather "what might have happened," inevitably demands that we incorporate our own experience into judgments of what constitutes a suitable historical account, we cannot expect to arrive at a single, unambiguous version of any episode in the apostle's life. Though this assertion regularly draws howls of protest from parishioners, they are quite content to hear conflicting versions of the lives of modern figures debated without any hope of resolution. When I challenged a neighbor with that observation one day, her response was quite revealing: "Yeah, but someone knows things like who was in on the assassination of John F. Kennedy, and everyone else is lying." "Someone knows" and "everyone else is lying." What the average Christian wants from biblical scholars is "what happened" as it is perceived by the ideal "someone" who knows what happened in the various events referred to. Such people are not very happy when I point out to them that from the Bible's point of view, only God has the kind of knowledge they are anticipating, and God did not put it down in the Bible.

At that juncture, the "everyone else is lying" reaction sets in. It is usually formulated as "so it's all just a story," where "just a story" means somehow it's less true and has less claim on my belief, my relationship with others, and with God. The story can make a case for its veracity when it resonates with human experience as in the account of Peter's denial of Jesus. At that point, members of a Bible-study group may bring out their own stories to illustrate situations, relationships and meanings that they observe in the biblical account. It is not at all uncommon for someone to ask, "How come they never read this part in church?" even when we have had the very same passage as a lesson a few weeks earlier.

Such correlation of biblical story and contemporary experiences forms the basis of most preaching on the Bible. When the Bible is effectively used, the congregation has the experience of a parishioner who said, "I really liked that meditation on Christmas. It brought the story right into today." As we have seen, "bringing the story into today" is also the point of any effective historical study. The difficulty with the "quick and easy" route taken in much spiritual writing, preaching, and do-it-yourself Bible study is that it lacks the discipline required to impart an understanding of the very different social, cultural, political, personal, and religious worlds that shaped the biblical writers and their audiences.

Correlation with our experience and knowledge of the world forms only one part of the job of asking historical questions. We need to know as much as we can find out about the first century. What would the stories being told about Peter look like to a first-century audience? Where we have multiple versions of a tradition, such as the fact that Peter abandoned his life as a fisherman to follow Jesus, we may be reasonably sure that we are dealing with a known event. Can the divergent accounts in the Gospels be shown to reflect different concerns at the level of the evangelist narrator? Sometimes there are linguistic or thematic associations with other passages in a particular Gospel or with well-known stories such as those in the Old Testament. Then it is possible to attribute changes in detail to the particular author. Changes may be associated with the narrative techniques of a given Gospel writer. Or they may reflect the religious significance which that Gospel attaches to a particular story.

As scholars attempt to reconstruct versions of stories and sayings that existed prior to those found in the Gospels, disagreements will inevitably become more pronounced. While it is relatively easy to observe differences and even parallels between biblical stories and those from earlier parts of the Bible or those found in literature of biblical times, ordering such observations into an account of how a particular story came to have the shape it does is much more problematic. Those who try to reconstruct the "historical Jesus" from the Gospel material speak of criteria like multiple, independent attestation, plausibility in the context of what we know of Palestinian Judaism in Jesus' time, divergence from views commonly expressed by others, and coherence with the overall picture of Jesus and his teaching. Arguments about whether or not a particular saying reflects an Aramaic substratum used to be common, but now carry much less weight. We are increasingly aware that first-century Palestine was multilingual. One cannot separate Jewish and Greek culture or language. "Jewish" and "Aramaic" should not be accorded the automatic presumption of being "early" or "authentic."[4] In every case, scholars must make the same kind of judgments of probability in terms of everything they know about the biblical narrative and its world that we have seen average people making when evaluating a story against their experience.

Scholars generally agree that Matthew and Luke used much of Mark's Gospel. They also shared a common collection of sayings and short episodes, which is designated "Q." These sayings and episodes do not refer to individual disciples, though some of them refer to the disciples as a group. One of them, "Whoever loves father or mother more than me is not worthy of me" (Matt. 10:37; Luke 14:26) describes the attitude displayed by Peter and the others when they leave their fathers to follow Jesus in the call story. We saw in the introduction that the Fourth Gospel has a completely different account of how Peter came to be a disciple of Jesus. His brother Andrew, already a disciple of John the Baptist, is said to bring Peter to Jesus (John 1:40–41). Though some scholars continue to hold that John was familiar with Mark and/or Luke, most agree that he was working with independent variants of the sayings and episodes which are similar to those found in the synoptics. When information from the Johannine tradition conflicts with that from the synoptic Gospels as in the case of how Peter came to be a disciple of Jesus, it is usually possible to find a theological reason for the divergence in the Johannine narrative. John emphasizes the role of John the Baptist as the one sent by God to witness to the presence of Jesus as savior. He has recast the account of the Baptist so that the reader sees the Baptist sending Jesus his first disciples, Andrew and the anonymous figure, who may be the narrative stand-in for the Beloved Disciple.

However, there is some historical plausibility in the suggestion that Jesus' first disciples had been influenced by the Baptist's preaching, since Jesus himself was baptized by John. Though they were probably not disciples of John the Baptist in a formal sense, their familiarity with his message of repentance and renewal would explain why they were ready to undertake such a radical change in their lives. Thus it is often possible to discover notes of historical plausibility in the Johannine account.

Literary analysis of the Gospel texts and comparison with what is known of the times is not the only basis for historical conjecture. In recent decades, scholars have turned to sociological models to understand the nature of the Jesus movement and its appeal in ancient Palestine. The histories of the period by the Jewish historian Josephus have provided a rich source of information about political divisions and social conflict. The disintegration of ancestral sources of authority in the priestly and royal line mirror a society in which established ties were generally fragile.[5] The execution of many of the established leaders when Herod came to power as well as the redistribution of lands to the new ruling-class left many persons displaced from the normal access to power. Even ties to the dead had been disrupted. Herod built the new city of Tiberias over an ancient cemetery, with the result that only Gentiles and destitute Jews were willing to live there.[6] The struggles of Herod's sons to succeed their fathers was mirrored on the lower levels of society in which the father's absolute power over his sons masked an equally precarious situation. Adult sons had to remain subservient and deferential.[7] Richard Fenn suggests that the Jesus movement broke through the constraints of an ailing social system: "The Jesus movement may have played a significant role precisely in this birth of new roles and networks through forms of speech that left little doubt as to what was said or done as well as through inspired forms of speech that crossed hitherto impassable barriers."[8] From the sociological perspective, the calling of Peter and the other disciples makes an indirect comment about the social system of its time.

PETER IN THE GOSPELS

When scholars speak of multiple attestation for a particular fact, episode or saying in reconstructing the life of Jesus, they mean independent versions. A passage that has been taken from Mark and reworked by Luke and Matthew is only attested once. The story of Jesus healing Peter's mother-in-law, for example, has been taken over from Mark 1:29–31 by Matthew 8:14–15 and Luke 4:38–39. We only have one original witness to the story. Paul's reference to Peter's wife (1 Cor. 9:5) provides a second witness to the fact that Peter was married. Since we hold the view that the Johannine tradition is independent of the synoptic Gospels, its claim that Peter's brother Andrew became a disciple along with Peter is a second witness for the Markan reference to Andrew in the call story (Mark 1:16–18; Matt. 4:18–20). Luke's account of the calling of Peter includes the sons of Zebedee but omits all reference to Andrew. Since the stronger tradition includes Andrew, we must conclude that Luke—or perhaps the source from which he took the episode—omitted him. The scene has been constructed to place Peter in the central role as the model disciple.

As a storyteller, Luke has made a number of changes to the Markan order. Mark situates this episode right at the beginning of Jesus' ministry. The reader has only been told in a single verse that after the Baptist's arrest, Jesus came into Galilee preaching repentance (Mark 1:15). Why should the disciples leave everything in order to follow Jesus? We have seen that such behavior would have been highly unusual. Sociologists have suggested that social conflicts and the new possibilities formulated in movements like that around Jesus might explain such behavior. In that case, as we have suggested, the disciples must have had some prior preparation for this move. Perhaps this preparation came through the preaching of John the Baptist or perhaps, as Luke suggests, through earlier experiences with Jesus himself. In Luke's account, before the disciples are called, they have already heard Jesus preach and have witnessed a number of miracles including the healing of Peter's mother-in-law (Luke 4:31–41).

The two chronologies cannot be harmonized. Mark depicts Jesus entering Peter's mother-in-law's house at Capernaum with a group whom he has already called to be disciples: Simon, Andrew, James, and John (Mark 1:29). In Luke, Jesus comes alone, since he has not yet called Peter and the others to be his disciples. Because Luke is following the sequence of Mark's narrative in the rest of this section, scholars commonly attribute the chronological shift and the expanded version of the calling of Peter to Luke.[9] The narrative plausibility of Luke's order would appear to be sufficient to account for the difference in sequence.[10]

Does the fact that Mark's account is the source which Luke modified imply that his sequence should be accepted as historically more probable? Should a list of events in Peter's life place his first encounter with Jesus at the sea where Jesus summons him to be a disciple and then proceed to the healing of Peter's mother-in-law? That might seem to be the logical conclusion if one were to assume that Mark's account is simply a record of the episode as it was remembered in the early church. However, Mark's version also contains a number of puzzles: (a) what happens to Andrew? (b) why pairs of brothers? and (c) in what context is the phrase "Follow me and I will make you fish for people" intelligible?

The more complex circumstances which the stories in Luke and John suggest for the calling of Peter have a plausibility that the brief Markan account lacks. First-century readers may have filled in assumptions based upon their understanding of society which are reflected in these later versions. It is also possible that brief call story in Mark has been formulated on the basis of earlier models. New Testament scholars are particularly aware of the importance of Old Testament stories as models for those in the New Testament. Mark's call story may have been based on a call story similar to that of Elisha's in 1 Kings 19:19–21. The disciple/successor is told to abandon his occupation in order to take up a new mission. This foundational call story may then have been expanded with the injunction to become "fishers of human beings" (Mark 1:17, Matt. 4:19, Luke 5:10). Gathering human beings for the Kingdom appears to refer more appropriately to the post-Easter preaching of the disciples.[11] John 21:11 has the risen Jesus direct Simon to a large catch, which appears to symbolize the future mission of the church. Earlier in John (4:38), Jesus tells his disciples that they are to become laborers in a harvest which they did not sow. Sending out pairs of missionaries may have been common in the early church. The Markan formulation of the call story focuses on pairs of brothers. Thus, elements in the Markan scene point to the role of Peter and the others in the later church. It is not simply a brief sketch of a historical fact.

The divergent traditions make it impossible give a single account of Peter's call. Several members of Peter's family figure in the story: his brother Andrew, his mother-in-law, who provides hospitality for the disciples after she is healed,[12] and Peter's wife, who accompanies him on his missionary journeys (1 Cor. 9:5). Whether or not Andrew became a follower of Jesus before Peter, Peter clearly belongs to a family which become supporters of Jesus and his movement.[13] Their house serves as the center for his activities in the region (Mark 2:1, 7:17, 9:33). Although Peter has to give up his occupation in order to follow Jesus and later to preach the Gospel, he does not entirely renounce the ties which he has to his family.

Another famous episode concerning Peter, which has both synoptic and Johannine variants, is the confession of Peter (Mark 8:27–30; Matt. 16:13–20; Luke 9:18–22; John 6:66–71). Matthew's version has been expanded with sayings about Peter that attribute his insight to God, that pronounce him the "rock" on which the community is built, and that convey the power of binding and loosing (Matt. 16:17–19). We have already seen in the introduction that these Matthean sayings have played a major role in the Roman Catholic argument for the primacy of Peter among the apostles. The Markan episode begins with a question in which Jesus asks his disciples who people say he is. They provide a list of possibilities, which the reader already knows is inadequate—John the Baptist, Elijah, or one of the prophets. Jesus then asks the disciples what they would say. Peter responds for the group: "the messiah" (Mark 8:29). In the Johannine variant, a number of followers have deserted Jesus after his teaching that his body is the manna of eternal life. Jesus turns to the Twelve and asks if they are going to leave as well. Again, Peter responds for the group: "You have the words of eternal life. We have come to believe, and know that you are the Holy One of God" (John 6:68–69). In both cases, Peter is merely acting as a spokesperson for all the disciples. The historical question posed by the episode does not concern Peter as an individual. It concerns the plausibility of the disciples' referring to Jesus as the eschatological agent of God during his lifetime.

This question is made more difficult by the Markan conclusion. The disciples are prohibited from making such a claim about Jesus (Mark 8:30; Luke 9:21). Since the beginning of the twentieth century, many scholars have concluded that this episode belongs with the group of post-Resurrection stories. Early creedal formulae like Romans 1:3–4 show that after the Resurrection, Jesus' followers recognized his exalted status. However, this sharp division resolves our modern discomfort only to create another one. It is very difficult to place the entire burden of christological claims about Jesus on the Resurrection. Jesus could not have claimed a hearing, let alone appeared to exercise the dangerous influence over the crowds that led to his death, if he had not been perceived to have a special relationship with God. He had no legitimacy in terms of the normal positions of religious or social authority.

Mark (followed by Luke) immediately qualifies the confession that Jesus is "messiah" with the first of three Passion predictions (Mark 8:31–33). When Peter protests, Jesus rebukes him sharply, "Get behind me Satan! For you are not on the side of God but of men" (v. 33; RSV). Again, Peter speaks as a representative of the disciples. They will follow him toward Jerusalem and the Passion, increasingly unable to understand what the insistence on suffering means. Although this sharp juxtaposition in Mark is frequently attributed to Mark's desire to keep the messiahship of Jesus secret until it can be seen in light of the Passion, most interpreters think that it is Mark's own creation. The traditions which he inherited did not follow the confession that Jesus is "messiah" with a sharp command to silence. The Passion prediction, Peter's protest, and Jesus' rebuke may have belonged to a separate unit of tradition.[14] The confession story as it stands in Mark would seem to demand a more positive response by Jesus than the command to silence. Matthew's beatitude not only elevates Peter by suggesting that his confession was inspired by God; it also resolves the dynamic tension inherent in Mark's version.[15]

Though many interpreters think that the command to silence has a merely symbolic function in Mark, Räisänen rightly insists that at least at the level of Mark's narrative it is understood to be a legitimate command of the historical Jesus.[16] Some scholars have suggested that the persecution suffered by Markan Christians required discrete speech about any claims for Jesus. Studies of the social conflict that occurred in Palestine between the death of Jesus and the Jewish revolt have made concerns about any forms of speech that might exalt an individual as a populist leader an important element in the historical ministry of Jesus as well. Groups bound together by symbolic speech that protected their critique of the illegitimate power exercised by those in charge evidently formed in diverse ways during this period. Any group might expect to have its "informers." The palace intrigues in the Herodian court and among the high priestly families are well documented in Josephus.[17]

This social phenomenon provides a historically plausible account of both the Markan command to be silent and the quite different ending taken by the Johannine variant, in which Jesus follows Peter's confession with an enigmatic saying that one of the Twelve is a devil (John 6:70). The evangelist immediately interprets the saying for us as a reference to Judas. The saying itself is a more generic comment on the treacherous social situation which confronted someone like Jesus. Multiple attestation and indications of historical plausibility make it possible to defend the claim that the confession of Peter is not entirely a post-Resurrection episode. Expansion of the christological title to "Son of the living God" as well as the sayings which confer on Peter the power of binding and loosing in Matthew 16:16–19 probably do reflect an expansion of the story with sayings derived from a post-Resurrection setting.[18]

The episode in which Jesus rebukes Peter as "Satan" for resisting the predictions of suffering to come in Jerusalem also has historical plausibility (Mark 8:31–33; Matt. 16:21–23; Luke 9:22). It provides an example of a criterion which some scholars refer to as "embarrassment"; incidents which reflect negatively on Jesus or the disciples are not likely to have been created in the early church. They must have been well-established in the tradition in order to be preserved.[19] As they stand, the Passion predictions have been worked into the narrative of a Gospel which will end with the death and the Resurrection of Jesus. The predictions of Jesus' Passion have been reworked accordingly. Peter's protest serves to highlight the resolve of Jesus to carry out what is really God's plan, not the inevitable result of paranoia and violence in first-century Palestine.

We have already seen that the story of Peter's denial of Jesus (Mark 14:53–54, 66–72; Matt. 26:57–58, 69–75; Luke 22:54b–62; John 18:15–18, 25–27) awakens a sympathetic chord in contemporary readers.[20] It has been integrated into the Passion narrative, since Jesus predicts the denial before it occurs in response to Peter's bold assertion that even if the others abandon Jesus, he will never do so (Mark 14:29–31; Matt. 26:33–35; Luke 22:31–34; John 13:36–38). Mark's version of Peter's initial claim, which is followed by Matthew, has the other disciples take up the challenge implicit in Peter's words. Though Jesus has predicted that the sheep would be scattered, the disciples as a group reject that prophecy. This episode parallels Peter's earlier response to the first Passion prediction. Even though they now recognize that Jesus might in fact die, the disciples allege that they too are ready to die rather than deny the Lord. The variants in Luke and John omit the participation of the disciples and focus on Peter himself. As we have seen, the Lukan promise that after Satan has "sifted him" Peter will turn to strengthen his brothers (Luke 22:32) plays a central role in contemporary reconstructions of the role of Peter in the community. It is taken as evidence that Peter reassembled the scattered disciples after his vision of the risen Lord. In that sense, Peter founds the post-Easter church.

In the Markan tradition, Peter's response singles him out from the other disciples. Unlike the others, he will not flee immediately (Mark 14:50). However, because Peter does not flee, he puts himself in the position of denying Jesus. The initial exchange may have been introduced into the pre-Markan Passion narrative in order to explain the events which it anticipates, the flight of the disciples and Peter's denial of Jesus.[21] Zephaniah 13:7 serves as a "proof text" for the flight of the disciples. It accommodates their behavior to the divine plan of salvation. Though there is no such text for Peter's denial, the precise temporal markers associated with the prophetic word of the Lord suggest that Peter, too, is playing out a divinely ordered script. Luke's revision of the episode shows even more interest in accommodating Peter's actions to a larger divine plan that will extend to Peter's leadership of the community after the Resurrection.[22]

The Johannine variant also contains an implied promise that Peter will later become what his brash words promise. Though Peter will deny Jesus rather than follow him to the death during the Passion, later he will follow Jesus (John 13:36). Thus, John and Luke provide evidence for a tradition of Jesus' promise to Peter that differs from the prediction of Peter's denial. This early tradition raises a question about the modern evaluation of the denial episode. Commentators commonly assume that because the early Passion narrative described Peter's threefold denial of Jesus, ancient readers would consider the apostle morally inferior to those who ran away.[23] By assimilating these events to the divine plan through appeal to a prophetic word of the Lord, the early Passion tradition seems to lift blame from the disciples. Luke treats the whole incident as a Satanic attack on the circle of disciples.

Historical analysis of the period reminds us that the disciples have good reason to fear for their own lives when Jesus is arrested on information given by one of their number. Peter's attempt to follow along and find out what has happened to Jesus is an act of some courage in itself. Further, any ancient reader familiar with the dangerous intrigue that was rampant among those who contended for power in royal or high priestly circles knew that lying and dissembling when faced with accusations was the only way to stay alive.[24] Peter's negative reaction to what he had done shows that he does not share the corruption of those who are plotting to execute Jesus. His response when reminded of Jesus' words shows that Peter knows that his relationship to Jesus is not that of those who seek to save their lives in this world at any price (Mark 8:34–38).[25]

We have already seen that some of the references to Resurrection appearances mention an appearance to Peter prior to those which involve the disciples as a group (e.g., 1 Cor. 15:3–5, Luke 24:34). These references play an important role in the argument that Peter's position in the post-Easter community is due to that experience of the risen Lord, not to a special status conferred on him by Jesus during the earthly ministry of Jesus. However, no early narrative traditions depict such an event. Scholars have proposed that sayings such as those in Matthew 16:18–19 belong to a church-founding commission given the apostle by the risen Lord.

PETER IN ACTS

Most of our images of Peter in the early church are shaped by the stories in Acts. While they provide valuable information about the image of Peter at the time the Gospel was written, their historical significance is difficult to assess. Scholars are sharply divided over whether it is possible to sift out reliable historical information from the Lukan narratives. When the picture of Paul in Acts is compared with that derived from the apostle's own letters, exegetes are forced to concede that either Luke or his sources were unaware of central events in Paul's ministry and major themes in his theology. Chronological hints contained in the Pauline letters cannot be forced to match those in Acts. There are such disagreements between the accounts of the key events involving Peter and Paul, the so-called "Jerusalem council" and the episode at Antioch (Gal. 2:1–14, Acts 15:1–33) that many interpreters even argue that Paul and Acts are referring to two different events.[26] I remain convinced that both refer to the same episode. The variety of hypotheses advanced to explain the divergence between Paul and Acts demonstrates the lack of criteria for establishing the historical traditions embodied in the narratives of Acts.

Comparisons between the speeches attributed to Paul in Acts and the apostle's letters lead to a similar conclusion. Acts shapes the speeches of its characters around a basic outline of early Christian preaching. Rhetorical conventions also shape the trial speeches attributed to the apostles when they are brought into court. The speeches of the apostle Peter in Acts (2:14–36, 3:12–26, 4:8–12, 5:29–32, 10:34–43,

11:2–18, 15:7–11) may reflect established patterns of early Christian preaching familiar to Luke. They do not provide evidence for the preaching of the historical Peter. Like other authors of his time, Luke provides words for his characters that are appropriate to the narrative context. The speeches in Acts 11:2–18 and 15:7–11 summarize the narrative account of Peter's divinely commanded baptism of the first Gentiles (Acts 10) for a Jerusalem audience. As he does with every episode which he repeats, Luke introduces variations in the retelling which situate each version in its setting.

The remaining speeches of Peter are mission speeches. They address the message of the gospel to non-believers. Scholars have long recognized that these speeches follow a set pattern which is repeated in Paul's address to the Jews of Pisidian Antioch as well (Acts 13:16–41).[27] However, Paul's speech distinguishes its audience of diaspora Jews from those in Jerusalem, who are held responsible for the death of Jesus. A Jerusalem audience is to be forgiven its complicity in the death of Jesus. To diaspora Jews, Paul can only speak of sins in general (13:38–39). Peter's Pentecost speech speaks directly to persons implicated in the death of Jesus. The sin which can still be forgiven if they repent is that of crucifying Jesus (2:23, 36). When Peter addresses the summons to repent to the crowd in the temple, he introduces a catalogue of motivations for conversion, such as forgiveness and the coming of the messianic age (3:19–26). In the Pentecost speech, repentance is the conclusion to the announcement that the crucified Messiah has been raised. In the temple speech, repentance forms the central subject of the address.

These variations are evidence that Luke has adapted each speech to fit the narrative context in which it is set. In Acts 5:30–32, Luke has provided the Jerusalem speeches with a short summary of their central themes. Through the apostles, God's gift of repentance can still be offered to Israel. The Sanhedrin's hostile reaction opens the way for the new initiative toward the Gentiles.[28] When the speeches in Acts summarize the career of Jesus, they refer back to Luke's Gospel. The main part of the speech to Cornelius includes such specifics as the message of peace (Luke 2:10–11, Acts 10:36), the Nazareth sermon (Luke 4:18, Acts 10:38), and the risen Lord's commission to his followers (Luke 24:46–48).[29] The first gentile converts must hear the whole narrative of the Gospel if they are to be incorporated into the community. No doubt, to those to whom he preached the gospel Peter did give information about the life of Jesus and God's offer of salvation through belief in Jesus. Paul tells us that Peter, James, and John carried on a mission among Jews (Gal. 2:9) comparable to that which he, Barnabas, and others carried on among Gentiles. On that point, the evidence of Acts and the Pauline letters agrees. But we cannot assume that the speeches attributed to Peter reflect the words of the apostle himself.

We have already seen in the introduction that the issue of Peter's position as leader in the Jerusalem community has critical importance for contemporary discussions of church order. Paul's comments about Peter in Galatians 2 suggest that his place in the leadership of the Jerusalem church changes. The narrative of Acts provides similar hints. In the earliest days of the community, Peter is the sole figure of authority. He determines what is to be done in crises facing the community. But when he returns to Jerusalem after baptizing Cornelius and his household, Peter has to defend his actions before the "apostles and brothers who were in Judea" as a result of accusations lodged by "those of the circumcision" (Acts 11:1–2). Peter's evangelizing activities appear to have separated him from the leadership of the community in Jerusalem.

The Acts tradition that Peter baptized Gentiles fits the picture of Peter as an ecclesial centrist which has been proposed to moderate the earlier dualism of Petrine versus Pauline Christianity. Although it conflicts with Paul's assertion that Peter and the others agreed to preach to the "circumcision" while Paul and his associates would go to the uncircumcised, Paul himself indicates that Peter's mission was not limited to Jews. The dispute over whether or not table fellowship in a mixed church could be divided to accommodate those Jews who felt uneasy about eating with Gentiles (Gal. 2:11–14) shows that Peter was associating with gentile Christians. The faction in Corinth which associated with Peter (1 Cor. 1:12) may be another indication that Peter's missionary preaching came to include Gentiles.

Thus the references to Peter in Paul's letters as well as the material in Acts provide a few clues about the apostle's career. Though some of the Resurrection stories suggest that the disciples all fled to Galilee, Peter is clearly established as the leader of an early Christian community in Jerusalem by the time of Paul's conversion some three years after the death of Jesus. When Paul visits Jerusalem three years after that, Peter is the principle person in the community, though James, the brother of the Lord, is also a leader in the church there. Sometime during the intervening years, Peter also participates in preaching outside of Jerusalem, perhaps even to Gentiles sympathetic to Judaism, as Acts suggests. By the time of the Jerusalem council (ca. A.D. 49) Peter, James and John seem to share leadership at Jerusalem. Paul also separates these "pillars" from those in a "circumcision" faction, who oppose admitting Gentiles to the community without requiring that they become full proselytes.

Jerusalem has some authority to make decisions that will be accepted in other prominent churches like that at Antioch. However, neither Peter nor any one of the other apostles has the sole responsibility of determining what the community shall or shall not do on crucial issues of practice and church discipline. Paul's comment that he had to secure the approval of Jerusalem lest his mission have been "in vain" (Gal. 2:2) shows that he could not unilaterally determine the conditions under which Gentiles would be considered members of Christ. If he had been unable to persuade those at Jerusalem to accept his gentile converts, then he would have labored in vain. Similarly, he now wishes to persuade the Galatians that if they add circumcision onto the faith they have in Christ, they will have believed "in vain" (Gal. 2:15–21). If Paul knows that Peter has already been converting Gentiles who were sympathetic to Judaism, he has good reason to suppose that Peter, James, and John can be persuaded to accept Gentiles as fellow Christians without demanding that they be circumcised.

At some point after the Jerusalem council, Peter comes to Antioch, where he apparently stays for some time. Acts 12:1–19 describes a severe persecution in Jerusalem prior to the Jerusalem council. During this persecution, which is attached to the Passover feast,[30] Herod executes James, the son of Zebedee, and imprisons Peter. After a miraculous escape from jail, Peter goes into hiding and eventually departs from the city (vv. 17–19). This episode is the third and most dangerous imprisonment faced by Peter in Acts (4:3–22, 5:17–42). Although it is not possible to derive historical details from any of the imprisonment stories, the fact of arrest and imprisonment for preaching about Christ is independently attested in the New Testament. Paul refers to his own activities as a zealous persecutor of the church (Gal. 1:13, 1 Cor. 15:9),[31] to beatings and imprisonments that he suffers at the hands of Jewish authorities (2 Cor. 11:23–25), and to the persecution of Christians in Judea (1 Thess. 2:14). Paul's letters also indicate that hostility frequently causes him to depart from a city in which he is preaching.

Although we cannot use the stories in Acts to provide details of arrests, interrogation, and imprisonment, the tradition that Peter suffered such persecution in Jerusalem is highly probable. The origin of the saying of Jesus about Peter's fate in John 21:18 might lie in the Jerusalem period. As an independent saying, it does not necessarily imply death on a cross.[32] The Johannine narrator interprets the saying as a prediction of the manner of Peter's death (v. 19b).[33] Sayings of Jesus which warn the disciples that they can anticipate being brought to trial before religious and civil authorities (e.g., Mark 13:9–13; Luke 21:12–19; Matt. 10:17–23) provide indirect evidence for the historical reality of such persecution.

Though individuals, like Paul and Peter, or groups, like the Jewish Christians in Rome under Claudius (Acts 18:2), might be driven from a city, they often return. We find Paul returning to Corinth, and a number of the Jewish Christians having coming back to Rome. Therefore, it is not impossible that Peter returned to Jerusalem after the persecution referred to in Acts 12. Further conflict stirred up by Peter's preaching may have led to his presence in Antioch and perhaps even to a decision to leave Jerusalem permanently. Peter may have visited other churches in Asia Minor and Greece. If the reference to Peter in 1 Corinthians 1:13 implies that Peter actually visited the church there, he must have done so in late A.D. 51 or 52. After that time, direct evidence concerning Peter's life runs out.

John 21:18–19 indicates that Peter died as a martyr but does not tell us when or where. The two letters attributed to Peter in the New Testament are pseudonymous. 1 Peter 5:13 provides our earliest indirect evidence for Peter's presence at Rome. The two persons, besides Peter, named in 1 Peter are associated with the Pauline mission, Silvanus (1 Pet. 5:12, 1 Thess. 1:1, 2 Cor. 1:19, Acts 15:40) and Mark (1 Pet. 5:13, Acts 12:25, 2 Tim. 4:11).[34] Elements in the form of these letters, their apostolic greetings, and their content follow Pauline models (1 Pet. 2:5; 3:16; 4:10–11; 5:10, 14).[35] Consequently, 1 Peter might be best understood as evidence for an adaptation of Pauline tradition in a Roman church which also revered Peter.[36] The image of Peter as pastor, "fellow elder" (1 Pet. 5:1) provides another glimpse of how Peter was remembered in the churches during the last decades of the first century. The exhortation "shepherd the flock of God" (1 Pet. 5:2) also recalls the commissioning of Peter in John 21:16, "tend my sheep." Thus, 1 Peter suggests that both the image of Peter as presbyter/shepherd and the tradition of his martyrdom were associated with

Roman Christianity by the end of the first century. When and under what circumstances Peter arrived in Rome we do not know.

ARCHAEOLOGY AND THE QUEST FOR PETER

Archaeological evidence also comes into the picture when we seek to discover what can be known about the historical evidence for Peter. We have seen that the New Testament suggests only that Peter was martyred at Rome. By the end of the second century A.D., Peter was commonly thought to be buried on the Vatican hill. Graffiti scratched on the walls of the site show that by the early fourth century, pilgrims offered prayers to Peter there.[37] Some form of tomb monument appears to go back to the beginning of the third century. However, it is not clear whether the monument designates the actual burial place of the apostle. His body might never have been recovered.[38] Other scholars who insist this monument was built on the site of Peter's burial as it was marked by an earlier tradition cannot be disproven.[39] Yet we have no evidence to support such a claim. The best one can say is that by Constantine's time a monument had been built over a site that was, as early as the third century, attested to be the burial place of the apostle.[40]

The second archaeological excavation connected with the Petrine tradition is the so-called "House of St. Peter" in Capernaum.[41] The site was later covered by an octagonal church and then a basilica. By the fourth century A.D., the site was occupied by a house church. Graffiti scratched in the mud and plaster walls mention Jesus as Lord and Christ. The complex had been cut off from the rest of the buildings in the block by a wall with entrances on the north and south. An arch across the center provided extra support for the roof. Broken pottery in the floor shows that this room was used by a normal family prior to the middle of the first century A.D. Once again, archaeological evidence demonstrates that the tradition which claimed this house as the place in which Jesus had lodged with his disciples could indeed be accurate. While nothing compels us to draw such a conclusion from this evidence, the house itself certainly reflects the type of house owned by Peter's family. Made of dry basalt, these houses had been grouped irregularly around a courtyard. Stairways ran up to the flat roofs.

Archaeologists have also looked for clues about the general prosperity of the region in the first century A.D. The houses in this block were poorer than some excavated elsewhere in Capernaum. Many scholars continue to think that Peter, Andrew, James, and John were poor fishermen. Yet the Gospels report that Zebedee had servants as well as his sons to assist him (Mark 1:20). Would the group of fishermen who became Jesus' first disciples have had an economic reason to abandon their occupation and follow him? Socio-historical information about Galilee in the time of Jesus does not provide an easy answer to this question. Neither the archaeological evidence, which now suggests considerable urbanization in lower Galilee,[42] nor the Gospels themselves refer to grinding poverty of the sort associated with the large urban areas.[43] The numerous tax-collectors, like Levi, responsible for collecting the revenues on commercial goods suggest a busy commercial life. Capernaum was the first town inside the border between Galilee and the Transjordan. Customs dues on goods crossing the border were collected there. Crossing the Sea of Galilee was easy and frequent. Galilean fishermen with hired servants were able to band together in order to avail themselves of the ready market for their product. They would have been higher on the social scale than the village farmers.[44] Therefore, one should not imagine that the stories of the miraculous catch of fish are intended as evidence of divine power coming to rescue "the poor" as in the story of Elijah (1 Kings 17:8–16) and the poor widow, for example.

As we have seen, both John and Luke provide a religious context for understanding why Peter and the others were willing to drop everything to follow Jesus. Archaeological evidence weighs against those modern theories which appeal to economic or social deprivation. If Andrew had been a disciple of John the Baptist, as the Fourth Gospel suggests, then the Baptist's preaching had already heightened expectations for a prophetic renewal of the people. If Luke's chronology is correct, then Jesus had engaged in some period of preaching and healing in the area before he acquired any disciples. We have also seen that other sociological analyses of Judean society emphasize the significance of such a religious renewal for a society in which the political and religious authorities were losing their claim to legitimacy.

THE NAME "PETER"

Archaeological evidence plays a role in another question concerning Peter, his name. Peter's given name, "Simon," is a Greek name, as are the names of his brother, Andrew, and another disciple, Philip.

Acts 15:14 apparently refers to Peter but uses a similar-sounding Semitic name, "Symeon." Some scholars have concluded that Peter followed the custom of other Jews in this period and used both a Semitic and a Greek form of his name.[45] However, this Semitic form appears only in Acts, which also gives two forms for Paul (Semitic, *Saul*; Greek, *Paul*). Therefore, other exegetes assume that Peter's given name was the Greek "Simon." John 1:40–44 links Andrew, Peter, and Philip with the region of Bethsaida. Hellenization in that area could easily lead to the use of Greek names among Jews.[46] As archaeologists continue to discover further evidence for the use of Greek in Roman Palestine, we have even less reason to follow Luke's lead and assume that unlike his brother Andrew, Simon also used a Semitic name.[47]

Most Christians know Simon as "Peter" or "Simon Peter." The double form is common in the Fourth Gospel (e.g., John 6:8, 68; 13:6, 9, 24, 36; 18:10, 15, 25; 20:2; 21:2, 3, 7, 11, 15). Otherwise it appears only in Luke 5:8, Matthew 16:16, and 2 Peter 1:1.[48] The name "Peter" was taken to be the Greek rendering of an Aramaic epithet, *Kephā'*, given Simon by Jesus (so Mark 3:16; John 1:42; Matt. 16:18). Paul routinely refers to Peter as "Cephas," even when writing to Greek-speaking churches (Gal. 1:18, 2:9; 1 Cor. 1:12, 3:22, 9:5, 15:5), though "Peter" appears in Galatians 2:7–8. Clearly the nickname "Cephas" had become the name used for the apostle in early Christian circles. Matthew 16:18 constructs a word-play on the Greek words "Peter" (*Petros*) and "rock" (*petra*) as the commissioning of the apostle. However, none of the other passages explain why Jesus named Simon "Cephas." Since Jesus also nicknamed James and John *Boanērges*, "sons of thunder" (Mark 3:17), the nicknames appear to be independent of the commissioning of Simon.[49]

Archaeological evidence provides some data on the meaning of the Aramaic word *kp'*. In all the examples from the Qumran, the word refers to crags or rocky cliffs which belong to a mountainous region.[50] Though it is often insisted that the Aramaic term *kephā'* never appears as a proper name, an Aramaic text from Elephantine (ca. 416 B.C.) refers to an individual as "son of *Kephā'*." Without further examples, we cannot tell whether *Kephā'* was being used as a name or nickname during the first century A.D.[51] How is the Aramaic name "Cephas" related to the Greek "Petros"? Unlike "Cephas," all of the pre-Christian evidence for the use of "Petros" as a name is debatable.[52] Consequently, the term may well have been created to provide a Greek translation for the Aramaic "Cephas." The use of roots with *petr* as a prefix—in Latin names which Caragounis emphasizes[53]—shows how this form might have easily been adopted as a proper name. Pending further evidence, we may conclude that "Cephas" was a nickname bestowed on Simon by Jesus. It may have been used as a name by others, though we lack evidence from the time of Jesus. Use of "Peter" as the Greek form was facilitated by the use of the stem in Greco-Roman names.

EXCURSUS: PETER AND ROME IN EUSEBIUS

Tradition holds that Peter had been martyred in Rome. *1 Clement* 4–5 refers to the recent deaths of Peter and Paul. The church at Rome had been founded by anonymous Christians by the 40s A.D. The large Jewish community in the city had provided the base for evangelization. 1 Peter 5:13 depicts Peter writing an authoritative letter from his Roman imprisonment. The only epithet used for the author is "fellow elder." Thus, Peter is not the founder of the Roman church in the way in which Paul could claim to be the apostle founder of his churches. How does Peter come to be the central figure in the Roman church? As we have seen, the New Testament does not provide us with any clues. Written early in the second century, Ignatius' letter to the Roman church does not refer to a single bishop there. The large Christian community was probably served by presbyter-bishops and deacons.[54] Eusebius' *Historia Ecclesiastica* contains references to a number of earlier authors which show that the process of converting Peter into the founding bishop of the Roman church began in the second century A.D.

Eusebius takes most of his information about the earliest period of the church from Acts and the letters of Paul. He uses later sources to deal with problems such as the ambiguity that surrounds the leadership in the Jerusalem community. As we have seen, Paul's epistles suggest that Peter, with James and John, was originally the central figure. Later, James appears to be the sole authority there. Eusebius cites a report that he has taken from the *Outlines* of Clement of Alexandria to show that the original group of three had elected James, the brother of the Lord, bishop of Jerusalem (1 *Hist. Eccl.* 2.1).

Second-century authors Justin Martyr and Irenaeus of Lyons both treat the Samaritan magician whom Peter opposes in Acts 8:18–23 as the founder of a second-century Gnostic sect. Legends of a further confrontation between Peter and Simon Magus at Rome are situated during the reign of Claudius in Eusebius' account (*Hist. Eccl.* 2.14). After reporting Peter's victory over the heretic, Eusebius claims that the Roman Christians prevailed upon Mark to record Peter's teaching. After Mark had completed his work, the apostle Peter allegedly authorized its reading in the churches. Eusebius appeals to Clement and to Papias as sources for this story. Papias, he tells us, demonstrated that Mark had based his Gospel on Peter's teaching at Rome by appealing to 1 Peter 5:13 (*Hist. Eccl.* 2.15, 3.39, 6.14). Eusebius assumes that Simon had actually reached the Roman church before Peter. God brings Peter to Rome for the providential purpose of combatting the heresy which was spreading there. He also draws a clear distinction between the oral preaching of Peter and the written Gospel. In order to insure the suitability of the Gospel as a representation of Peter's teaching, the story has Peter approve the completed work.

Eusebius indicates that Peter and Paul were martyred by Nero, whose madness was so extreme that he even killed members of his own family. A quotation from the late second-century presbyter Gaius intended to counter Montanist claims identifies the tomb monuments of Peter on the Vatican hill and of Paul on the Ostian Way. Gaius refers to both as "founders" of the Roman church. Eusebius supplements that information with a letter from Dionysius of Corinth that had been written to the bishop of Rome, Soter (ca. A.D. 170). Dionysius refers to the common missionary effort of Peter and Paul in both Corinth and Rome. He then observes that they were martyred in Rome at the same time (*Hist. Eccl.* 2.25). The legend that Peter's crucifixion took place head downwards appears attached to Eusebius' list of the regions to which each of the Twelve had gone to preach (*Hist. Eccl.* 3.1). Yet another legend, taken from Clement's *Stromateis*, reports an encounter between Peter and his wife, who goes to be martyred before him (*Hist. Eccl.* 3.30). Eusebius apparently follows the lead of Irenaeus in assuming that Peter actually came to Rome before Paul. All of these early traditions develop clues taken from the New Testament or reflect later legends about Peter's martyrdom. Dionysius' emphasis on the fact that Peter and Paul had sowed the seed of the gospel together—first in Corinth and then in Rome, where they had both died at the same time—appears to be a piece of ecclesial polemic. The seed sown by the apostles in Corinth is identical to that sown in Rome. Therefore, Dionysius can address its bishop as an equal.

After treating the deaths of Peter and Paul, Eusebius begins to note the succession of bishops in the Roman church. In order to provide the record of the succession in Jerusalem, Eusebius draws upon Hegesippus for the list of Jewish Christian successors to James (*Hist. Eccl.* 3.11). By the end of the second century, major sees had begun to construct succession lists. Jerusalem, Corinth, and Rome all claim some share in the Petrine ministry. Though without ancient authorities to back up this assertion, Eusebius also presumes that Peter had been bishop of Antioch before Ignatius (*Hist. Eccl.* 3.36).[55] Clearly, every major see sought to begin its ecclesiastical history with apostolic founders. If one adds the association between Mark and Egypt (Alexandria), then no less than five cities claimed some connection with Peter. The church founded on Peter's rock was hardly encompassed by the Roman See alone!

The quest for a life of the apostle Peter takes us from a family of apparently prosperous Galilean fishermen to an ancient tomb monument in the city of Rome. Although Paul persists in referring to the apostle by the Aramaic form of his nickname, "Cephas," both the apostle Simon, and his brother, Andrew, had Greek names. The family may have been accustomed to dealing with the Greek-speaking populace in the region as well as Aramaic-speaking Jews. We later see Peter dealing with both Aramaic-speaking and Greek-speaking Christians within the Jerusalem community (e.g., Acts 6:1) and preaching in churches like those in Antioch, Corinth, and Rome where Greek was the common language. Perhaps, his brother, Andrew, was already a follower of John the Baptist before the two became disciples of Jesus. In addition, Jesus and his disciples were welcomed in the family home in Capernaum.

The prominence which Peter appears to have enjoyed among the disciples of the earthly Jesus may be partially due to the long-standing involvement of his entire family with the religious movements around John the Baptist and Jesus.[56] Consequently, Peter's conviction that Jesus is God's "anointed" probably reflects a view that he shared with other followers of Jesus. At the level of the historical Jesus, this confession must be understood in first-century Jewish terms, not as a reflection of post-Easter developments in Christology. Similarly, the real dangers confronting populist preachers like the Baptist and Jesus, especially if they undertake actions challenging the legitimating symbols of power, provide sufficient historical background for the debate and anxiety which accompany Jesus' move to Jerusalem. Peter's assertion that he will be more loyal than the others, his attempt to carry out that promise, and his denials when identified by by-standers—all reflect plausible social relationships.

Peter's role in the post-Easter community may have been supported and shaped by his experience of the risen Lord, but it also derives from a close relationship with the historical Jesus. Jesus did not establish a line of succession such as one associates with philosophical schools in which Peter became the "head" of the movement and was thus able to govern or teach in Jesus' name independently of the other disciples. Instead, we find those who had been closest to the historical Jesus—Peter, the sons of Zebedee, and the brother of the Lord—providing the leadership needed in the Jerusalem community. When authorities in Jerusalem became suspicious of the Christian group, they arrested, interrogated, and even executed persons who were perceived to be creating trouble by preaching about Jesus. Peter probably suffered both arrest and imprisonment before he was forced to leave the city.

Since leadership was shared among those who had known Jesus, Peter's apparent loss of personal authority in Jerusalem should not be attributed to ideological conflict. Peter was able and willing to preach to and associate with Greek-speaking, gentile Christians. As far as we can tell, he did not oppose the missionary efforts directed primarily at Gentiles that were sponsored by the Antioch church and that later became the basis for Paul's independent missionary efforts. Though Paul's polemic against Judaizing in Galatians created an impression that Peter had been responsible for dividing the community at Antioch, one suspects that Peter himself would have been baffled by the charge. In the matter of table fellowship, Peter and the others have merely acted as any Jew—ancient or modern—might. The observance of the stricter party takes priority in determining commensality. Peter's continued association with gentile Christians was required by his subsequent visits to churches like Corinth and Rome. How Peter came to be in Rome we do not know. We have seen that late second-century tradition associated his arrival with Paul's. By the end of the first century, both Peter and Paul were known to have died as martyrs in Rome under Nero (ca. A.D. 62).

Evidence for our sketch of Peter's life is fragmentary and subject to widely different evaluations. Historians must create much of the framework in order to give a plausible account of persons and events in the distant past. We must admit that at almost every turn, we lack sufficient evidence to decide between conflicting interpretations. Historians make their judgments based on the credibility of their overall understanding of the development of early Christianity. Both information about ancient society as well as contemporary understandings about the dynamics of social and religious groups play a role in such constructions, as we have seen.

The ecclesial assertions about Peter which have shaped the self-understanding of different Christian churches do not depend upon detailed, historical arguments. The images of Peter embodied in the New Testament narratives form the basis of Christian sentiments about the apostle. Even though our historical reconstruction suggests that Peter should be understood as an ecclesial centrist rather than as the foundation for an ideological party in the early Church, the New Testament portraits may convey a different message. When we investigate the use of the Peter/Paul conflict to focus divisions within the community, we will see that ideological understandings of the apostle have a long history.

We have also seen that one cannot ask about the historicity of a particular Gospel passage without assessing the relationship between the text and the overall literary and thematic emphases of a particular writer. Increasing emphasis on individual Gospels as narrative wholes rather than as collections of variously edited sources reminds scholars that all episodes should be considered in their relationship to the larger whole. Emphasis on the rhetorical conventions in New Testament Epistles reminds scholars that assertions about persons and events must be evaluated in the context of the agenda in a particular passage. We will turn to a reading of the Gospels and the Epistles as evidence for the divergent visions of Peter in the early Christian communities. Such study picks up those narrative details which an historical reconstruction must omit. We have already seen that Luke shapes the confrontation between Jesus' disciples and religious authorities on the model of the early Passion narrative. Though such details cannot be admitted as historical evidence, they provide the reader of Luke's narrative with an unspoken reassurance about Peter's character. Not only has Peter turned to "strengthen his brothers" by establishing the Jerusalem community;[57] he has recovered from the fear evident in the denial of Jesus. Peter becomes the model for other disciples as they confront civic and religious authorities.

NOTES

1. See, e.g., Raymond E. Brown, Karl P. Donfried, and John Reumann, eds., *Peter in the New Testament* (New York: Paulist Press, 1973), 90–93. The editors have adopted a formal classification of Resurrection stories which assumes that some were church-founding, as here, and others mission-inaugurating, as in the call of the apostle Paul. They further presume that community-founding on the part of the historical Jesus is improbable even though the Dead Sea Scrolls provide evidence for the use of similar expressions by a group which did engage in re-founding the elect remnant of Israel (CD 3, 19; 4 Q flor 6; 4 Q pPs 37, 3, 15f.). Matthew is responsible for casting the saying as one which concerns founding a "church." See Joachim Gnilka, *Das Matthäusevangelium. II Teil. Kommentar zu Kap. 14,1–28,20*, HTKNT 2 (Freiburg: Herder, 1988), 61–63. It may be impossible to reconstruct a primitive tradition behind this saying. However, the impossibility of community-founding by the historical Jesus that is assumed by many earlier discussions of this tradition rests on presumptions that are not widely shared today. At least those scholars who think that we can reconstruct some picture of the historical Jesus on the basis of the surviving traditions about him generally concede that Jesus sought to re-establish the people of God. The boundary- and convention-breaking egalitarianism of the ministry of Jesus—who reached out to the sinners, the marginal, and the poor, and extended to them a more prominent place in the Kingdom than the righteous (see J. D. Crossan, *The Historical Jesus: The Life of a Mediterranean Jewish Peasant* [San Francisco: Harper Collins, 1991], 263–91)—provides a context within which such a tradition might be reinterpreted. Peter is not being credited with either the religious insight of a scribe or the juridical authority of a vizier. Jesus' community of those who belong to the Kingdom of God will not be based upon the sort of persons and power typical of the religious and political institutions of his time (or ours). Rather, it is to be built upon persons like Peter—someone whose background, education, trade, class, and status make it virtually impossible that he could occupy a position of authority, leadership, or power in the social and religious world. If some variant of this saying does go back to the historical Jesus, then it must embody the irony of reversal so typical of Jesus' sayings and parables. The ironies are invisible to moderns who no longer understand the restrictions that social origins placed on individuals in the ancient world. They are also invisible to readers whose religious upbringing has taught them to identify as successors to the apostles persons who do occupy the educational, socio-economic, and religious positions of power that are sanctioned by the larger society.

2. See Rudolf Pesch, *Simon Petrus*, Geschichte und geschichtliche Bedeu-

tung des ersten Jüngers Jesu Christi, Päpste und Papstum Bd. 15 (Stuttgart: Anton Hiersemann, 1980), 2–7.

3.   Pesch, *Simon Petrus*, 147 n. 8.

4.   For a detailed discussion of the criteria used in historical Jesus research, see John P. Meier, *A Marginal Jew, Rethinking the Historical Jesus 1: The Roots of the Problem and the Person* (Garden City: Doubleday, 1991), 167–95.

5.   The two most important recent studies of this phenomenon are Marvin Goodmann, *The Ruling Class of Judea: The Origins of the Jewish Revolt Against Rome AD 66–70* (Cambridge: Cambridge University Press, 1987); and Richard Fenn, *The Death of Herod: An Essay in the Sociology of Religion* (Cambridge: Cambridge University Press, 1992).

6.   Fenn, *The Death of Herod*, 41.

7.   *The Death of Herod*, 16–20, 70–72. Luke's Gospel deals with the apparent rejection of this normative relationship between sons and their father by showing that Jesus dutifully accepted his obligations to his earthly father even though he was aware of his eventual calling to be about the business of his heavenly Father (Luke 2:41–52).

8.   Fenn, *The Death of Herod*, 89.

9.   See, e.g., Joseph A. Fitzmyer, *The Gospel According to Luke (I–IX)*, AB 28 (Garden City: Doubleday, 1981), 541–42.

10. Fitzmyer speaks of the healing of Peter's mother-in-law as "part of the psychological background for the call of Simon, the fisherman." The narrative does not reflect on Peter's motivation. The only "psychological background" at issue is what the reader might consider plausible motivation. See *Luke (I–IX)*, 549.

11. Pesch, *Simon Petrus*, 15–20.

12. Fitzmyer suggests that the story of Peter's mother-in-law served as a paradigm for the stories about the Galilean women who serve Jesus in Luke (8:1–3; 23:49, 55); see *Luke (I–IX)*, 549.

13. Pesch, *Simon Petrus*, 21–22.

14. See Heikki Räisänen, *The Messianic Secret in Mark*, trans. C. Tuckett (Edinburgh: T. and T. Clark, 1990), 174–84. Räisänen rejects the historicizing explanation which moves from Mark's story to the assertion that the historical Jesus rejected Peter's use of the title Messiah because of its nationalist associations.

15. See the discussion in Räisänen, *The Messianic Secret*, 175–76.

16. *The Messianic Secret*, 182–83.

17. See Fenn, *The Death of Herod*, 7–8.

18. See Fitzmyer, *Luke (I–IX)*, 774–75.

19. See Meier, *Marginal Jew*, 168–71.

20. For a history of the interpretation of this pericope, which challenges modern readings that treat it as polemic against the disciples, see Robert

W. Herron, *Mark's Account of Peter's Denial of Jesus: A History of Its Interpretation* (New York: University Press of America, 1991).

21. See, e.g., Rudolf Pesch, *Das Markusevangelium II. Teil Kommentar zu Kap. 8,27–16,20*, HTKNT II/2 (Freiburg: Herder, 1977), 2:377–84.

22. Joseph A. Fitzmyer, *The Gospel According to Luke (X–XXIV)*, AB 28A (Garden City: Doubleday, 1981), 1422–23.

23. Fitzmyer's remark is typical of the assumption that many modern readers make in response to this story: "Simon Peter is clearly being singled out by the Lukan Jesus; though he is part of the apostolic group that will be tested by the coming satanic plot, *and though he will sink lower than the rest of them*, Jesus has prayed for him" (*Luke (X–XXIV)*, 1422; italics mine).

24. Fenn, *The Death of Herod*, 98–100.

25. Herron, *Mark's Account of Peter's Denial*, 142–44. Herron treats the "failed" discipleship of Peter as an opening in Mark's narrative for a theology of reconciliation. This literary dimension of the narrative fits the emphasis on failure and repentance common in the ancient commentaries on this text.

26. For a detailed defense of the position that Galatians 2:1–10 refers to the so-called "famine visit" in Acts 11:27–30, and that the Antioch episode referred to in Galatians 2:11–14 was the occasion for the Jerusalem council of Acts 15, see Richard Longenecker, *Galatians*, WBC 41 (Dallas: Word Books, 1990), lxxiv–lxxxiii. This position attempts to reconcile the chronological difficulties created by Paul's references in Galatians with the chronology of Acts by presuming an early date for the composition of Galatians as well as Paul's conversion and assuming that the "fourteen years" refers back to the conversion. These assumptions create other problems for understanding the Pauline letters, such as Paul's reference to his flight from Damascus at the time of Aretas (2 Cor. 11:31); the chronology of the collection for the poor at Jerusalem; and the clear similarity between the issues which spark the Jerusalem meeting in Galatians 2:2–5 and in Acts 15:1.

27. See Robert Tannehill, "The Functions of Peter's Mission Speeches in the Narrative of Acts," *NTS* 37 (1991): 401.

28. "The Functions of Peter's Mission Speeches," 407–10.

29. "The Functions of Peter's Mission Speeches," 411.

30. This chronological notice may be part of Luke's literary interest in shaping the stories of the trials and deaths of early Christians along the lines of the Passion narrative. The account of the death of Stephen even contains some parallels to the Markan Passion, which are not found in Luke's Gospel: the false witnesses (Mark 14:56–57; Matt. 26:60–61; Acts 6:13); the prediction of the destruction of the temple (Mark 14:58; Matt. 26:61; Acts 6:14); the temple "made with hands" (Mark 14:58; Acts

7:48); the blasphemy charge (Mark 14:64; Matt. 26:65; Acts 6:11); and the high priest's question (Mark 14:61; Matt. 26:63; Acts 7:1). See Craig C. Hill, *Hellenists and Hebrews: Reappraising Division within the Earliest Church* (Minneapolis: Fortress Press, 1992), 58–60.

31. Though the suggestion made by Luke that Paul's activities were centered in Jerusalem (Acts 8:1–3) seems to be without any historical basis, given Paul's own testimony that he was unknown to the church there (Gal. 1:22), see the discussion of this point in Hill, *Hellenists and Hebrews*, 32–40.

32. The reference to stretching out and binding of hands with a belt appears in the prophecy of Paul's arrest in Acts 21:11–12. See, e.g., Raymond E. Brown, *The Gospel According to John (XIII–XXI)*, AB 29A (Garden City: Doubleday, 1970), 1107.

33. As a reference to crucifixion, the image of binding the hands could refer to the prisoner's carrying the crossbar to the site. This reading avoids the difficulty of our assuming that the idea of bound hands indicates the act of crucifixion itself—an assumption which would make the saying refer to Peter's being crucified prior to his being compelled to go where he does not wish. See George R. Beasley-Murray, *John*, WBC 36 (Waco, TX: Word Books, 1987), 408–9.

34. Raymond E. Brown and John P. Meier, *Antioch and Rome: New Testament Cradles of Catholic Christianity* (Ramsey, NJ: Paulist Press, 1983), 135.

35. James D. G. Dunn, *Unity and Diversity in the New Testament: An Inquiry into the Character of Earliest Christianity* (Philadelphia: Westminster Press, 1977), 116.

36. R. E. Brown and Meier, *Antioch and Rome*, 130–32. The addressees may have been congregations in rural Asia Minor that had been founded as a result of the Jerusalem-based mission with which Peter was associated.

37. See Daniel Wm. O'Connor, *Peter in Rome*: The Literary, Liturgical and Archaeological Evidence (New York: Columbia University Press, 1969), 180–82.

38. Attempts to identify one of the skeletons found in the structures which make up the early monument under the Vatican as the remains of the apostle are extremely hypothetical. For an account which favors the view that such a skeleton may be identified as Peter's, see John E. Walsh, *The Bones of St. Peter* (Garden City: Doubleday, 1982). In order to maintain this claim, scholars have to make a virtue of the lack of markings indicating that the bones are those of the apostle by claiming that the danger of persecution required an unmarked grave.

39. Pesch, *Simon Petrus*, 131f.

40. See, e.g., D. W. O'Connor, *Peter in Rome*, 205.

41.   See Jerome Murphy O'Connor, *The Holy Land: An Archaeological Guide from Earliest Times to 1700*, 2d ed. (New York: Oxford University Press, 1986), 189–91.

42.   J. Andrew Overman, "Who Were the First Urban Christians? Urbanization in Galilee in the First Century," in *Society of Biblical Literature Seminar Papers 1988*, ed. D. Lull (Atlanta: Scholars Press, 1988), 160–68; Douglas R. Edwards, "First Century Urban/Rural Relations in Lower Galilee: Exploring the Archaeological and Literary Evidence," in *Society of Biblical Literature Seminar Papers 1988*, 169–82.

43.   Sean Freyne, *Galilee, Jesus and the Gospels: Literary and Historical Approaches* (Philadelphia: Fortress Press, 1988), 38–40.

44.   Freyne, *Galilee*, 154f. Capernaum appears to have been a center for the production of salted fish, which was exported from the region (*Galilee*, 159f).

45.   See, e.g., Joseph A. Fitzmyer, "Aramaic *Kephā'* and Peter's Name in the New Testament," in *To Advance the Gospel* (New York: Crossroad, 1981), 112f.

46.   Oscar Cullmann, *Peter: Disciple—Apostle—Martyr*, 2d ed., trans. Floyd V. Filson (London: SCM, 1962), 22.

47.   I also see no reason to assume that Acts 15:14 refers to a person other than Simon Peter. Rudolf Pesch suggests that Luke may be "hebraizing" James' speech by using the form "Symeon"; see R. Pesch, "Πετρος," in *Exegetisches Wörterbuch zum Neuen Testament*, Bd. 3, ed. H. Balz and G. Schneider (Stuttgart: W. Kohlhammer, 1983), 195.

48.   As we have already seen, Luke 5:8, the story of the miraculous catch, may be a variant of the tradition behind the episode in John 21:1–14.

49.   Chrys C. Caragounis argues against the common view that "you are *Petros*" is intended to introduce a play on Simon's name that would show him to be the *petra* on which the church is founded. The sentence is a solemn pronouncement that Peter's confession of Jesus as Messiah is the "rock" on which the church is founded. See *Peter and the Rock*, BZNW 58 (New York: Walter de Gruyter, 1990), 109–11. However, the linguistic evidence Caragonis introduces to show that the terms *petros* and *petra* are interchangeable seems to support the view which he himself rejects; see the review of *Peter and the Rock* by Gérard Claudel in *Biblica* 71 (1990): 570–76.

50.   Fitzmyer, "Aramaic *Kephā'*," 115.

51.   "Aramaic *Kephā'*," 116–18.

52.   "Aramaic *Kephā'*," 119; Claudel, *Biblica* 71 (1990): 573.

53.   Caragounis, *Peter and the Rock*, 18–23.

54.   R. E. Brown and Meier, *Antioch and Rome*, 202.

55.   See Pesch, *Simon Petrus*, 105.

56.   If this suggestion is correct, then the family of Peter forms a striking

contrast to the dangerous divisions within families that were evident in the social and political struggles for power at the time, as well as in the experience of disciples "turned in" by relatives—e.g., Matthew 10:21, 34–36 (see Fenn, *The Death of Herod*, 91 n. 6). Peter's family appears to be even more receptive to Jesus' preaching than members of Jesus' own family (Mark 6:1–6; John 6:42 preserves an independent variant of this tradition).

57.   See Fitzmyer, *Luke (X–XXIV)*, 1423.

CHAPTER 2

Peter in New Testament Narratives
Mark and Matthew

PETER AS A NARRATIVE CHARACTER

Most readers respond to Peter and the other figures in the Gospels as they do to persons described in news stories, biographies, documentaries, or historical novels. Even though the individuals and events depicted in such sources may be presented from a definite point of view, people assume that they are getting a "real picture" of the persons involved. One member of our Bible-study group provoked a heated discussion when she wanted to know if the Taylor Caldwell novel *Dear and Glorious Physician* gave her an accurate picture of Luke. In fact, most Christians have constructed a mental representation of Jesus and his disciples made up of favorite incidents from the various Gospels and such favorite books or works of art that create images of what the world of Jesus was like. Even though they are distressed by the suggestion that the evangelists were working with their own images of figures they did not know through direct experience, many parishioners are more upset when the Gospels clash with one another in their personal stories about Jesus and his disciples.

It is easy to show parishioners that the Gospel writers cannot be collapsed into a single point of view. We have already seen that there are major differences between Mark on the one hand, and both Luke and John on the other. The differences between Mark and Matthew are less evident to the casual reader. We have seen that Matthew heightens the significance of Peter's confession that Jesus is Messiah by incorporating a beatitude that affirms the divine origin of Peter's insight and sayings that confirm his later role in the community. This addition also moderates the severity of juxtaposing Peter's confession with the rebuke by Jesus when Peter fails to accept the prediction of Jesus' Passion (cf. Mark 8:27–33; Matt. 16:13–23). Luke's version omits the rebuke of Peter altogether (Luke 9:18–22). Matthew adds an incident with Peter to the story of Jesus' walking on water. Mark concludes the episode with a sharp denunciation of the disciples as being without understanding and hard-hearted (Mark 6:45–52). In the Gospel of Matthew, Peter himself begins to walk toward Jesus on the water. When Peter becomes fearful of the storm, Jesus must rescue his sinking disciple. Jesus comments on Peter's "little faith," but as they enter the boat, the wind ceases and the disciples worship Jesus as "Son of God" (Matt. 14:22–32). Thus the episode demonstrates that the disciples have some faith and that they are able to grasp the truth manifest in the miracle itself.

Since most readers do not consider walking on water a credible event, they are willing to concede that the evangelist has reshaped the Markan miracle story in order to convey a different understanding of Peter and the other disciples than that in Mark. Most Christians find that Matthew's version fits their image of Peter better than the harsh Markan conclusion does. If one presumes that the unflattering details about Jesus' disciples are historical facts which later Christians erased from the record, then Matthew's Gospel appears to have shifted from the real, fallible, uncomprehending Peter to a more admirable follower. Peter trusts Jesus enough to risk leaving the boat and fails only when overwhelmed by the storm.

The ancient tradition that the material in Mark's Gospel came to the evangelist directly from Peter might suggest that we should give priority to the Markan evidence whenever the Gospels diverge. Scholars today recognize that Mark is not based upon memories of the apostle Peter.[1] By the second century, a tradition had arisen which alleged that Mark had written down Peter's recollections (see Eusebius, *Historia Ecclesiastica* 3.39.15). Had Peter been the proximate source of Mark's tradition, uncertainty about Jewish customs or Palestinian geography would not exist. Peter is absent from several of the most vivid, theologically significant scenes in the Gospel. Finally, the unfavorable elements attached to Peter in Mark would hardly be found in a Gospel dependent upon his testimony.[2] Thus, Mark's Gospel cannot be given priority over other early traditions on the grounds that its author was writing down what Peter had told him.

Redaction criticism has taught us to look for the unique perspective which informs the way in which each evangelist shapes his material. The unexpectedly harsh portrayal of Jesus' disciples in Mark plays a crucial role in redaction-critical studies of Mark. The evangelist is not just reporting. Rather, the portrait of the disciples is an important clue to his point of view.[3] In more recent years, redaction criticism has been challenged by the emergence of narrative criticism.[4] One cannot determine an author's point of view by focusing on his or her editing of sources and the repetition of dominant themes. Too often, the source against which an interpreter defines the evangelist's redactional work is itself a scholarly creation. Identification of dominant themes or theological tendencies frequently depends upon judgments based on criteria external to the text. Narrative criticism uses the insights of literary criticism and the study of ancient rhetorical practice to treat the Gospel as a literary whole. Who is Peter as a character in a specific Gospel? What responses does the evangelist expect from his audience when they hear the various sections about Peter? Is the reader expected to identify with Peter or to adopt the omniscient perspective of the narrator?[5]

Literary analyses that appeal to the text as a whole are more accessible to general readers than the complex reconstructions of tradition-history and redaction found in historical-critical treatments. However, we have seen that sociological and historical information about first-century Palestine frequently challenges the adequacy of our modern reactions to the human interactions depicted in the New Testament. Literary analyses are even more dependent upon the critic's sensitivity to the cultural codes inherent in the actions of characters than are traditional methods of historical criticism. Therefore, many exegetes insist on an eclectic method of analysis that combines results of redaction criticism and narrative criticism.[6] Our surveys of the figure of Peter in the narratives of the New Testament will combine insights derived from newer literary studies of the evangelists with the results of historical-critical interpretation.

Earlier redaction-critical theories frequently reinforced the antagonistic, dualistic views of early Christian origins that we have seen in discussions of Peter and Paul. We have seen that Mark silences Peter's messianic confession and immediately introduces the necessity of Jesus' suffering. Exegetes often suggested that Mark's emphasis on the cross corrects the theology of divine power that Mark inherited from one of his sources, the collection of Jesus' miracles.[7] More recently, scholars have moved away from the version of redaction criticism which sets the evangelist in tension with his sources to one which stresses the function of the disciples as examples in a didactic narrative.[8] This type of redaction criticism provides an opening for the insights of literary analysis.[9] Ernest Best connects Peter's inability to accept the word of the cross with the two-stage healing of the blind man (Mark 8:22–26). The lessons which the disciples learn are those which Mark expected his readers to apply to their experience: "all understanding of discipleship begins with the cross," Best writes, "and it never moves to any other point of orientation."[10]

Both redaction criticism and literary analyses can evaluate the significance of particular incidents and details only within the context of the narrative as a whole. Redaction criticism incorporates statements about the narrative as a whole by speaking of the author's intentions and the situation of the community that he addresses. Literary methods may describe the plot as a whole, or they may emphasize the perspective taken by the ideal reader. Reader-response criticism argues that the text creates an implied author and a narrator as well as an ideal reader and narratee. The ironies in the story, such as the enigma of the blindly perceptive Peter, depend upon a reader who knows more than the characters know about its overall plot.[11]

The tension between the plot that is actually narrated in the words of the text and the plot that the author expects the reader to construct is particularly evident in Mark. Even though Peter and the other disciples consistently resist Jesus' Passion predictions, Mark's readers know that Jesus' mission leads to the cross. References to the death of Jesus are introduced early in the story (Mark 2:19–20; 3:6).[12] The rash promises of Peter and the others that they will suffer with Jesus rather than deny him are entwined with Jesus' words about their mutual fate (Mark 14:27–31). The certainty of Jesus' death and Peter's denial is matched by a promise that Jesus will be raised and go before the disciples to Galilee (v. 28). The reader is intended to recognize the Easter references in this promise.

When Mark comes to a sudden conclusion with the frightened women fleeing the tomb (Mark 16:7–8), the reader is reminded of the earlier prediction. The angel sends the women to "tell his disciples and Peter that he is going ahead you to Galilee; there you will see him just as he told you" (v. 7). The phrases "his disciples and Peter" and "he goes before you into Galilee" clearly indicate that the episode in 14:27–31 is the one to which the angel alludes. Though exegetes sometimes argue that "you will see him" refers to the Parousia in Galilee, a Resurrection appearance such as that supplied in Matthew 28:16–20 is clearly what Mark expects his reader to supply in completing the plot of the narrative.[13] On the one hand, the reader recognizes that Jesus' own prophetic words about his Resurrection have been fulfilled. On the other, the fear, silence, and flight of the women repeats and reinforces the pattern already established by the other disciples and Peter.[14] Debates over the ending of Mark are fueled by the thwarted expectations of success. Jesus had told the disciples, for example, that the vision of the Transfiguration could be told "after the resurrection" (Mark 9:9).[15]

Another indication that the text of Mark presumes a reader who will expand the story and interpret the actions of its characters in light of a later story which is not narrative appears in the so-called "Markan apocalypse" (Mark 13). Mark 13:9–13 describes the trials of the disciples as they preach the gospel before "all the nations." The reader implied by the narrative knows that this shocking conclusion is not the final word. Mark's actual readers, ancient or modern, know that if Jesus' promise had not been fulfilled, we would not be listening to the gospel.

The Gospels themselves provide evidence that later readers "filled in" the narrative gaps in Mark's text. Matthew adds two Resurrection appearances to the tomb story. Jesus appears to the women (Matt. 28:9–10). Then he appears to the disciples in Galilee (28:16–20). Additional endings were also supplied for Mark's Gospel itself (Mark 16:9–20). However effective the dramatic irony of Mark's original ending, later Christians have insisted on spelling out the reversal in the disciples wrought by Easter. Matthew's additional material is relatively brief. Luke and John are considerably more extensive. John 21:15–17 has the risen Lord extract a threefold profession of love from Peter. Thus, Peter is able to reverse his earlier denial. The hints of future mission are spelled out in Luke's second volume, which depicts the witness of Jesus' disciples.

Some modern interpreters reject the readings of Mark embodied in later Gospels as irrelevant to a decision about the way the ambiguities in the Markan narrative are to be resolved by the ideal reader. They assume that since Matthew and Luke make Peter a model of Christian discipleship, one cannot credit the softening of the harsh statements about the disciple found in their narratives. John, on the other hand, stands closer to the anti-Peter tradition that such interpreters detect in Mark. Though John appears to rehabilitate Peter, chapter 21 is often viewed as the final redactional ending to the Gospel. The final editor may have sought to accommodate the unique Johannine tradition to the Petrine Christianity of the larger church.[16] As indicated above, the presumption of ideological dualism in the reconstruction of early Christian history appears to be a modern methodological assumption. The later evangelists can provide a valuable example of how the Markan narrative was read in the first century.

PETER IN THE GOSPEL OF MARK

References to Peter frame Mark's account of Jesus' disciples. Jesus' ministry opens with the calling of Peter and Andrew at the Sea of Galilee (Mark 1:16–20). It concludes with the angel's message to "his disciples and Peter" (Mark 16:7). We have also seen that episodes concerning Peter spotlight the general issue of discipleship in Mark. Though Peter recognizes that Jesus is God's Messiah, he is unable to grasp the message of the cross. We have also seen that some hints provided in the text suggest that the reader should know that Peter and the other disciples will overcome the apparent deficiencies of their behavior within the narrative.

Mary Ann Tolbert takes the allegory in the parable of the sower as the key to the narrative situation of the disciples in Mark. Seeds without roots wither when the hot sun strikes them (Mark 4:6, 17). The first half of the Gospel demonstrates that the disciples do not comprehend Jesus' mission. When the Passion finally arrives, they show that they have no roots. The disciples flee (Mark 14:50).[17] Peter's attempt to distinguish himself from the other disciples (14:29) fails when he denies Jesus (Mark 14:66–72). The flight of the women in Mark 16:8 completes the picture of failure. None of Jesus' followers stands up to the testing imposed by the Passion.[18] The individual episodes which involve Peter belong to the story of Jesus' followers. The question about how the actions of the disciples and other characters will relate to the divine necessity that the Son of man suffer forms a crucial element in the plot.[19] By bringing about the suffering which is the fate of the Son of man, Jesus' enemies unwittingly help him accomplish his divine destiny. Jesus' disciples, on the other hand, would stop Jesus from undertaking that mission if they could. Peter represents their opposition (Mark 8:31–33).[20]

Exegetes have suggested that this tension between the failures of Jesus' disciples and the success of Jesus' ministry that is evident in the centurion's confession (Mark 15:39)[21] points to the interplay between human weakness and divine power in Mark.[22] Since Peter is referred to either as an individual or as a member of the inner group with James and John in every section of the narrative which deals with the disciples, the reader builds up a complex picture of the apostle.[23] One must remember that the evangelists do not create their characters as novelists might, since even Mark is constrained by traditional material about the apostle.[24] But we may ask how the character of Peter is developed as the narrative proceeds. Do the final scenes interpret the earlier ones as a plausible outgrowth of what the reader has already learned about Peter? Or are they intended as a shock which leads the reader to question the image of Peter that she or he has developed?[25]

Unlike many of the minor characters whose faith in Jesus is exhibited when they ask for healing (e.g., Mark 5:21–43; 9:14–29),[26] his disciples are called away from their daily occupations. First-century readers acquainted with the Old Testament might interpret such a sudden interruption along the lines of familiar call stories. The prophet Samuel takes the young David from tending his father's sheep (1 Sam. 16:1–13). Elijah finds his successor, Elisha, plowing with his oxen (1 Kings 19:19–21). In such cases, the prophet, who possesses God's Spirit, commands an individual, who will play a crucial role in the future, to leave a relatively obscure position and to follow him. Mark's reader knows that Jesus possesses the Spirit (Mark 1:10) and is preaching repentance in view of the impending reign of God (Mark 1:14–15). Since the two pairs of brothers immediately leave fishing and follow Jesus, the reader may conclude that they recognize that Jesus possesses the Spirit. The reader might also expect that, like Elisha, they will come to share the Spirit possessed by their master.

The story reinforces this expectation with the commissioning saying that Jesus addresses to Peter and Andrew, "Follow me, and I will cause you [pl.] to become fishers of human beings" (Mark 1:17; my translation). Read against prophetic sayings in which Yahweh sends "fishers" to catch a sinful Israel on the day of the Lord (e.g., Jer. 16:16; Amos 4:2; Hab. 1:14–15),[27] the saying picks up the call to repentance in the notice about Jesus' preaching. Read against the Christian's experience of the later missionary efforts of the disciples (Mark 13:9–10), it points forward to future greatness.

The next episode, the healing of Peter's mother-in-law (Mark 1:29–31), contributes to the reader's positive expectations. Unlike the longer healing narratives in which Mark explores the issues of Jesus' identity and the faith of those who seek healing, this story is not developed at all. The exorcism which Jesus has just performed in the synagogue will establish his reputation as a healer throughout the region (Mark 1:28,

32–34). As soon as Jesus enters the house of Peter and Andrew with his four disciples, someone tells him about the sick woman (v. 30b). Jesus heals her, and she, in turn, serves the group (v. 31b). Such service could be understood as the appropriate hospitality shown to a visitor who bears God's power. Because the impoverished widow uses her last grain and oil to provide for the prophet, Elijah's presence in her house enables the woman, her son, and her prophet to survive the famine (1 Kings 17:8–24). Early Christian readers might also have recognized "serving" as part of their own experience as a community. However, the traditional form of a miracle story requires some evidence that the healing has occurred. Reference to "serving" may have been no more than the traditional evidence that Peter's mother-in-law had been healed.[28] Unlike the males in her household, she returns to her routine activities.

Our expectations that Jesus' new disciples will participate in their master's activities are confirmed in the next references to Simon and the others. Jesus has withdrawn to the desert to pray without them (1:35). With hindsight, the reader may link this scene to the prayer in the garden of Gethsemane. There, although Jesus takes the disciples as a group and then the inner circle, he is finally isolated from his disciples by their failure to keep watch with him (14:35, 39). The other instance in which Jesus withdraws to pray alone (Mark 6:46) sets up the second rescue at sea miracle. Jesus comes on the stormy waters to rescue the frightened disciples (Mark 6:45–52). Mark ends that episode with the ominous remark that the disciples' "hearts were hardened" (v. 52). Thus, they are suddenly thrust into the same category as Jesus' opponents (Mark 3:5) and the crowds who cannot penetrate Jesus' parables and so be saved (Mark 4:11–12).[29]

Such ironies occur to the Markan reader or audience who knows what is coming. Repeated performance enables audiences to make such connections. But the irony plays off initial scenes which confirm the established pattern of teacher/disciple relationships. Jesus has withdrawn to pray. His disciples, referred to as "Simon and those with him" (Mark 1:36), seek Jesus to report that everyone is looking for him. Jesus then departs with his disciples to preach throughout Galilee (vv. 38–39). The disciples have access to Jesus which the crowds do not. In this instance, the others can be referred to as those who are with Peter. Thus, in two short passages Mark has moved Peter out of the group of four into the foreground. Though the house belonged to Peter and Andrew, Peter's mother-in-law was healed by Jesus. Now

Peter appears to be the leader of the group in the absence of Jesus.[30] Geographically, this scene marks a transition away from the events that occurred in the vicinity of Peter's house.[31] But the initial episodes that occur in and near Peter's house give Peter and his family a prominent place in relationship to Jesus.

These stories depict Jesus with four disciples from the same region. In our discussion of the life of Peter, we saw that the evidence suggests that Peter's family (and perhaps, the family of Zebedee) supported the renewal movements associated with John the Baptist and then Jesus. The calling of Levi, the toll collector, also occurs by the sea. As in the earlier case, it is followed by a meal in Levi's house. There the meal has a new focus. Instead, of healing, Jesus eats with tax collectors and sinners, thus solidifying the suspicious anger of the Pharisees (Mark 2:13–17). After the cycle of controversy stories is completed, Jesus selects the group of disciples to be known as "the Twelve" (Mark 3:13–19). As anticipated, they are entrusted with a share of Jesus' mission, which includes his power over demons (vv. 14–15). The list includes two "nicknames." Jesus names Simon "Peter" (v. 16), and James and John "Boanerges, that is, sons of thunder" (v. 17). The nicknames single out the three disciples who will constitute an inner circle.

Mark provides no further information about the significance of these names. He may be presuming that his audience knows why the names are appropriate. Perhaps, they are indications of the missionary function of these disciples.[32] Mark has referred to Peter as "Simon" prior to this point in the narrative. From now on, he will be "Peter."[33] The Twelve are chosen to be "with Jesus" as well as to participate in his mission. The significance of "being with Jesus" becomes evident in the next episode. It contrasts disciples with hostile opponents and unbelieving relatives. The disciples around Jesus are now his true relatives (Mark 3:20–35).[34] The fact that Jesus has abandoned his own family for this new one is underlined by Jesus' movements. After choosing the Twelve on a mountain away from the crowds, Jesus goes into a house and is immediately surrounded by such a mob that he and the Twelve cannot eat. The statement of Mark 3:20a "and he went home" suggests that the crowd as gathered at Jesus' house. Since his mother, brothers, and other relatives have to come to seek him (vv. 21, 31), the house cannot be Jesus' family home. The reader may be intended to identify this house as Peter's.[35] If so, the reader gains an even stronger sense that Peter, his family, and associates are the most significant members of the circle gathered around Jesus. The definition which Jesus gives for those who constitute his family, "whoever does the will of God" (Mark 3:35), strengthens the reader's expectation that this group of disciples will be faithful followers of Jesus. Mark says that Jesus spoke these words "looking at those seated around him in a circle" (v. 34a). These persons replace Jesus' biological family.[36]

Even though we might assume that those seated in this circle of disciples have superior insight to that exhibited by Jesus' family, Mark raises questions about the disciples' ability to understand Jesus' teaching. They receive private instruction on the parables (4:10–12, 34), a fact which also poses a question about their capacity to understand (v. 13). The first rescue at sea episode raises the question of their faith as a group (4:39–41). Since Mark's readers know that Jesus has power over the elements, the blindness of his disciples is problematic.[37] Jesus takes the inner group to witness the raising of Jaïrus' daughter (5:37). Yet the disciples continue to witness Jesus' miracles without understanding (Mark 8:21). A two–stage healing of a blind man (Mark 8:22–26) separates that comment from Peter's confession that Jesus is Messiah (Mark 8:27–30). Scholars see this healing as an ironic comment on the healing which will be required if Jesus' blind disciples are to perceive his true identity. Some interpreters have suggested that the increasing alienation between Jesus and his followers destroys any sympathy which the audience might feel for the disciples.[38] Such a judgment assumes either that readers come to Mark's Gospel without prior knowledge of the later witness by the disciples or that Mark has an ideological interest in undermining the position of the disciples of Jesus in early Christianity. If the Markan reader identifies with the disciples, then such episodes must be viewed as encouragement to maintain one's fidelity to the Lord even in the face of persecution.[39]

Positive identification with the disciples on the part of Mark's reader is fostered by the alternation between scenes in which the disciples fail to understand and those in which their closeness to Jesus is affirmed. Peter's confession initially seems to indicate a positive growth in understanding. The other disciples answer Jesus' question about what the crowds are saying (8:28). Peter answers the question about what the disciples say of Jesus (v. 29). He speaks for the group and is the first human being in the Gospel to state Jesus' identity. This confession, along with the command to "tell no one about him" (v. 30), separates the disciples from other characters in the narrative.[40] The reader knows that Jesus is the Christ. Consequently, Peter's immediate rejection of teaching about God's divine plan given by the Messiah comes as a shock to the reader (8:31–33).[41] Jesus' rebuke once again challenges the understanding of a disciple: "Get behind me, Satan. You do not think the things of God but of human beings" (v. 33; my translation). Human beings, allied with Satan, would consider the suffering Son of man a contradiction to Jesus' role as Messiah. But he has just told the disciples that the Passion and Resurrection of the Son of man is God's plan. Peter has proven unable to hear that word.[42]

Peter's role in this section anticipates his role in the Passion account. Mark 8:27–33 could serve as an introduction to the Passion of Jesus. With the Transfiguration which follows, the three titles which emerge as the center of the Sanhedrin trial have been introduced: Messiah (8:29), Son of man (8:31), and Son of God (9:7).[43] A similar catalogue of popular opinions about Jesus (Mark 6:14–16) introduces the account of the Baptist's execution. Those around Herod identify Jesus with Elijah or one of the prophets; Herod insists that Jesus is the Baptist returned. Catalogues of opinions followed by the true identity of Jesus may have been familiar to early Christians.[44] The command to all the disciples not to make the fact that Jesus is Messiah known not only sets the disciples apart as a group; it also indicates that Jesus accepts this confession.[45]

Since Peter represents the whole group of disciples in making the confession, his rejection of the Passion in the next episode also represents the community of disciples.[46] One might expect that "Satan" would reappear in the Passion account. Mark does not refer to Satan as responsible for the failure of the disciples. Both Luke and John attribute Judas' betrayal to Satan (Luke 22:3; John 13:27). Luke also considers the flight of the other disciples as a testing that God has permitted (Luke 22:31). Mark's reader might recall the interpretation given the parable of the sower. Satan snatches the word from the hearts of some persons as soon as they hear it (Mark 4:15).[47] By casting Satan/Peter behind him, Jesus shows that he is the one being "tested." Will Jesus fulfil his divinely appointed destiny? Peter's counsel would effectively take the word of God from Jesus. Jesus' sharp response indicates that the Son of man will not be deterred from his way.[48]

After further instruction on the necessity of suffering (Mark 8:34–38), Jesus is transfigured before the core group of disciples. The baptismal address to the Son (Mark 1:11) is now conveyed to them along with the divine command to listen to him (9:7). The divine voice follows upon a peculiar notice about Peter's reaction. He proposes to construct three tents—one for each of the divine figures, Moses, Elijah, and Jesus (v. 5). A reader might consider this gesture an appropriate response to a theophany, set up a shrine at the spot. The narrator breaks in to warn us that Peter's response was motivated by confusion and fear (v. 6). The core group exhibits similar confusion when they are caught sleeping in Gethsemane (14:40).[49] The extraordinary revelation has no impact on the actions of the characters inside the narrative. It does shape the reader's judgment about Jesus' disciples, however. God himself directs them to listen to Jesus. The particular teaching at stake would appear to be the words about suffering discipleship. By presuming that the heavenly figures of Moses and Elijah could be in need of such earthly "tents" and that Jesus can attain to heavenly glory without first going the way of suffering, Peter has demonstrated how far the disciples are from understanding what Jesus said.[50]

As Jesus continues to instruct his disciples, Peter's questions elicit comments that point toward their future participation in Jesus' destiny. Despite the depth of misunderstanding exhibited by the disciples, it seems wrong to attribute to Mark the view that Jesus' disciples are examples of faith which fails completely. As Christopher D. Marshall rightly observes: "Mark introduces the element of growing conflict with Jesus. Yet he also continues to foster the readers' identification with them in two ways: by still portraying positive features in their behavior . . . and by attributing to them the kinds of failings and weaknesses his audience could identify with."[51] Peter's question about the rewards for those who have left everything to follow Jesus elicits both reassurance and warning (Mark 10:28–31). Whatever a person leaves behind for the sake of the Kingdom, he or she will receive back in abundance. However, disciples must also expect to receive persecution (Mark 10:30). The episode reminds the reader that Peter and the others had left family and occupation to follow Jesus (1:16–20).[52] The question and response also remind Mark's readers of the early Christian missionary effort.[53]

Peter's next intervention points out the withered fig tree (Mark 11:21). This remark elicits from Jesus a significant block of teaching on faith, prayer, and forgiveness (Mark 11:22–25). Juxtaposed to the symbolic withering of the old place of prayer, the Temple, these sayings point toward the post-Easter community as the new place of prayer. Jesus' sayings reinforce the reader's confidence that prayer and forgiveness are more effective in the new community than they

had been in the old.[54] The content of these promises appears to have
been drawn from a compilation of sayings of Jesus that circulated
independently of one another.[55] Mark has simply used the introductory
question by Peter as a vehicle for this important teaching. The promises are directed to the community of believers as a whole.

The prayer sayings emphasize the fact that what human beings might
consider impossible is possible for God.[56] Mark first introduces the
theme in Jesus' response to his incredulous disciples after the rich
young man has declined Jesus' invitation to become a disciple (Mark
10:27). Human probabilities do not constrain what God can do for the
faithful community. This perspective also moderates the reader's perception of Jesus' disciples. Their apparent weaknesses do not limit the
power of God. Both the end of the old order and the new position of
the disciples are predicted in Jesus' discourse in Mark 13. Jesus
delivers these words to the four disciples who were first called to
follow him (Mark 13:3). However, the list of names follows the order
which we find in the listing of the Twelve (Mark 3:16–17). The core
group—Peter, James, and John—are listed before Peter's brother,
Andrew.

The final scenes in which Peter figures occur during the Markan
Passion narrative. We have seen that Peter's initial boast that he will
never be scandalized by Jesus even if the other disciples desert him
(Mark 14:27–31) is contradicted when Peter denies knowing Jesus
(14:66–72). Peter's protest recalls his earlier rejection of the Passion.
There, he rejected suffering. Here, he claims a heroism that he does
not possess. The best he will be able to do is to follow Jesus longer
than the others who flee the garden (Mark 14:54).[57]

Though Jesus' teaching on prayer assures the disciples that all things
are possible through prayer, the Gethsemane scene demonstrates that
the disciples have not yet learned to pray. Jesus takes the inner group
of three apart and tells them to remain awake and watch (14:34). Later,
even though Jesus is in agony a little way off, the disciples are unable
to remain awake (14:36–42). By this point in the narrative, the reader
probably anticipates the fact that the disciples will fail Jesus.[58] He or
she has learned that the only person who is completely reliable is Jesus
himself. Jesus' prayer begins with the affirmation that God is able to
do all things. The proper response to God's power is to submit to
God's will.[59] When Jesus finds the disciples asleep, he addresses Peter
directly (v. 37). Despite his earlier boast, Peter cannot even stay awake.
Despite the warning that he should pray to avoid temptation, clearly

an instruction later disciples are to take to heart, Peter and the others fail once again (vv. 38–42). In contrast to his disciples, Jesus continues to pray (v. 39).[60] The weakness of Jesus' followers serves to highlight his own example of steadfast devotion to God's will.[61]

After the Gethsemane scene, Peter's denial hardly comes as a surprise. The disciples fled, just as Jesus had predicted (Mark 14:27, 50). Since Jesus had also predicted Peter's denial (14:30), the reader must anticipate that Peter will deny Jesus. The threefold repetition, a common element in story-telling, makes it evident that Peter's behavior is no accident. He does not remember the Lord's words to him until the final challenge, in which he claims that he does not even know the man about whom they are speaking (vv. 71–72). Mary Ann Tolbert challenges the common assumption that Peter's tears imply repentance on his part. She suggests that they should be read as a variation of the sadness of the rich young man (Mark 10:22).[62] In this reading, Jesus would appear to have lost to his opponents even before his death, since those with whom he had established the new family (Mark 3:31–35) have now been scattered. However, the tension between divine necessity and human action emphasized by the predictions in the narrative makes it difficult to accept the claim that the reader is to see the denial of Peter as a failure at the level of the divine purpose.

Readers of Mark know that the disciples went on to testify about Jesus before hostile authorities. We have also seen Jesus make repeated efforts to rescue and enlighten his failing disciples. If the repeated emphasis on persecution is analogous to the experiences of Mark's audience, then readers may also be familiar with flight, fear, equivocation, and denial as commonplace. Driven back to Jesus' own prophecy by Peter's denial, we discover that failure has been followed by a promise of renewed community between Jesus and his disciples (Mark 14:27–28).[63] Though the Gospel never depicts its fulfillment, the Easter message reminds Peter and the others that Jesus' word will be fulfilled (Mark 16:7). Since Jesus predicted the flight and denial of the disciples, even those events give the reader evidence to believe the word of promise.

As we have seen, Peter is singled out from the other disciples when the angel delivers the message. That reference has been taken to indicate Peter's primacy among the disciples. Since we have seen that while Peter is the central figure among the disciples, the narrative does not set him above the other disciples. The expression "his disciples and Peter" (Mark 16:7) provides the answer to the tears the apostle

shed after the denial. Jesus will take Peter back. The Christians of
Mark's day were to look to Jesus as the model of a strong confession
(cf. 1 Tim. 6:13). At the same time, any who have lapsed were to be
encouraged by the story of Peter.[64] The difficulty faced by scholars in
interpreting the ending of Mark shows how quickly a set of assumptions about the actual situation of the churches for which the evangelist
wrote is required to determine the most plausible interpretation of the
text.

PETER IN THE GOSPEL OF MATTHEW

We have seen that Mark depicts Peter as the most prominent of
Jesus' disciples. Peter's flawed character serves to both warn and
encourage a community under persecution. We have also seen Matthew soften the harsh edges in Mark's depiction of the disciples. The
walking on water incident (Matt. 14:22–32) uses Peter to show that the
"little faith" of the disciples might fail under stress. Peter becomes
afraid and begins to sink. However, Jesus is present to rescue the
disciple. The presence of the Son of God as the basis for the community founded on his teaching is affirmed in the post-Resurrection
commission which brings Matthew's narrative to its conclusion (Matt.
28:16–20).

The final commission involves making disciples of the nations and
teaching them to observe "all that I have commanded you" (v. 20a).
The uncertainty and misunderstanding associated with the disciples
that Matthew found in Mark's Gospel could not provide an adequate
basis for disciples who will carry out this injunction. Matthew has the
disciples as a group state that they have understood the parables of
Jesus (Matt. 13:51). However, Peter is the primary figure whose understanding guarantees that the teaching preserved in the church represents what the Lord has commanded.[65]

Matthew designates him "first" in the list of Jesus' disciples (Matt.
10:2). He is the first to be called (Matt. 4:18).[66] His name "Peter" is
associated with the solid foundation for the Kingdom of God in the
teaching of Jesus. Peter's grasp of Jesus' teaching is made evident in
incidents in which he elicits and receives special instructions from the
Lord in matters of *halachah*: payment of the temple tax, which Jesus
pays both for himself and for Peter (17:26–27); forgiveness within the
community (18:21); explanation of Jesus' saying concerning clean and
unclean (15:15). This last exchange is particularly significant because

it follows a discussion between Jesus and his disciples about the authority of the Pharisees:

> And he called the people to him and said to them, "Hear and understand: not what goes into the mouth defiles a man, but what comes out of the mouth, this defiles a man." Then the disciples came and said to him, "Do you not know that the Pharisees were offended when they heard this saying?" He answered, "Every plant which my heavenly Father has not planted will be rooted up. Let them alone; they are blind guides. And if a blind man leads a blind man, both will fall into a pit." But Peter said to him, "Explain the parable to us." And he said, "Are you also still without understanding?" Do you not see that whatever goes into the mouth passes into the stomach. . . . (Matt. 15:10–17; RSV)

Though Peter's request for an explanation draws an initial rebuke, Jesus does interpret the saying. Unlike the Pharisees, Peter (and the other disciples) will not be blind guides leading the people to disaster.

Two of the three items of *halachah* associated with Peter in Matthew—the temple tax and the purity rules associated with eating—directly affect the relationships between Jews and Gentiles within the Christian community. Unlike the Markan source from which he drew the sayings about "what defiles" (Mark 7:1–23), Matthew has moderated the condemnation of the traditions of the elders and the Pharisees. The problem with the Pharisees lies in their inability to perceive the real meaning of these traditions. Consequently, Matthew leaves room for Jewish Christian to continue observing them while not insisting that gentile converts to Christianity do so. Similarly, the temple tax episode, however it might have applied to Matthew's community, maintains the principle of "the sons are free" along with a willingness to pay in order not to offend those who must collect the tax (Matt. 17:24–28). The episode also demonstrates that Peter has the authority to teach because he has turned to Jesus to resolve the question.[67]

As we have seen, the special sayings which Matthew has attached to Peter's confession (Matt. 16:17–19) have traditionally been the basis for later claims that Peter was to enjoy a unique role as the interpreter of Jesus' teaching. For Roman Catholics, this passage implies that there could be no true teaching or practice which contradicted the understanding of the apostle and his successors. One should not infer

from the disagreement between Peter and Paul referred to in Galatians
2:11–14 that Peter had erred in understanding the Gospel.

Matthew has combined three distinct traditions in the passage in
question: (a) a beatitude in verse 17; (b) the naming of Simon as the
"rock" in 18, and (c) the power of the keys in verse 19. Each of these
three has an independent history in the tradition, which can be con-
strued apart from their combination in the Gospel narrative.[68] We have
already discussed the name "Peter" in our examination of the life of
Peter. The beatitude follows the pattern of other sayings which assert
that Jesus' disciples are recipients of divine revelation. When the
disciples are sent out to preach the Kingdom, they are told that what
is hidden will be revealed. Their preaching proclaims what they have
heard in secret (Matt. 10:26–27; Luke 12:2–3).[69] Jesus thanks God for
having hidden "these things" from the "wise and understanding" and
revealed them to babes (Matt. 11:25; Luke 10:21). Before beginning to
explain the parable of the sower to his disciples, Jesus pronounces
them "blessed" because they have seen and heard what many prophets and righteous persons longed to see and hear (Matt. 13:16–17).[70]
We have already seen that some exegetes think that some affirmative
response by Jesus must have concluded the initial story of Peter's
confession. By supplying a saying which highlights the revealed character of Peter's confession, Matthew continues a pattern that he has
already established with the other references to Jesus' disciples as the
recipients of the message about the Kingdom which is hidden from
others. Jesus' word to Peter is a special instance of the more general
principle that God has made the truth about the Kingdom available to
the "little ones" of the world.

The second saying provides an additional interpretation of the name
change from "Simon" to "Peter." We have seen that other traditions
attach the name change to the calling of Peter as a disciple (John 1:42)
or to the selection of the Twelve (Mark 3:16). They do not provide any
explicit interpretation of the name. Since Matthew has been using the
name "Peter" in the narrative prior to this passage (e.g., Matt. 14:28),
the evangelist probably did not create the saying about Peter's name
as central to this passage. However, the ecclesial understanding of the
name as a reference to a "foundation rock" for the community may
derive from the evangelist. The rock foundation echoes the parable of
the two foundations which closed the Sermon on the Mount (Matt.
7:24–27).[71] Like the episode in which Peter walked on water, the
"rock" saying reassures a church under assault that it cannot be

destroyed. By combining this saying with the beatitude, Matthew indicates that Jesus is confident because the Father has revealed Jesus' identity to Peter.[72]

The Old Testament examples of renaming Abraham (Gen. 17:1–8) and Jacob (Gen. 32:22–32) provide a possible background for this reinterpretation. The new names given the patriarchs are both references to their roles as ancestors of the people. At the beginning of Matthew, the Baptist warned the scribes and Pharisees that God could raise up new children for Abraham from the rocks (Matt. 3:9). As the "rock," Peter becomes the foundation for the renewed Israel.[73] Some Qumran texts also speak of the "Teacher of Righteousness" as a pillar from which God builds the new congregation.[74] The term "church," which appears in the Gospels only in Matthew, is used here to refer to the universal church. Matthew's other example (18:18) uses the term to indicate the local congregation. It is difficult to determine whether or not Matthew understands the false teachers and prophets to which he refers as the basis for the assault of Hades on the community. Isaiah 28:15–19 refers to the foundation stone of the new Zion as one able to survive the attacks of those who have made a covenant with Sheol.[75]

The final saying about the keys also refers to Isaiah. The key to the house of David is to be given to Eliakim. What he opens, no one can shut. What he shuts, no one can open (Isa. 22:22). The oracle implies succession to divinely sanctioned authority, which no one can challenge. Keys appear in apocalyptic contexts in Revelation 3:7 and 2 Baruch 10:18. Revelation depicts the exalted Son of man as possessor of this key of David. 2 Baruch is not an allusion to the Isaiah passage. In 2 Baruch, the priests toss the keys of the temple to God while confessing that they have been false stewards. In both instances, the keys imply that the possessor has authority for the welfare of the community or one of its central institutions.[76] Matthew 16:19 combines the gift of the keys with another saying that conveys the authority to bind and loose (v. 19b). The latter appears independently in Matthew 18:18 as a confirmation of judgments which the community renders when it excludes from its ranks those who will not heed the church.

The issues referred to in Matthew 18 are disciplinary: how to deal with members of the community who sin. The sayings on binding and loosing convey to Peter and to the early community an authority for which Jesus himself was challenged, forgiving sin (Matt. 6:15; 9:8; 16:19; 18:18). Matthew underlines the permanence of this gift by shifting the crowd reaction to the healing from what he found in Mark. Instead of being amazed (e.g., Mark 2:12), the people praise God for giving such authority to human beings.[77] Matthew 18:15–18 describes how this power is to be exercised within local Christian communities. The disputes referred to in Matthew 18:15–18 may not have been limited to those considered "sinful," that is, violations of the ethical and religious standards of the community. When Josephus describes the political authority enjoyed by Pharisees under Alexandra, he comments that they were at liberty to "banish and recall, to loose and to bind" (*War* 1.5.1–3, sec. 111).[78] Matthew may have understood "binding and loosing" to refer to a more generally exercised judicial authority exercised by the local community. The Sermon on the Mount contains two sayings of Jesus that exhort persons to resolve disputes without resorting to the civil courts (Matt. 5:25, 40).[79] The formulation "if your brother sins against you"[80] (Matt. 18:15) suggests that general disputes between members of the community are at issue.

These examples provide a political, judicial, and communal background for the saying about the keys and binding/loosing in Matthew 16:19. Peter's authority provides the legitimation for the community's practice of mediating disputes between members, disciplining sinners, and even excluding some from the community. Peter appears in Matthew 18:21–22 as the disciple who asks how often one is to extend forgiveness to the fellow Christian who sins against him. He is instructed that there are no limits to forgiveness. The importance of Peter as arbiter for concrete issues of community practice informs another episode in which Peter serves as mediator between local Jewish officials and Jesus, the question of whether or not Jesus will pay the temple tax (Matt. 17:24–27). We are not concerned here with the question of whether or not the story legitimates Jewish Christian compliance with a particular tax assessment. The story clearly depicts Peter as the person approached by the local authorities to answer a question about Jesus' practice. Since Matthew treats Capernaum as Jesus' place of residence, this question is not motivated by the fact that Jesus resides in Peter's family house. Further, when Jesus does pay the tax, he includes Peter in the payment.

We have seen that our evidence for the historical position of Peter in the Jerusalem community does not present the apostle as the sole successor to Jesus. Although the opening chapters of Acts depict Peter as the one who determines community practice, we soon find others involved in crucial decisions. Matthew's presentation of Peter shows a similar oscillation. In some instances, Peter appears merely to represent the larger group of disciples (e.g., Matt. 14:28–32, Peter's "little faith"; and Matt. 16:5–12, the disciples' "little faith"). In others, Peter occupies a unique position in relationship to Jesus. Jesus' words in Matthew 16:17–19 single out Peter as the foundation for the new community which cannot be overwhelmed by the forces of Hades that will be arrayed against it. The reader knows from Matthew 7:15–22 that those dangers to the community are internal as well as external. False teachers and prophets can threaten the community if they lead others away from doing the will of God. The sharp warnings against the practice of the Pharisees which echo throughout the Gospel (e.g., Matthew 15:3, 7–9; 16:12; 23:2–28) also remind the reader of the dangers of a practice based on false teaching. The Pharisees and scribes are said to "shut the kingdom of heaven" so that neither they nor others can enter (23:14). Consequently, the establishment of Petrine authority as the basis for the church's practice assures the reader that the Christian community will survive the dangers facing it.

The correlation between the commission to Peter and the injunctions to the whole community in Matthew 18 suggests that one should not describe Peter as a "chief rabbi."[81] Peter is the basis for the tradition of Christian practice in the Matthean community. But Peter does not establish an "office" within the church to which others may succeed. Matthew 23:8–12 warns Christians against adopting the authoritative positions to which competence in interpreting the Law entitled others. Nor does Peter take over the function of teaching except in the more limited sense of determining how Christians are to "keep" the words which they have heard from Jesus. Peter's christological confession forms the basis for Matthew's insisting that to follow Jesus' commands is to do the will of God. Thus, it is *halachah*, practice, not doctrine that is founded on the apostle.[82]

As the walking on water episode suggests, Matthew does not cancel out that side of the tradition which speaks of the apostle's weaknesses. By adding the additional material, Matthew has reinforced the positive picture of Peter suggested by his place as "first" (Matt. 10:2) among the disciples. He does retain the rebuke issued by Jesus when Peter protests the prediction of the Passion. He even sharpens that rebuke somewhat by having Jesus describe Peter as a "stumbling block" (*skandalon*) to him. This expansion develops a hint that we find in Mark's narrative, that Peter's protest serves as a testing of Jesus. The wording creates an ironic contrast between the foundation rock of verse 17 and the stumbling stone of verse 23.[83]

Despite the exalted role which Peter fills as spokesperson for the disciples and authoritative interpreter of the traditions handed down from Jesus, Matthew never separates him completely from the larger group of disciples. His persistent need for correction and instruction draws the reader's attention to his weaknesses as well as his strengths.[84] Modern readers are often attracted by the rich ambiguity of Peter's character. His "little faith" makes him easier to understand and even to admire. However, such a depiction would not have drawn the same response from a first-century reader. Flaws of character might serve as the cracks which would lead to later tragedy. If there is a tragedy of Peter and the disciples from Matthew's point of view, it can only be in their flight and Peter's denial. Peter shows himself superior to the rest in initially following those who had arrested Jesus. Once again, fear overtakes him and without the possibility of divine assistance, he flees.

Matthew intensifies some of the elements that he has taken over from Mark.[85] Peter insists that he will never fall away (Matt. 26:33; cf. Mark 14:29). When Peter denies Jesus, he does so before all who are in the courtyard (Matt. 26:70). He already swears an oath and claims not to know Jesus with the second denial rather than the third (Matt. 26:72; cf. Mark 14:70). Finally, Peter is said to weep "bitterly" (Matt. 26:75). Peter's personal responsibility both for a boast that he could not keep and for the denial of Jesus have been sharpened by the evangelist. Matthew also omits Peter's name from the Easter message given to the women by the angel. This omission may stem from the fact that the final vision of the risen Lord restores the whole group of disciples at the end of the Gospel.[86] The Gospel concludes with Jesus' promise to remain with his church until the end-time. For Matthew, one of the concrete ways in which this promise is fulfilled is in the figure of Peter.

Our study of the figure of Peter in Mark and Matthew shows that Peter was remembered as the central figure among Jesus' disciples. No other disciple figures as prominently in the narrative traditions about the followers of Jesus. However, the characterization of the apostle in the Gospels is both complex and ambiguous. Peter always exemplifies what it means to be a follower of Jesus. But when the weaknesses of Peter and the other disciples are progressively underlined as they are in Mark's narrative, some interpreters question the assumption that Markan readers would identify with the apostle. Instead, they have understood the image of Peter as a flawed disciple to be directed against all of Jesus' disciples. Even though Mark initially treats the group of disciples as the replacement for Jesus' natural family and leads the reader to assume that they will be "hearers and doers of the word of God," their failure at the end of the narrative serves to undermine the reader's confidence in them.

Although such interpretations have highlighted important ambiguities and ironies in Markan narrative, we have suggested that Mark does not intend to undermine the position of Peter and the other disciples. Early in the narrative, their failures serve to highlight the forces arrayed against Jesus if Jesus is to accomplish his mission. During the Passion, their flight and Peter's denial confirm the fact that everything which occurs has been fixed in God's plan. Jesus' prophetic word about their fate and his own is confirmed. Since it is verified by the disciples' actions during the Passion, the reader also recognizes that the Easter promise will also be fulfilled. Mark's narrative plays the weakness of the disciples off against the knowledge which his Christian readers have of the later witness that the disciples gave to Jesus. For a persecuted community, this depiction of radically flawed disciples serves as reassurance that they too can endure to the end.

Further evidence that Mark's picture of Peter and the disciples does not suggest ironic hostility to the Twelve is evident in Matthew's redaction of Mark. Combining Mark with other traditions about the apostle enables Matthew to provide an additional facet to the image of Peter. Peter becomes the foundation of community because he provides the basis for its claiming to "keep the word of God." To this end, Peter has received special instruction from the Lord. However, Peter's relationship to Jesus does not elevate him above the other disciples. Nor does it provide the basis for a hierarchical communal structure based on teachers and disciples. The content of Jesus' teaching against which the community must measure its own good or bad fruit remains the words of Jesus embodied in the Gospel.

Although Matthew has moderated the harsh language about the disciples that he finds in some Markan episodes, the evangelist is not unwilling to ascribe weaknesses to Peter and the others. He revises passages in Mark which might imply that the disciples are completely without understanding so that the perplexity which the disciples show at the beginning of an episode is clarified at its conclusion. The most dramatic example of this clarification occurs at the end of the Gospel. We are not left, as in Mark, with frightened disciples and a promise. Instead, the risen Lord appears first to the women outside the tomb (28:8–10) and then to the Eleven on a mountain in Galilee (28:16–20). The final commission assures the reader that Jesus' disciples will carry his teaching to the nations. It promises the true basis for the community's ongoing life in this age, the Lord who remains present (28:20).

NOTES

1. Raymond E. Brown and John P. Meier, *Antioch and Rome: New Testament Cradles of Catholic Christianity* (Ramsey, NJ: Paulist Press, 1983), 195–201.
2. *Antioch and Rome*, 196.
3. For a detailed study of redaction criticism and the understanding of Mark's treatment of the disciples, see Clifton Black, *The Disciples According to Mark: Markan Redaction in Current Debate*, Journal for the Study of the New Testament, Supplement Series 27 (Sheffield: JSOT Press, 1989). Black concludes that the standard redaction critical treatments of Mark come to such divergent conclusions that the method itself must be considered flawed when applied to Mark (*The Disciples According to Mark*, 248–53).
4. Narrative criticism combines modern literary criticism with an understanding of ancient authors and their methods of composition. See Christopher D. Marshall, *Faith as a Theme in Mark's Gospel*, SNTSMS 64 (Cambridge: Cambridge University Press, 1989), 8–30.
5. The particular methodology known as reader-response criticism is especially attentive to the way in which texts generate an implied reader and author. This method seeks to describe the "response" which the dynamics of the narrative require of the ideal reader. This method also warns scholars to be wary of naive judgments about a Gospel's actual author or audience. See the reader-response commentary on Mark by J. P. Heil in *The Gospel of Mark as a Model for Action: A Reader-Response Commentary* (New York: Paulist Press, 1992).
6. See Black, *The Disciples According to Mark*, 241–48.
7. See the survey of the debate over Markan Christology as a counterweight to emphasis on Jesus as a "divine man" in Sharyn Echols Dowd, *Prayer, Power and the Problem of Suffering: Mark 11:22–25 in the Context of Markan Theology*, SBLDS 105 (Atlanta: Scholars Press, 1988), 6–24.
8. Dowd, *Prayer*, 24–26.
9. Black finds Ernest Best's methodology, which adopts this approach, the best way of accounting for the mixed treatment of the disciples in Mark; see *The Disciples According to Mark*, 100–25.

10.   Ernest Best, *Mark: The Gospel as Story* (Edinburgh: T. and T. Clark, 1983), 85.

11.   See Marshall, *Faith as a Theme in Mark's Gospel*, 21–23. On the Markan disciples, see Robert Tannehill, "The Disciples in Mark: The Function of a Narrative Role," *JR* 57 (1977): 386–405. For a literary analysis which focuses on how character is created in the Lukan narrative, see John A. Darr, *On Character Building: The Reader and the Rhetoric of Characterization in Luke-Acts* (Louisville: Westminster/John Knox Press, 1992).

12.   Best, *Mark*, 20.

13.   Andrew Lincoln, "The Promise and the Failure—Mark 16:7, 8," *JBL* 108 (1989): 285.

14.   Lincoln, "The Promise and the Failure," 286–90.

15.   "The Promise and the Failure," 294.

16.   A modified view of this redactional history is espoused by Raymond E. Brown in *The Gospel According to John (XIII–XXI)*, AB 29A (Garden City: Doubleday, 1970), 1078–82. Brown rejects the view that the material about Peter added in John 21 was intended to domesticate a radically anti-Peter stance in the earlier edition of the Gospel, which ended with John 20:30–31.

17.   Mary Ann Tolbert, *Sowing the Gospel: Mark's World in Literary-Historical Perspective* (Minneapolis: Fortress Press, 1989), 130.

18.   See Elizabeth S. Malbon, "Fallible Followers: Women and Men in the Gospel of Mark," *Semeia* 28 (1983): 29–48.

19.   Robert M. Fowler speaks of a tension between two plots in the story: (a) the divine necessity which appears to predetermine the action, and (b) the freedom and contingency of the actions of Jesus and the other disciples. Mark's construction violates the Aristotelian dicta about unity of plot. See *Let the Reader Understand: Reader-Response Criticism and the Gospel of Mark* (Minneapolis: Fortress Press, 1991), 138–39.

20.   See Robert Tannehill, "The Gospel of Mark as a Narrative Christology," *Semeia* 16 (1979): 57–95.

21.   Fowler insists that the reader recognizes the claim that Jesus is "Son of God" as the truth. At the level of the story, the centurion can only be speaking ironically, just as the soldiers who had "mocked" Jesus earlier. See *Let the Reader Understand*, 206–8.

22.   Marshall, *Faith*, 75–78; Dowd, *Prayer*, 161–65; Lincoln, "The Promise and the Failure," 295; Dorothy A. Lee-Pollard, "Powerlessness as Power: A Key Emphasis in the Gospel of Mark," *SJT* 40 (1987): 173–88.

23.   A full treatment of characterization in Mark would require analysis of minor characters as well. They often act as foils to Jesus' disciples and to his enemies by exhibiting virtues that the major characters lack. See Marshall, *Faith*, 77.

24. See the caution against excessive enthusiasm for literary critical catego-
    ries in Gospel analysis that neglects both redaction criticism and the
    effort to situate the Gospels within the context of early Christianity by
    Best in *Mark*, 109–22. Best considers it misleading even to speak of
    Mark as an "author." He prefers the imagery of an artist creating a
    collage or a composer a piece of music to describe the interplay between
    traditional materials and composition.
25. Just as scholars now recognize it is impossible to show that the figure of
    Jesus is intended to contradict an opposing Christology, so it is impossi-
    ble to demonstrate that the portrayal of Peter and the disciples has been
    formulated to call into question some extra-textual picture of the disci-
    ples that was prevalent in Mark's community.
26. Marshall, *Faith*, 94–122.
27. Joseph A. Fitzmyer notes that the element of eschatological warning
    need not be erased from the New Testament use of this image; see *The
    Gospel According to Luke (I–IX)*, AB 28 (Garden City: Doubleday,
    1981), 569.
28. Robert Guelich, *Mark 1–8:26*, WBC 34A (Dallas: Word Books, 1989),
    61–63.
29. Guelich, *Mark*, 352–54. Guelich describes these scenes as Markan irony.
    The disciples are "insiders" who remain "outsiders" in their under-
    standing. This charge is made even more sharply in Mark 8:14–21.
30. Guelich notes that Peter appears to be responsible for the action of
    pursuing Jesus into the wilderness (*Mark*, 69).
31. Guelich, *Mark*, 70.
32. Guelich thinks that Mark saw "Peter" as a name without any particular
    significance. The parallel with the nickname given the sons of Zebedee
    seems to imply that Mark knew the name had some metaphorical
    significance. See *Mark*, 161.
33. The other Gospels begin to use "Peter" as soon as Simon appears in the
    narrative (John 1:42, where the name change occurs; Matt. 4:18; Luke
    5:8). As we have seen, he is known to Paul as both "Cephas" and
    "Peter."
34. Guelich, *Mark*, 156.
35. *Mark*, 172.
36. Readers who are aware of the later tensions between Jesus and the
    disciples may see an irony in this replacement of Jesus' mother and
    brothers with the "mother and brothers" who constitute the circle of
    disciples. Both groups initially fall short in their understanding that Jesus
    "does the will of God."
37. Tolbert treats this episode as an example of situational irony; see
    Sowing, 101.
38. Tolbert, *Sowing*, 103.

39. Heil's understanding of the Gospel as a model for action highlights the importance of our identification with the disciples in the process of reading through the narrative. See, e.g., Heil, *Mark*, 180–81, on the rebuke of Peter.

40. The rhetorical function of the command in separating "insiders" who know who Jesus is from outsiders who remain ignorant of that identity depends upon the Markan alternations between the disciples, who are around Jesus and receive private instruction, and the crowds and opponents of Jesus. This function is independent of the question of a "messianic secret" in Mark, which views the numerous commands to silence (e.g., Mark 1:44) as a break from christological perceptions of Jesus based on power without the cross.

41. Tolbert, *Sowing*, 200–202.

42. This emphasis appears to have been created by Mark's bringing together three traditional pieces into a single unit: Peter's confession, the Passion prediction, and Jesus' rebuke. Passion predictions clearly circulated independently and are formulated in terms of the Son of man rather than "Messiah." See, e.g., Joachim Gnilka, *Das Evangelium nach Markus*, EKK II/2 (Neukirchen-Vluyn: Neukirchener, 1979), 10–12.

43. Rudolf Pesch, *Das Markusevangelium*, HTKNT II/2 (Freiburg: Herder, 1977), 28.

44. John 1:19–23 contains the list in descending order of importance: Christ, Elijah, the prophet, a voice crying out. See Pesch, *Markusevangelium* 2:31–32.

45. Pesch, *Markusevangelium* 2:33.

46. *Markusevangelium* 2:35.

47. Tolbert sees the interpretation of the sower parable as central to Mark's depiction of Jesus' disciples (*Sowing*, 122–24). They are the "rocky ground" on which the seed may sprout but will fail to mature (*Sowing*, 154–55).

48. Gnilka, *Evangelium nach Markus* 1:17.

49. Gnilka, *Evangelium nach Markus* 2:35.

50. Pesch, *Markusevangelium* 2:75.

51. Marshall, *Faith*, 211.

52. Pesch, *Markusevangelium* 2:144.

53. *Markusevangelium* 2:145.

54. Marshall, *Faith*, 160–72.

55. Mark 8:23–24; cf. Luke 17:6//Matt. 17:20; Mark 8:25; cf. Matt. 6:14; Gnilka *Evangelium nach Markus* 2:133.

56. Dowd, *Prayer*, 64.

57. Pesch, *Markusevangelium* 2:382.

58. Dowd, *Prayer*, 154f.

59. Pesch, *Markusevangelium* 2:391.

60. *Markusevangelium* 1:393.
61. Jesus exemplifies prayer and trust in God; the disciples exemplify human weakness. The episode underlines the warning to Christians that they must watch in the last days (Mark 13:33–37). See Pesch, *Markusevangelium* 2:396.
62. Tolbert, *Sowing*, 218. This suggestion would be more persuasive if there were verbal parallels between the two stories.
63. See, e.g., Pesch, *Markusevangelium* 2:451.
64. *Markusevangelium* 2:453.
65. Since Matthew warns his readers that they must avoid false teachers within the Christian community (Matt. 7:15–17) and the discord between teaching and practice evident among the Pharisees (Matt. 23:2–3), they know that communities must guard the integrity of religious teaching and practice.
66. J. D. Kingsbury, "The Figure of Peter in Matthew's Gospel as a Theological Problem," *JBL* 98 (1979): 67–83.
67. Michael J. Wilkins, *The Concept of Disciple in Matthew's Gospel*, NovTSup 59 (Leiden: E. J. Brill, 1988), 199–200.
68. I disagree with Davies and Allison that verses 17–19 of Matthew 16 were taken as a whole from a variant form of Peter's confession. The two authors adduce allusions to this tradition scattered throughout the Fourth Gospel as indications that it was known to the Fourth Evangelist, who used fragments of it in different contexts. See W. D. Davies and Dale C. Allison, *Commentary on Matthew VIII–XVIII*, vol. 2 of *The Gospel According to St. Matthew*, ICC (Edinburgh: T. and T. Clark, 1991), 605–9. I would argue that the Johannine evidence ought to be understood as evidence for the independent history of the three traditions.
69. Matthew has transformed the second saying in the Q pair—which originally spoke of the impossibility of "hiding" what those addressed have said in secret—into a missionary commission. The disciples are to make the hidden things known. This shift anticipates the great commission which concludes the Gospel.
70. Luke 10:23–24 preserves this saying independently of the setting which Matthew supplies in his Gospel.
71. Chrys C. Caragounis, *Peter and the Rock*, BZNW 58 (New York: Walter de Gruyter, 1990), 107–11. Caragounis attempts to deny any ecclesial significance attached to Peter in this passage. He insists that no New Testament passage thinks of Peter as the foundation of the church. Its only foundation is Christ (e.g., 1 Cor. 3:11).
72. Rudolf Pesch, *Simon Petrus*, Geschichte und geschichtliche Bedeutung des ersten Jüngers Jesu Christi. Päpste und Papstum Bd. 15 (Stuttgart: Anton Hiersemann, 1980), 97.

73. Davies and Allison, *Matthew VIII–XVIII*, 624.

74. 4QpIsa (= 4Q164); the people of God are described both as a "temple" (1 QS 5.5–7; 8.4–7; CD 3.18–4:10) and as a house (4 QpPs 1–10 2 14). See Davies and Allison, *Matthew VIII–XVIII*, 628–29.

75. Davies and Allison, *Matthew VIII–XVIII*, 630. Parallels with Qumran imagery suggest an apocalyptic context for the origins of this saying (see *Matthew VIII–XVIII*, 634).

76. Overman, *Matthew's Gospel and Formative Judaism: A Study of the Social World of Matthew's Community* (Philadelphia: Fortress Press, 1990), 138–39. Though Overman initially describes the Petrine authority as guaranteeing understanding and teaching, he does recognize the juridical elements in this passage.

77. *Matthew's Gospel*, 130–32. "Binding and loosing" appears in Josephus as a political and judicial power that the Pharisees exercised during the chaos of the Jewish War (*War* 1:5.1–3). The injunctions to avoid courts (Matt. 5:25, 40) suggest that Matthew's community also drew back from established social and civic institutions; see *Matthew's Gospel*, 105–7.

78. Josephus may be projecting into the past the political and judicial power exercised by the Pharisees in his own time; see, e.g., Overman, *Matthew's Gospel*, 105f.

79. Overman, *Matthew's Gospel*, 106f. 1 Corinthians 6:1–8 shows an awareness that lawsuits between Christians are contrary to ideal Christian practice. Given the fact of such lawsuits, Paul also opts for resolution within the community (v. 8). However, there is no hint that Paul is familiar with a saying of the Lord authorizing such practice.

80. The "against you" does not appear in a number of early manuscripts, which indicates uncertainty about the nature of the reference. The Q version of the injunction (Luke 17:3–4) contains both "sins" and "sins against you." It appeals for unlimited forgiveness between Christians but does not presume that the community will take a role in resolving disputes.

81. Often, the position that one should not describe Peter as a "chief rabbi" is upheld by those who emphasize the unique position given the apostle—e.g., Davies and Allison, *Matthew VIII–XVIII*, 639: ". . . Jesus replaces the Jewish academy with his own 'chief rabbi.' "

82. This view, while self-evident to Jewish readers, was already eclipsed in early Christianity. The Fourth Gospel appeals to its communal founder, the Beloved Disciple, for a doctrinal claim, the unique position of Jesus as Son of God. I also see no evidence in the narrative to over-interpret the name change and make Peter the "new Abraham" for the church as Davies and Allison propose (*Matthew VIII–XVIII*, 642–43), even though I agree with their desire to situate Peter between the traditional Protestant view that Peter is "one of the disciples" and the traditional Roman Catholic view that he is the first holder of an ecclesial office.

83.   Wilkins, *The Concept of Disciple*, 202–3.
84.   This dual element in the portrayal of Peter as well as in his association
      with the larger group of disciples is emphasized by Wilkins in *The
      Concept of Disciple*, 208–16.
85.   Kingsbury, "The Figure of Peter," 70.
86.   Wilkins, *The Concept of Disciple*, 208.

CHAPTER 3

Peter in New Testament Narratives
Luke and John

PETER AMONG THE APOSTLES

Along with the stories of Peter's attempt to walk on water, his commissioning by Jesus as the rock on which the church is founded, and his denial of Jesus, the Lukan images of Peter fill out the picture of Peter for most Christians. In our study of the life of Peter, we have already seen that the association of Peter's call with a miraculous catch of fish in Luke (5:1–11) is related to the manifestation of the risen Lord in John (21:1–14). Luke's version of the prophecy that Peter would deny Jesus has been moderated by the prophecy that Peter would turn and strengthen his brothers (Luke 22:31–34). Jesus' prayer will protect Simon from being destroyed by Satan's attack. In John's Gospel, the risen Lord restores Peter and commissions him to care for the flock (John 21:15–17). Both Luke 22:31 and John 21:15 have Jesus address Peter with his proper name, "Simon" (Luke) and "Simon, son of John" (John). This formulation supports the suggestion that the two variants may go back to a single account of the commissioning of Peter by the risen Lord.[1] Luke refers to that tradition in his account of the Easter appearances (Luke 24:34).

Luke also refers to a visit by some of the disciples to check Jesus' tomb after the women report that it is empty (Luke 24:24). John 20:2–10 describes such a visit by Peter—to whom Mary Magdalene reports finding the tomb empty—and the Beloved Disciple. Many early manuscripts of Luke also contain a concise version of Peter's visit to the tomb (Luke 24:12). The verbal parallels between this verse and the longer Johannine account lead many text critics to omit the verse from the text of Luke. Even though it is found in ancient witnesses, Luke 24:12 appears to be a summary statement based on knowledge of the Johannine tradition.[2] Both Luke and John presume that the disciples remained in the vicinity of Jerusalem and that the initial appearances of Jesus to the disciples took place there. John 21, on the other hand, concurs with the tradition attested in Mark and Matthew that Jesus appeared to his disciples in Galilee. Both the miraculous catch and the commissioning of Peter as shepherd are attached to a Galilean setting.

The historical problems created by the dual traditions cannot be definitively resolved. Exegetes often point out that from the beginning of the Gospel, Luke uses Jerusalem as a focal point for the events of salvation history. The apostles are explicitly told to remain in the city to await the coming of the Spirit at Pentecost (Acts 1:4). This literary emphasis also reflects the historical evidence that the Jerusalem community with Peter as its preeminent leader was the center from which Christianity spread to diaspora communities. Although Paul's pre-conversion encounters with the movement take place outside of Jerusalem, he knows that "those who were apostles before me" (Gal. 1:17) are in Jerusalem.

Yet the commissioning which concludes Matthew's Gospel, as well as the miraculous catch and the other allusions to the commissioning of Peter by the risen Lord, is strongly linked to Galilee. It is these Galilee traditions about Peter which form the basis for John 21. Luke has drawn much of the special material about Peter in the Gospel from a variant of this Galilean tradition. Unlike the final redaction of the Fourth Gospel, which attaches the Galilean traditions as though they were chronologically posterior to the Jerusalem appearances,[3] Luke presumes that the disciples remain permanently in the vicinity of Jerusalem. Thus, Peter's activities as leader of the Jerusalem community in the opening chapters of Acts are continuous with the assumption made in Luke 22:31–34 and Luke 24 that he is the one around whom the disciples gather after the Crucifixion.[4]

The issue of Peter's position among the apostles, which is resolved by Luke's treatment of Peter in the Gospel and Acts, was a problematic one for the Johannine tradition. The community's founder, who is invoked as the implied narrator in the Gospel as well as the authoritative voice that guarantees its tradition, is not Peter or one of the Twelve.[5] Throughout the Passion and Resurrection accounts, the Beloved Disciple appears as a counterpoint to Peter. He is closer to Jesus (John 13:23–25) and always responds with the fidelity and insight that the reader expects of a true disciple. However, the Beloved Disciple material stands in tension with many of the traditional pieces into which John has incorporated it. Though Jesus predicts that all the disciples will be scattered and leave him alone (John 16:32), the Beloved Disciple is present at the foot of the cross and witnesses to Jesus' death (John 19:25–27, 33–35). Though Peter is the one to investigate the tomb itself, the Beloved Disciple arrives first and is able to discern the significance of the tomb and its grave wrappings (John 20:4–5, 8). If we did not have chapter 21, we might assume that the Johannine community has simply substituted its relatively unknown founder for Peter. The Beloved Disciple's insight and fidelity to Jesus proves that the Johannine tradition is superior to that of churches which trace their founding tradition to Peter.

The rehabilitation and commissioning of Peter as shepherd in John 21:15–17 complicates the picture. The shepherd discourse in John 10:1–21 leaves no doubt about the communal as well as the christological significance of the shepherd image in Johannine tradition. Just as Matthew uses "rock" and "foundation" to refer both to the word of Jesus and to the apostle, so the Johannine author uses "shepherd" primarily in reference to Jesus, who sacrifices himself for the sheep, and now, secondarily, in reference to Peter. For Peter to stand in Jesus' stead, he must be more than the flawed disciple, who fails at every point when compared with the Beloved Disciple. Raymond Brown's reconstruction of the history of the Johannine community resolves this dilemma by analyzing the point of view taken by the Gospel's narrator as well as the tradition-history that has been postulated for the sources of the Gospel itself. Johannine Christianity is depicted by Brown as possessing superior insight into the truth about Jesus' relationship to the Father when contrasted even with other Christians. When Jesus refers to "other sheep" who also belong to his fold (John 10:16), the Johannine reader recognizes a reference to churches which derive their tradition from Peter.[6]

This interpretation provides a way of reconciling the Johannine and Lukan pictures of Peter's relationship to the other apostles. Johannine Christians acknowledge the legitimacy of the Petrine traditions in other churches while preserving the unique authority of their own founder. The Pauline mission provides a historical example of churches whose foundation is only loosely related to Petrine authority. Their apostle founder must claim to stand on the same basis as Peter and the others in view of his own commissioning by the risen Lord (Gal. 1:15–17). Where they have employed variants of a common tradition, Luke and John develop the picture of Peter in two different directions. Luke looks to the unity of the early Christian movement as it spread from

Jerusalem; John, to a distinctive perception of Jesus in a community that seeks to establish itself alongside other versions of Christianity. Luke moves Peter more forcefully to the center of the community. John incorporates the material dealing with the Beloved Disciple in order to move Peter off center.

PETER IN THE GOSPEL OF LUKE

We have seen that Luke makes a major modification in the Markan picture of Peter at the outset. Peter's call, the miraculous catch (Luke 5:1–11), occurs only after those summoned to be disciples have had experience of both Jesus' teaching and healing. Luke also modifies the tradition of Peter's confession. Both Matthew and Luke provide the reader with an explanation for the insight that Peter demonstrates. Matthew had insisted that Peter's confession came through divine revelation. In Luke, Jesus poses the question to his disciples after the feeding of the multitude.[7] Therefore, Peter's answer is based upon what he has witnessed (Luke 9:18–22).[8] Luke assumes that the teaching and miracles of Jesus are clear evidence that God's Spirit is acting in Jesus (e.g., Luke 4:16, 36; 5:17). When Peter responds to the miraculous catch with the confession of his own sinfulness (Luke 5:8), he acknowledged the holiness of God present in Jesus (cf. Isa. 6:5).[9] The confession that Jesus is the Messiah of God demonstrates a growing insight on the part of the disciples. Luke omits Peter's protest and Jesus' subsequent rebuke. He merely attaches the sayings on discipleship to Jesus' first Passion prediction (Luke 9:22, 23–27).

Luke not only omits negative comments about the disciples from his Markan source material; he also adds explanations for their actions. In the Transfiguration scene (Luke 9:28–36), Luke recasts his Markan source (Mark 9:2–8) so that there are two moments of revelation.[10] The first—witnessed only by the reader, since the disciples have fallen asleep—has Moses and Elijah discuss Jesus' coming departure (crucifixion) with him (Luke 9:29–32a). The disciples awaken just in time to see the two figures and Jesus' own glory (v. 32b). When used with reference to Jesus, the term "glory" appears to signify the risen Lord (e.g., Luke 24:26). Jesus' disciples have heard predictions of his Passion and suffering. Now they witness the glory which lies beyond the Passion.[11]

The second episode in the Transfiguration scene centers in Peter's response to the vision. In Mark, he was said to have reacted out of ignorance and fear. Luke shifts the fear to a theophanic appearance, the cloud from which the voice of God speaks (vv. 34–35). Peter's initial response that it would be good to build three booths is explained with a simpler statement, "not knowing what he said." Peter is not rebuked for misunderstanding in speaking these words. The disciples have just awakened from a sound sleep and have not been privy to the conversation between Jesus and the others.[12] The reader, who does hear that conversation, knows that this is not the time to retain these heavenly figures on earth. They have already discussed Jesus' departure with him. The christological importance of the scene is clear. God's voice teaches the disciples, including Peter, that Jesus replaces the old sources of authority, the Law, and the prophets.[13] The double scene allows Luke to show the reader the full interpretation of the Transfiguration event without revealing its full meaning to the disciples in the story.

Luke's tendency to exonerate the disciples comes through strongly in the Passion narrative. Satan, who has been absent from the narrative up to this point, attempts to gain control over the apostles (Luke 22:31–34; Mark 14:26–31). Jesus has prayed for Peter so that Satan has been defeated. The Lukan reader has already seen a miniature variant of this type of scene. Jesus announces that he has seen Satan fall from the heavens (Luke 10:17–20). His words are followed by the return of the seventy-two. The narrative hints that the extraordinary success of their mission is linked to Satan's fall from power.[14] The returning disciples report that even demons are subject to them. Since Jesus has broken Satan's power, the reader knows that Jesus' prayer for Peter will be answered. Peter's bold announcement that he would even die with Jesus leads Jesus to predict Peter's denial.

Luke's version of this episode looks forward to Peter's future role in the community. Jesus addresses Peter. He refers to Satan "sifting" the disciples as a group and then to his own prayer that Peter's faith will not fail (v. 31). However, the "sifting" will involve a falling away, since Jesus speaks of Peter's turning again and strengthening his brothers (v. 32). Peter responds by asserting that he is willing to go to prison and to death with Jesus (v. 33). Within the context, this response shows that Peter understands the implication of Jesus' words. Luke has recast Peter's assertions that he will not "fall away" or deny Jesus but will go to death (Mark 14:29, 31) so that they point toward Peter's own later imprisonment and death. Peter's imprisonments will be described in Luke's second volume, Acts. Jesus then predicts that

Peter will deny him three times before the cock crows (v. 34). Mark's version has Peter and the others protest their readiness to die with Jesus after the words about the denial. Luke ends with the saying of Jesus.

By treating Peter's denial in this fashion, Luke moderates the impact of the exchange between Jesus and Peter. Satan is responsible for the initial sifting of the disciples—not a flaw in their character. Though Peter is to be tested with the rest, he will be the agent of their restoration. As the reader knows, Peter will go to prison and later suffer death for Jesus. However, Jesus' warning shows that he will not do so during the events which are about to unfold. Peter never misunderstands or rejects the words which Jesus speaks about his fate. A reader might even conclude that Peter's initial reply shows that he relies upon Jesus as Lord and so rejects the suggestion that he might lose faith.[15]

The prophetic saying in verses 31–32 may have been independent of the Passion material into which Luke has incorporated it. "Brothers" is a common expression for Christians in Acts (1:15; 15:23, 32). Consequently, the prediction could have referred to Peter's future role in the community as witness to the Resurrection (24:34), as the one who reconstituted the Twelve (Acts 1:15), and as the leader of the early community.[16] The saying fits a general pattern of sayings about Peter's place in the community, as we have seen. The play on Peter's name and the foundation of the community in Matthew 16:16b–19[17] and the commissioning of Peter as shepherd over Jesus' sheep in John 21:15–17 both fit this pattern. Both Luke and John juxtapose Peter's denial with the new role that he is to assume. Therefore, the tradition from which Luke draws his additional Peter material may have linked a reversal of the denial scene with the commission to re-establish the community.

The reader will hardly be surprised to discover that Luke has also softened the characterization of Peter in the denial scene itself. Mark's account makes each of the three denials more pointed. Peter finally swears an oath that he does not know Jesus (Mark 14:71). In Luke, the series of Peter's denials moves from "not knowing him" (v. 57), to not being one of Jesus' Galilean followers (v. 58), to not understanding what the questioner is talking about (v. 60). All three responses are sufficiently equivocal for us to regard Peter as not denying Jesus directly. When Jesus looks at him, Peter then remembers Jesus' prediction.[18] The reader, who is reminded of the exchange between

Jesus and Peter at the Last Supper, will recognize that Peter's tears are a sign of repentance. Even though Luke has modified the verbal harshness of Peter's words to show that the apostle makes an attempt to avoid rejecting the Lord, there is no ambiguity about Peter's intent. His remorse acknowledges his failure to remain loyal to Jesus.

Other small details indicate that Luke's characterization of Peter is essentially positive. We have seen that the testing of the disciples in Mark corresponds with the evangelist's interpretation of the parable of the sower. A similar case might be made for this section of Luke. Luke treats the seed on rock as an example of those who believe for a while and then under "testing" fall away (Luke 8:13). In this episode, Peter is "tested." Though he fulfills Jesus' predictions by denying him, Peter does not fall away. He has not lost his faith in the Lord.[19] During Jesus' prayer in Gethsemane, Mark has Jesus rebuke Peter specifically for sleeping (Mark 14:37) and then has Jesus rebuke the whole group (14:40f.). Luke shortens the episode, omits any mention of Peter, and explains that the disciples were sleeping "for sorrow" (Luke 22:45). They may be viewed as not disobeying Jesus' command to "watch" lest they enter into temptation, since the arresting party arrives immediately (Luke 22:46–47). Luke also omits any reference to the flight of the disciples.

Peter does not figure prominently in the Easter stories of Luke 24. As we have seen, small details indicate that Luke considers him a leader among the disciples during this period. We have seen that some ancient manuscripts include a short reference to Peter's visit to the tomb (Luke 24:12).[20] This verse probably did not belong to the original text of Luke, since it conflicts with the rejection of the women's report attributed to the apostles in Luke 24:11. The Johannine variant makes it possible to assert that Peter and the Beloved Disciple are witnesses to the empty tomb as well. Luke 24:24 asserts that some of the disciples do verify the women's report. The notice in Luke 24:34 echoes a tradition that Peter is the first to see the risen Lord. By including this notice at the end of the Emmaus episode, Luke has incorporated Peter into the second section of chapter 24. The final section describes the appearance to the whole group in Jerusalem (24:36–49). Peter is not explicitly singled out. The disciples are commissioned to preach repentance in Jesus' name to all the nations. This renewed apostolate refers back to the original selection of the Twelve in Luke 6:12–16. After praying on a mountain, Jesus selected twelve of his followers to be apostles. They will be entrusted with their mission by the coming of the Spirit at Pentecost.[21]

The commissioning scenes provide the reader with the schema of the divine purpose which guides Luke's narrative. Those like Jesus, Peter, and Paul, who are designated as agents for God's plan, also come to function as reliable spokespersons. They are able to interpret key events in the narrative.[22] Luke has recast traditions about Peter so that the reader accepts Peter's witness to the Gospel and his central role in the early church. The disciples as a group have learned how the Scriptures predict the suffering of the Messiah from the risen Lord himself (Luke 24:44–46). The divine plan which led to the Crucifixion and Resurrection now leads forward to the testimony of these witnesses (v. 47). The connection between this mission and the instruction the disciples receive during the ministry of Jesus is evident in the speeches of Peter. Peter's summaries of the gospel message in Acts refer back to key passages in the Gospel of Luke. Peter's words to the crowds on Pentecost echo the preaching of the Baptist (Acts 2:38, 40; see also Luke 3:3, 5–6).[23] The restoration of Israel, a hope that was disappointed and delayed by the Crucifixion (Luke 24:21, Acts 1:6), might still come if Israel repents at the apostle's preaching (Acts 3:21).[24] In words which echo Jesus' first sermon (Luke 4:18–19, 43–44),[25] the summary in Acts 10:36–38 speaks of the Spirit in Jesus' healing as well as the geographical range of that healing. Thus Peter's speeches in Acts confirm the impression of Peter that is established in the Gospel. He is an authentic witness to Jesus' ministry.

PETER IN THE ACTS OF THE APOSTLES

Although it is difficult to evaluate the historical significance of the stories about Peter in Acts, they leave no doubt about his importance as the leader in the earliest community. By echoing words in the speeches of Peter in Acts, Luke is able to show that the message of the apostles parallels that of Jesus, himself. The miracles performed by Peter also correspond to those of Jesus: healing paralyzed persons, curing crowds, and restoring the dead to life (Acts 3:1–10; 5:15; 9:32–34, 36–42). Such activities demonstrate that the mission of the apostles corresponds to the instructions given the Twelve during Jesus' lifetime (Luke 9:1–2).[26] The Peter who denied knowing Jesus in the Gospel of Luke confesses him now before the Sanhedrin and the high priest. Peter insists that God's Spirit remains with those who obey God (Acts

5:27–40). Thus the close association between the Spirit, miracles, and preaching in the ministry of Jesus has been transferred to the apostles who are his witnesses. Luke's second volume makes explicit the perspective of later Christian readers. Any failures shown by the apostle during Jesus' lifetime have been eradicated by his post-Resurrection transformation.

Peter comes closer to stepping into the place of Jesus than any of the other apostles. In order for the core group of disciples to fulfil the mandate which Jesus had originally given the Twelve, the place left by Judas must be filled. Peter takes the initiative (Acts 1:15–26). He knows the scriptural passages that predicted Judas' betrayal. He recognizes the necessity of restoring the group to twelve in number and proposes the criteria for selection. Even before Pentecost initiates the disciples' mission to others, Peter is sufficiently inspired by the Spirit to interpret God's plan and to provide for the community.[27] Like Jesus, Peter is able to discern what is in a person's heart. Ananias and Sapphira cannot deceive the Spirit when they attempt to lie to the apostle (5:1–11).[28]

However, Luke makes it evident that whatever powers the disciples enjoy, they owe them to God's activity in the Spirit. Those who are healed experience the saving power of Jesus' name (3:6). Though Peter's activities are closely modeled on those of Jesus, he does not act alone. Throughout the account in Acts, other apostles are present with Peter. John shares his healing, imprisonment, and testimony before the Sanhedrin (3:1, 11; 4:2–7; 5:29). When the church is faced with an internal crisis between Hebrews and Hellenists (6:1–6), a preliminary to the Jew/Gentile tensions (10:1–11:18; 15:1–35),[29] the issue is resolved by the Twelve acting as a group. Though Peter decides that God's will requires him to baptize the gentile centurion and his household, he cannot establish the change of practice on his own. Peter must account for his actions to persons from the "circumcision party" in Jerusalem (11:1–18).[30] Luke may have deflected the serious danger of division in the primitive church by shifting the issue away from whether Peter should have baptized the Gentiles to whom God gave the Spirit. The charge to which Peter must answer is that of eating with Gentiles.[31]

Though Peter's speeches to the Jerusalem crowds open up the possibility that Israel may repent now that they have learned that the one who was crucified has been exalted (2:24–36),[32] God's promises are to go beyond Israel (3:17). Just as those who crucified Jesus unwittingly played a role God's plan for redemption (Acts 3:17–18), so the persecution that scattered Christians from Jerusalem will spread the gospel to the nations. The first outbreak of persecution forces out of the city those whose preaching in the Greek-speaking synagogues had led to disruption (Acts 8:1–4).[33] After the persecution which included the martyrdom of James, the son of Zebedee, and another imprisonment of Peter, the apostle himself is forced to leave the city (Acts 12:1–17).

Luke builds his narrative on repetitions of the same pattern. Each exemplar introduces variations that are specific to the context in Acts. These variations also provide additional instruction for the reader in interpreting the characters and events associated with that pattern.[34] The persecution scenes involve successive arrests and releases of Peter and the other apostles (Acts 4:3–22; 5:17–42; 12:1–17) that are inter-locked with two episodes in which witnesses to Jesus are martyred, Stephen (Acts 6:8–7:60) and James (12:1–2). Luke repeatedly reminds the reader that Peter and the others spoke boldly both in proclaiming Jesus and in accusing the Jewish leaders of disbelief.[35] Though the first two episodes culminate in the apostle's release and continued activity in Jerusalem, the third, which follows the two martyrdoms, ends with a divinely assisted escape. This time, Peter does not stay in the city. Luke reminds the reader of the events of Jesus' death in Peter's opening speeches (e.g., Acts 3:13–15). Other details from the Lukan Passion narrative color the imprisonment and martyrdom stories.[36] Peter's final Jerusalem imprisonment occurs during Passover. The church's prayer for the apostle is said to spark the divine rescue mission (12:5). When Herod finds Peter missing, the guards are exe-cuted instead (12:18–19). Thus the reader has no doubt that without God's intervention, Peter would have died. Peter's boast that he was ready to go to prison and die with Jesus (Luke 22:33) has been tested and proven true.[37]

In addition to his steadfast witness to Jesus in the face of hostility, Peter plays a crucial role in the emergence of a gentile mission. His responsibility for the apostolic mission was suggested when he recon-stituted the number of apostles. The Pentecost scene as well as Peter's own words (Acts 2:39) suggests a mission that will expand outside the boundaries of the Jewish people. Driven from Jerusalem by the first persecution, Philip makes converts in Samaria and later baptizes an Ethiopian proselyte on the road to Gaza. Peter and John are sent to confirm the Samaritan mission by conferring the Holy Spirit on the new converts (Acts 8:14–17).[38] As we have seen, Peter is not alone in this action. Both apostles confer the Spirit through the laying on of hands. This sequence prepares the ground for the Cornelius episode by making reception of the Spirit the decisive mark of Christian believers. When God confers the Spirit on those in Cornelius' household, Peter can hardly deny them the lesser sign of baptism (Acts 10:44–48, 11:15–17). When Peter defends his action back in Jerusalem, he refers the audience to the Gospel account of the Baptist (Luke 3:11). But Peter alters the circumstances. John's saying about the one to come after him becomes a saying of the Lord: "I remembered the word of the Lord, that he said, 'John baptized with water, but you will be baptized with the Holy Spirit,' " (Acts 11:16). This shift has been facilitated by Jesus' reference to the saying in Acts 1:4–5 in order to indicate that the Pentecost episode will fulfil that promise. He also invokes the theological principle, which the reader first learns from Gamaliel's intervention before the Sanhedrin (Acts 5:38–39), that no one can resist what God wills (Acts 11:17).[39]

Luke attaches a legendary story about Peter's confrontation with the Samaritan magician, Simon Magus, to the bestowal of the Spirit (Acts 8:9–11, 18–24). Later tradition will use Simon Magus as the archetype of the heretic. Peter's victory over Simon demonstrates the superiority of orthodox Christianity. In Acts, this episode initiates a series of encounters between those who preach the gospel and representatives of superstitious idolatry. As here, the pagans often have financial interests at stake.[40] Prior to Peter's arrival, Philip had outdone the magician by exorcism and healing. Ironically, Simon seeks to purchase the power to bestow the Holy Spirit on others that is possessed by the apostles (8:18–19). The reader knows from the earlier story of Ananias and Sapphira that Peter's curse (v. 20) means probable death. Though Peter exhorts Simon to repent, hoping that the Lord will save him (v. 22), Peter's description of Simon's heart (v. 23) suggests that this will not be the case.[41]

Susan Garrett has pointed out that this episode exploits stereotyped portraits of persons who belong to Satan, the use of magic, self-glorification, the ability to seduce the people, and secret sinfulness. The story with its evidence that both Philip and Peter are superior to Simon Magus demonstrates that the Lord's witnesses have authority over Satan. The fall of Satan envisaged in the Gospel continues to be effected through the disciples' mission.[42] The description of Simon Magus' heart evokes passages from the Old Testament that refer to the bondage of idolatry. The "gall of bitterness" and "bond of iniquity" have hold of Simon Magus. The "gall" refers to the wrath with which the Lord will punish those who commit idolatry (Deut. 29:17–19) Septuagint, the "bondage" to the "bonds of wickedness" (Isa. 58:6) which Jesus came to break (Acts 10:38). Simon Magus is completely trapped in iniquity while he offers money to obtain the Spirit, which he would have to receive as a gift from God.[43] Simon's initial entry into the Christian community (8:13) is as fraudulent as the deceit of Ananias and Sapphira. Ananias and Sapphira and Simon have hearts that are filled with Satan (Acts 5:3). Peter's ability to discern what is hidden in such hearts demonstrates that he is acting as the agent of the Spirit.

This agency underlines a difference between the apostle and the magician. The apostle acts in the name of Jesus or through the power of the Spirit, which he does not control. Were Simon to repent, for example, God might rescue him from the evil to which he is subject. The healing miracles are performed in the name of Jesus (Acts 3:6, 12, 16; 9:34) or through prayer (9:40). Simon thinks that the power of the Spirit can be bought and sold by its human recipients. The apostles never exalt themselves as Simon does. The extraordinary power evident in their miraculous deeds always turns others to the Lord (e.g., 9:35, 42). Peter quickly prevents Cornelius from worshiping him because he, Peter, is a mere mortal (10:26).[44]

Obedience to the will of the Lord and the guidance of the Spirit characterizes all the actions of the apostles. The Cornelius episode turns upon this fact of divine agency. With the conversion of the persecutor, Paul (Acts 9:1–31), the reader knows that prayer and visions accompany major shifts in the story. Jesus speaks with the divine voice to direct the course of events. Both episodes pave the way for the mission to the Gentiles.[45] Peter's initial reaction to the vision (10:14) shows that he is no more willing than Paul to violate the Law of God. However, he is constrained by the divine command to see what God has in store. Similarly, Paul is not commissioned immediately. He must go into the city, where he will be told what God intends (9:5f.). Both apostles act on a "riddle" which they expect future events to resolve.[46] Thus, Luke insists that no human considerations motivate either Paul or Peter. Neither acts alone. God sends Ananias to heal Paul's blindness and reveal God's plan for him (9:10–19). When the Holy Spirit comes upon those who are listening to Peter's summary of the gospel, "believers from the circumcised" who have accompanied Peter recognize that the Gentiles are experiencing the Spirit just as they themselves have experienced it (10:44–46a).

The legitimation of this mission to the Gentiles is not complete until Peter convinces the Jerusalem community that he has acted according to God's will. We have seen that Luke shifts the narrative away from the divisive issue of whether or not non-Jews can be members of the new movement. Instead, the protest resembles the dispute referred to in Galatians 2:11–14. Peter should not have eaten with Gentiles. The historical question of whether or not Jews would share meals with non-Jews has been the subject of extensive dispute. The evidence suggests that practices in this regard varied widely.[47] The vision of clean and unclean animals suggests to the reader of Acts that the problem centered on the likelihood that eating in a Gentile's home would force the Jew to violate the Law concerning pure and impure food.[48]

Though scholars agree that such concerns over maintaining kosher when eating with Gentiles could have led to the problems in Antioch, Peter's defense of his actions in Acts does not turn on that question. His vision of the animals was first interpreted as evidence that he should consider no person "unclean" (10:28–29). He tells Cornelius that because of that vision, he came willingly to the house. However, the version for the Jerusalem audience does not apply the vision to that question. Peter states that the Spirit told him to go with the men without making any distinction (11:12). The authorization for his actions comes from the fact that the promised Spirit came upon the Gentiles. Peter expands this motif by referring to a saying of the Lord. To act differently would have been an attempt to resist God, which the reader knows is impossible (11:15–17).

Though it is common to speak of the Cornelius episode as the first conversion of Gentiles, Robert Tannehill notes that the narrative does not support this interpretation. Philip has already baptized an Ethiopian eunuch as well as numerous Samaritans (8:26–40). Cornelius himself is an extremely "Jewish" Gentile. His piety rivals that of the relatives of Jesus in the infancy narratives to the Gospel. The angel attests that his prayer and good works ascend before the Lord (10:4).[49] The consequences of the Cornelius story can be seen in the mission of the apostles. Rather than wait for private encounters with individual pious Gentiles, Jewish Christian missionaries may associate with Gentiles in general. God is opening the door to all people. His apostle witnesses must go to preach among all people.[50]

On the one hand, Luke recasts events in the early community so that Peter's response to God's directive initiates the mission to the nations. On the other, Luke recognizes that conversion of the Gentiles has not followed the fixed order depicted in Acts 8–10. The initial missionary efforts among Jews has already spilled over into Gentiles who live in the same cities (Acts 11:19–21). Peter's final appearance in the narrative of Acts occurs at the "Jerusalem Council." We have seen that such a meeting clearly did take place and that it was well enough known for Paul to use it to support his argument against Judaizers in Galatia (Gal. 2:6–10). We are not concerned with resolving the conflicts between the two accounts. The only question is what Luke's version tells the reader about Peter. As in the earlier speech, Peter must persuade an assembled group of apostles and elders that the Pharisee Christians who demand that Gentiles be circumcised are wrong (15:1, 5–6). Neither he nor James can simply decide the issue.[51]

Peter refers back to God's decisive actions in the Cornelius episode (15:7–9). God is the subject of every statement about those events. Consequently, Peter can then turn and charge his opponents with attempting to resist what God has already done. Peter reaches the conclusion that both Jews and Gentiles are saved because of the grace received from the Lord. The Law does not determine whether or not God has cleansed a person's heart (vv. 10–11).[52]

We have seen that the historical evidence suggests that leadership in the Jerusalem community shifted from Peter to James. People associated with James sparked the change in meal practices at Antioch, a fact which set Peter at odds with Paul (Gal. 2:12). Acts reflects a similar shift away from Peter's position in its opening chapters. At the Jerusalem council, the final decision is not pronounced by Peter but by James. James provides yet another interpretation of the Cornelius episode by highlighting the ecclesial significance of that event. God has not just chosen some individual pious Gentiles to receive grace. Rather, God has chosen a new people for himself (15:14). James backs up this conclusion by referring to the prophetic vision of the rebuilding of the city of David as a place for all to seek the Lord (15:15–18). Though Peter was God's agent in the crucial events which taught the early Jerusalem community to view the conversion of the Gentiles as God's will, he is not the instrument by which the policy is carried out. Peter disappears from the narrative. The rest of Acts focuses on Paul.

Luke's portrayal of Peter remains consistent throughout Acts. Echoes of the Gospel account of Jesus' ministry shape much of the early narrative about the apostles. As agents of the Spirit, Peter and the others repeat paradigmatic miracles of Jesus. As we have seen, the contents of the Gospel also form the basis for summaries in the apostle's preaching. Peter is clearly the central character among the apostles in Jerusalem. He is usually the spokesperson for the group. However, he does not enjoy supremacy over the other apostles. Indeed, such a position would violate the sayings about greatness which Luke has attached to the Last Supper (Luke 22:24–27). Instead, Peter always acts with others from the apostolic group. They, in turn, recognize that God has continued to act decisively through Peter. The reader also knows that Peter has fulfilled the promise he made at the Last Supper. He has spoken boldly before the authorities when imprisoned. Juxtaposition of Peter's imprisonment and the stories of the martyrdoms of Stephen and James suggests that the reader is to infer that Peter too will suffer this fate. Only an extraordinary divine rescue saves Peter from death at Herod's hands (Acts 12:11).

Like the other apostles, Peter never exalts himself. The extraordinary miraculous powers that he possesses are sharply curtailed. They serve only to provide evidence of the truth of what the apostles are preaching concerning Jesus. The "name" of Jesus carries healing power. Divine power also leads persons to respond in faith to the apostle's preaching. The careful narrative structures woven into Luke's account show that he is not primarily interested in describing Peter as a historical figure. Peter, James and later Paul show heroic and unwavering dedication to the mission which God has directed them to carry out. Even the weaknesses in Peter's character which Luke derives from the sources that he uses for the Gospel are missing in Acts. Luke's readers can look back to the earliest community and its leaders as an inspiration for the future.

PETER IN THE GOSPEL OF JOHN

We have already seen that the Fourth Evangelist draws upon a synoptic-like tradition about Peter: (a) Jesus gives Simon the nickname "Cephas," which means "Peter" (John 1:42); (b) Peter is spokesperson for the Twelve in an episode which recalls the confession of Peter (6:67–69); (c) Jesus predicts that Peter will deny him (13:36–38); (d) Peter denies Jesus three times (18:15–17, 25–27). Other items in the Johannine account probably contain elements of historical memory. Though Andrew drops out of the core group in the synoptics, John credits him with a crucial role in bringing his brother to Jesus (1:40–

42). We have also seen that Jesus' prophecy of Peter's destiny has been interpreted by the Gospel narrator as evidence that he died a martyr's death. John appears to be responsible for naming Peter as the disciple who cut off the ear of one of the high priest's servants (18:10–11; cf. Mark 14:47; Matt. 26:51–54; Luke 22:49–51).[53] In addition to those episodes which are variants of the general synoptic tradition, others seem to be divergent strands of traditions that are found in Luke. Peter's visit to the tomb after the women report it empty is recounted in detail (John 20:2–10; cf. Luke 24:12). The miraculous catch of fish, used as a call story in Luke, occurs as a Resurrection appearance story in John (21:1–11; cf. Luke 5:1–11). That episode has been combined with a story about Jesus as a mysterious stranger who is recognized by his disciples at a meal (John 21:12–13) which is more distantly related to the Lukan Emmaus tradition (Luke 24:28–30).[54]

Since the commissioning of Peter as the one to tend Jesus' flock echoes a central image used for Jesus himself, one might presume that the Johannine tradition saw Peter as the leader of the early community. However, as we have noted, Peter will be shadowed by the Beloved Disciple in the second half of the Gospel. The Beloved Disciple, the source of the Johannine tradition, clearly has both loyalty to Jesus and insight into his person that surpasses Peter's. The variants in the synoptic tradition show that the Resurrection stories of the visit to inspect the tomb and the miraculous catch originally had Peter as their central character. The Fourth Evangelist has introduced the Beloved Disciple. This figure first appears at the Last Supper, where he is closer to Jesus than Peter. Peter must ask him to ask Jesus for an explanation of his words about the disciple who is going to betray him (13:23–25). Peter does not understand the significance of the empty tomb or recognize the figure on the shore. The Beloved Disciple does. We have also seen that John 21:15–19 depicts a commissioning of Peter to be shepherd of the sheep and predicts Peter's death. The following verses contrast Peter's death as a martyr with the long life of the Beloved Disciple, who is the source of the Johannine church's tradition (21:20–24). Peter raises the question about the Beloved Disciple's fate (v. 20).

The contrast between Peter and the Beloved Disciple highlights the irony with which the Fourth Evangelist treats Jesus' disciples. The Beloved Disciple provides a reliable testimony to events concerning Jesus because the Beloved Disciple is never the subject of such irony. He is closest to Jesus. He does not flee but is present with Jesus' mother at the foot of the cross and is able to bear witness to the events of Jesus' death. He is also able to recognize that Jesus has returned to the Father in glory when he sees the empty tomb. To a greater or lesser degree, all of the other characters in the Fourth Gospel fail to perceive the revelation of God's glory in Jesus.[55] Peter's boasts of faithfulness (6:68) and willingness to lay down his life for Jesus (13:37)[56] are sharpened by the presence of the Beloved Disciple. Peter is no longer the "best" among a weak, frightened, uncomprehending group of disciples as we see him in Mark.

Matthew and Luke reshaped the Markan image of Peter so that Christians could see Peter as a model for discipleship. John departs from this trend. Peter is not the first disciple. He is called by his brother, Andrew, who with an unnamed disciple had come to Jesus on the testimony of the Baptist (John 1:40–42). Andrew confesses that Jesus is the Messiah. Though Peter does confess loyalty to Jesus in the name of the Twelve (John 6:68–69), Jesus responds to his words with a reference to Judas' betrayal (v. 70). This response alerts the reader that Jesus' disciples are not trustworthy.[57]

The disciples do not figure prominently in the public ministry of Jesus. Their preparation and instruction occur during the Last Supper. It is initiated by the foot-washing (John 13:3–20). The Fourth Evangelist has used irony and misunderstanding throughout the Gospel. A character's challenge to Jesus' words or actions enables Jesus or the narrator to explain the true meaning of what is occurring. Peter's reaction to Jesus' washing the disciples' feet follows this pattern (John 13:6–10). It does not provide information about character traits of Peter as an individual, such as his alleged impulsiveness.[58] Given the implied rebuke or even threat in Jesus' response, "If I do not . . . you will have no share with me" (v. 8), some interpreters think that this episode is similar to Peter's rejection of the Passion prediction in Mark 8:32–33.[59] Beginning at the Last Supper, Peter's deficiencies are highlighted as he is consistently contrasted with the Beloved Disciple.

Since the risen Jesus rehabilitates Peter with the threefold profession of love in John 21:15–17 and simultaneously entrusts him with caring for his sheep, the evangelist clearly acknowledges the ongoing significance of Peter in the larger Christian community.[60] When Jesus predicts Peter's martyrdom (21:18–19), Peter raises a question about the fate of the Beloved Disciple. In recounting this episode, the evangelist takes pains to remind the reader of the special relationship between Jesus and the Beloved Disciple: "Peter turned and saw the disciple whom Jesus loved following them; he was the one who reclined next to Jesus at the supper and had said, 'Lord, who is it that is going to betray you?' When Peter saw him, he said to Jesus, 'Lord, what about him?' Jesus said to him, 'If it is my will that he remain until I come, what is that to you? Follow me!' " (John 21:20–22). Jesus' final word to Peter, "Follow me," repeats the final sentence of the martyrdom prediction (v. 19). At this point, the reader of John is able to decipher Jesus' enigmatic response to Peter's ill-timed promise to follow Jesus "where he is going" during the Passion: "Where I am going you cannot follow me now; but you will follow me afterward" (13:36).[61] The evangelist's comment that people later misunderstood Jesus' saying about the Beloved Disciple to mean that he would not die before the Second Coming (v. 23) indicates that by the time chapter 21 is written, both disciples have died.

Why then the contrast between the two? Most exegetes today assume that Johannine Christians recognized the pastoral importance of Peter while defending the uniqueness of the traditions they had inherited from the Beloved Disciple. The view of the Johannine tradition as accommodating the esteem Peter enjoys in other churches indeed seems to be correct. However, some scholars insist that such readings are merely harmonizing John with the synoptic Gospels or accommodating contemporary ecumenical sensibilities.

These challenges to the usual interpretation demonstrate the uncertainty which attends any claim to determine the intentions behind ambiguous features in a narrative. They also demonstrate the difficulty of those forms of literary analysis which claim to specify how the text projects the response of its ideal reader. Two peculiar details of the Johannine narrative have been the focus of such arguments: Peter as the one who cuts off the servant's ear (John 18:10–11, 26),[62] and Peter's leaping into the sea when the Beloved Disciple recognizes the stranger on shore as the Lord (John 21:7).[63] It is argued that both reflect negatively on Peter's status as a disciple. In the first instance, Jesus rebukes Peter for failing to recognize that Jesus is doing the Father's will: "Put your sword into its sheath. Am I not to drink the cup that the Father has given me?" (v. 11). Peter's response is particularly wrong-headed in the Johannine narrative because Jesus has just stopped a huge arresting party in its tracks with his divine "I am" (v. 6: "When he said to them, 'I am He,' they stepped back and fell to the ground"). This episode is attached to the third denial, since the man who questions Peter is said to be a relative of the servant. But the most damning evidence of Peter's failure occurs during Jesus' trial before Pilate.[64] In response to a question about his kingship, Jesus replies: "My kingdom is not from this world. If my kingdom were from this world, my followers would be fighting to keep me from being handed over to the Jews. But as it is, my kingdom is not from here" (18:36). Both the violence with which Peter acts and the fear evidenced in his denial are alleged to demonstrate that Peter is not among the "servants" of Jesus. He does take up the sword to resist Jesus' arrest.

If we recognize that the tradition of Jesus' appearance at the Sea of Galilee was originally not the third in a series as it is now (21:1) but an independent account of Jesus' manifestation to the disciples, then Peter's action there appears more ominous. The text does not tell us why Peter grabs his clothes and leaps into the sea when the figure on the shore is identified as Jesus. In the "great catch" call story of Luke 5:1–11, Peter responds with a confession of sinfulness and attempts to separate himself from Jesus. Rather than assume that Peter's action represents eagerness to get to the Lord,[65] D. H. Gee proposes that this detail reflects Peter's intention to flee from the presence of the one he has denied. The fire Jesus has built on the shore (v. 9) recalls the fire in the courtyard of the high priest's house (18:18).[66] Fear, guilt, and panic motivate Peter. However, he apparently remains clothed and paralyzed in the water. When the disciples bring the boat near the shore, Peter has unhooked the net and climbs up on shore dragging it behind him (vv. 9–11).[67]

If we accept the suggestions of these scholars, then the tragedy of Peter's flawed character is highlighted by the Fourth Evangelist. The presence of the Beloved Disciple in the Gospel highlights Peter's failures by demonstrating what is possible for a disciple of Jesus. The Resurrection scene at the Sea of Galilee does what ancient tragedies could not do. It forces Peter to confront the Lord, whom he has denied knowing after all of his earlier professions of loyalty. Peter's subsequent rehabilitation and position in the church owe nothing to his own character or merits. They are simply and only a gift of the risen Lord.

As Rudolf Schnackenburg has pointed out, Peter's restoration in John 21 includes both a pastoral function, "feed my sheep," and the injunction to follow Jesus in death. There are no indications of the missionary image so typical of other trajectories in the Peter story.[68] Jesus' words about Peter's martyrdom also have an ironic edge when set against the scene we have just witnessed of Peter in the boat:[69] "When you were young, you girded yourself and walked where you would; but when you are old, you will stretch out your hands; and another will gird you, and carry you where you do not want to go'' (John 21:18; RSV). Peter had girded himself with his outer garment and lept into the sea. The image of Peter with outstretched hands being gird by others and led where he does not wish to go suggests the notion of the apostle as a prisoner. The evangelist tells the reader that these words refer to Peter's death (v. 19). However unpromising Peter's situation appears to be at the beginning of the chapter, readers are reminded that he does complete his mission as shepherd of Jesus' flock.

If the Fourth Evangelist or the final editor who attached the final chapter to the Gospel intends the reader to look back to the earlier narrative, then Peter's death is part of his function as shepherd. Peter becomes the shepherd of Jesus' flock only because he has learned to ''love the Lord.'' The boast that he would ''lay down his life for Jesus'' (13:37–38) contains an ironic claim to act like the good shepherd, Jesus (10:15). Jesus' own willingness to lay down his life for his followers establishes the new relationship that makes them his friends (15:13).[70] Peter and the other disciples who have shared the final meal with Jesus all belong to this circle of friends. Though it is possible to observe a decentering of Peter in John, the evangelist is not hostile to Jesus' disciples.

Unlike Matthew or Acts, the Fourth Gospel does not indicate how Peter carried out his mission as shepherd. Since the Johannine churches trace their ancestry and tradition to the Beloved Disciple, such traditions may have had little relevance. Other traditions show that ''shepherd'' soon came to designate the elders or bishops who had to care for the local churches (see, e.g., Acts 20:28; 1 Pet. 2:25; 5:2).[71] The Beloved Disciple has performed that role within the Johannine community. However, this passage appears to acknowledge that Peter exemplifies that office in the larger church. The tradition of Peter's martyrdom has concluded Peter's career with a final testimony to his love for the true shepherd, Jesus.

Though many exegetes think that John 21 was a later addition to the Gospel, there is no reason to treat its Petrine material as an effort to moderate an anti-Peter tradition in the earlier edition of the Gospel, as is sometimes suggested. The portrayal of Peter in John 21 fills out hints that are contained in the earlier chapters. Peter is the most prominent member of the group which has followed Jesus from the beginning of his ministry in Galilee. He continues partly to understand the truth of

Jesus' words. In that respect, he continues to be overshadowed by the figure of the Beloved Disciple. However, Peter's love for the Lord remains despite his earlier failures. The reader of the Fourth Gospel knows that Jesus is never ignorant of human character (e.g., John 2:23–25). Therefore, the pastoral charge which the risen Lord gives to Peter will be carried out as Jesus intended.

EXCURSUS: PETER AND THE TWELVE

Ecumenical discussions of the papacy have focused attention on the relationship between Peter's role and that of the Twelve as a group. The church fathers and later Catholic exegetes often read John 21:15–17 as evidence that Peter was given authority over the other apostles as well as the faithful. As Schnackenburg points out, the passage itself does not support that reading.[72] Nor does the use of "shepherd" for those charged with pastoral responsibility in the New Testament suggest that the expression refers to the primacy of a particular disciple. For the Fourth Gospel, Jesus is the exemplary shepherd. 1 Peter 2:25 also speaks of Jesus as "shepherd and guardian." The exhortation to the elders in Acts 20:17–35 presents the departing apostle, Paul, as a model for the care of the flock.

John 6:68 assumes that the reader is familiar with a group of disciples known as the Twelve, even though no account of their appointment is given in the Gospel itself. The list in Mark 3:16–19 begins with Simon and James and John, the sons of Zebedee. As we have seen, this group, all of whom are given nicknames, forms an inner circle during the ministry of Jesus. We have also seen that the historical evidence for leadership in the early Jerusalem church that we have in Galatians 1–2 is somewhat ambiguous. Paul's first visit is with Peter, though he also meets James, the brother of the Lord (Gal. 1:18–19). His later visit includes James, Peter, and John as "pillars" of that church (Gal. 2:9). Finally, when Paul is visiting Antioch, he is constrained to change his practice of eating with Gentiles by "certain persons from James" (Gal. 2:12). There is no indication here that the Twelve was a functioning group of authorities in the early community.

Since the discovery of the Dead Sea Scrolls, some scholars have compared the institution of the group of Twelve to the group of twelve laymen who, along with three priests, are designated leaders of the sect in the Qumran rule (1 QS 8, 1). Though Acts 1:15–26 depicts Peter reconstituting that group after the betrayal by Judas, it is not restored when James is martyred (Acts 12:2). Even in the narrative of Acts, it does not form an institutional structure. Ernst Haenchen insists that scholars should not mistake a symbolic group of witnesses to Jesus' life and Resurrection for a governing structure.[73]

The Twelve apparently symbolize the renewal of Israel through the preaching of Jesus. The eschatological symbolism of the number appears in sayings about the Twelve as judges of Israel (e.g., Matt. 19:28; Luke 22:30). Luke appears to be responsible for the confusion between the group of disciples referred to as the Twelve and the apostles. He adds the term "apostles" to the call of the Twelve (Luke 6:13).[74] It also appears in Matthew 10:2 and Revelation 21:14. The formulae in 1 Corinthians 15:5 and 7 distinguish Peter and the Twelve, followers of Jesus, from others—James and the apostles— whose position like that of Paul stems from an appearance of the risen Lord.

Peter's prominence in the Gospel narratives is not a function of his position within a group of Twelve. He is a spokesperson within the more limited group of three disciples. And his relationships with the other prominent leaders shows considerable variation. Acts 11:1–18 suggests that Peter has to win over others in Jerusalem. Haenchen notes that although Peter is first among the apostles, the whole apostolic church is greater than he is.[75] The two commissioning stories which are sometimes said to exalt Peter's place in the community, Matthew 16:18–19 and John 21:15–17, point to the apostle's significance in early communities, not to his relationship to the Twelve.

Both Luke and John have preserved independent traditions about Peter's life and position in the early church. The extensive reshaping of early traditions about the apostle by each of the evangelists indicates the prominence of Peter traditions in early Christian churches that were of very different heritage. We have seen that both authors also provide evidence that Peter's death was understood to be following the pattern established by Jesus. The final chapter of the Fourth Gospel makes this parallel clear. Because Peter fulfills his role as shepherd over the flock, he will eventually make good on the promise to follow the Lord even in death. Though Luke never tells the reader of Acts about the deaths of either Peter or Paul, readers can recognize the indirect clues that the apostles will share the fate of their Lord. In Peter's case, each arrest is more ominous. In each instance, Peter shows unyielding courage when confronted by the authorities. The fearful equivocations in the Gospel story of Peter's denial never appear in Acts.

The Johannine account highlights Peter's weaknesses as a disciple when it contrasts him with the community's own revered founder, the Beloved Disciple. But that very sharp outline also shows the reader the drama of Peter's transformation by the risen Lord. The Gospel does not end as a tragedy of Jesus' followers or with the ambiguity of Mark's promise to disciples who remain in disarray. The risen Lord has secured the unity of his diverse flock by providing those who do not belong to the Johannine community with a reliable shepherd.

However, neither Luke nor John provide any evidence to support the claim that Peter is shepherd or successor to Jesus in a way that other apostles are not. Acts depicts the changing leadership in the Jerusalem community. Its primary figures have not clashed with each other because they all recognize the power of God guiding the church in its crucial decisions and the divine plan behind events such as death and persecution which have also shaped its history. In the Johannine tradition, we see a community with an apostle founder who is not one of the Twelve. This follower of Jesus has given Johannine traditions a distinctive picture of Jesus and of salvation. Though the Johannine church has not derived the legitimacy of its tradition from Peter, it recognizes the validity of the witness to Jesus in other communities. Peter, the martyr-shepherd, guarantees that other Christian churches also belong to Jesus' flock.

NOTES

1. Rudolf Schnackenburg argues that the commissioning of Peter stems from a tradition that was originally independent of the miraculous catch and may reflect the original narrative of the Lord's appearance to Peter. See *Commentary on Chapters 13–21*, vol. 3 of *The Gospel According to St. John*, trans. David Smith and G. A. Kon (New York: Crossroad, 1982), 348. Since the designation "son of John" occurs only in the Fourth Gospel (John 1:42), Schnackenburg does not think that the formal address "Simon, son of John" stems from the older tradition (*Commentary on Chapters 13–21*, 362).

2. Joseph A. Fitzmyer argues for the inclusion of the Lukan variant in the Greek text of the Gospel; see *The Gospel According to Luke (X–XXIV)*, AB 28A (Garden City: Doubleday, 1981), 1547–48.

3. This juxtaposition of the Galilean traditions and the Jerusalem appearances continues the awkward series of jumps between Galilee and

Jerusalem that occur in the narrative throughout the Gospel. John presumes that Jesus' ministry occurred over a period of three years, during which he alternated between Galilee and Jerusalem.

4. As I have already suggested in discussing Edward Schillebeeckx's interpretation of Peter's conversion, this later construction of events is not to be understood as a historical foundation for the centrality of Peter's experience in re-establishing the group of disciples.

5. Attempts to avoid the possibility of a disciple other than one of the Twelve as being the Beloved Disciple are unpersuasive. Likewise is the argument of those who conclude that the so-called "Beloved Disciple" is a symbolic figure because the Beloved Disciple appears as a character only in the Passion and Resurrection accounts and always embodies the ideal response to Jesus. See the extensive discussion of the literature on this topic in George R. Beasley-Murray, *John*, WBC 36 (Waco, TX: Word Books, 1987), lxvi–lxxv; and Schnackenburg, *Commentary on Chapters 13–21*, 375–87. The parallels between the Qumran Teacher of Righteousness and the Beloved Disciple provide evidence for the use of a symbolic designation for the authoritative founder of a community's tradition. See J. Roloff, "Der johanneische 'Lieblingsjünger' und der Lehrer der Gerechtigkeit," *NTS* 15 (1968–1969): 129–51.

6. Raymond E. Brown, *Community of the Beloved Disciple* (New York: Paulist Press, 1979), 81–88.

7. This order results from the omission of a block of Markan material. As a result of that omission, Luke frames the feeding with two confession scenes: Herod's opinion of Jesus (9:7–9), the feeding (9:10–17), Peter's opinion of Jesus (9:18–21). See Joseph A. Fitzmyer, *The Gospel According to Luke (I–IX)*, AB 28 (Garden City: Doubleday, 1981), 770.

8. Robert Tannehill, *The Gospel According to Luke*, vol. 1 of *The Narrative Unity of Luke-Acts: A Literary Interpretation* (Philadelphia: Fortress Press, 1986), 98.

9. Fitzmyer, *Luke (I–IX)*, 567. Wofgang Dietrich emphasizes the theophany character of the miraculous catch; see *Das Petrusbild der Lukanischen Schriften* (Stuttgart: W. Kohlhammer, 1972), 53–54.

10. For the argument that Luke is dependent on Mark and not a variant tradition, see Fitzmyer, *Luke (I–IX)*, 791–94.

11. *Luke (I–IX)*, 794.

12. *Luke (I–IX)*, 801.

13. *Luke (I–IX)*, 803.

14. Susan Garrett, *The Demise of the Devil* (Minneapolis: Fortress Press, 1989), 48–50.

15. Dietrich, *Das Petrusbild*, 135f.

16. *Das Petrusbild*, 134; Fitzmyer, *Luke (X–XXIV)*, 1423.

17. Oscar Cullmann makes too great an effort to harmonize these traditions

in his proposing that Matthew 16 originally belonged in a Last Supper context; see *Peter: Disciple—Apostle—Martyr*, 2d ed., trans. Floyd V. Filson (London: SCM, 1962), 191.

18. Dietrich, *Das Petrusbild*, 137, 144–53.
19. *Das Petrusbild*, 128–31.
20. Fitzmyer, *Luke (X–XXIV)*, 1547f.
21. Dietrich, *Das Petrusbild*, 163.
22. See Tannehill, *The Gospel According to Luke*, 22.
23. *The Gospel According to Luke*, 49.
24. *The Gospel According to Luke*, 35.
25. *The Gospel According to Luke*, 81–82.
26. Rudolf Pesch, *Simon Petrus*, Geschichte und geschichtliche Bedeutung des ersten Jüngers Jesu Christi. Päpste und Papstum Bd. 15 (Stuttgart: Anton Hiersemann, 1980), 147.
27. See Robert Tannehill, *The Acts of the Apostles*, vol. 2 of *The Narrative Unity of Luke-Acts:: A Literary Interpretation* (Minneapolis: Fortress Press, 1990), 20–21.
28. *The Acts of the Apostles*, 79.
29. *The Acts of the Apostles*, 81.
30. Dietrich, *Das Petrusbild*, 288.
31. Ernst Haenchen suggests that Luke wishes to avoid having the primitive community opposing the will of God; see *The Acts of the Apostles*, trans. B. Noble and G. Shinn (Philadelphia: Westminster Press, 1971), 359.
32. Tannehill, *The Acts of the Apostles*, 36–41.
33. See the historical assessment of this notice about severe persecution in Craig C. Hill, *Hellenists and Hebrews: Reappraising Division within the Earliest Church* (Minneapolis: Fortress Press, 1992), 32–40. Hill argues that the scholarly convention of over-interpreting Acts 8:1 as though Jewish officials launched a selective persecution against Greek-speaking Christians because of an anti-temple ideology found in Stephen's speech is without merit. The text most naturally alludes to the type of incident that Paul's preaching in diaspora synagogues would cause. "Hellenist" does not designate an early Christian party but a Greek-speaking Jew, whether Christian or not. Luke has reformulated the notice to fit the geographical demands of Acts 1:8b. Before the mission moves into the diaspora, Philip, under the authority of Jerusalem, makes converts in Samaria and then converts a proselyte, the Ethiopian eunuch, on the road to Gaza. Peter himself will convert the first Gentiles.
34. See Tannehill, *The Acts of the Apostles*, 74–77.
35. *The Acts of the Apostles*, 60–63.
36. *The Acts of the Apostles*, 68–70.
37. Dietrich, *Das Petrusbild*, 299–300. Though Luke does not narrate the

deaths of the major apostles, Peter and Paul, these narrative parallels remind the reader that the other apostles will also die because they are witnesses to the Lord.

38.   Tannehill, *The Acts of the Apostles*, 104–5.
39.   *The Acts of the Apostles*, 62.
40.   *The Acts of the Apostles*, 106–7.
41.   Dietrich, *Das Petrusbild*, 252–55. Dietrich thinks that since Simon does not perish as in the previous story, Luke intends to hold out the possibility of Simon's repentance. Though Garrett admits the possibility that Luke expects the reader to know that Simon is condemned, she also concludes that his fate remains open (*Demise*, 74).
42.   Garrett, *Demise*, 68–78.
43.   *Demise*, 71–72.
44.   Dietrich, *Das Petrusbild*, 267f.
45.   *Das Petrusbild*, 256–66.
46.   *Das Petrusbild*, 276.
47.   See the extensive survey of the literature in Hill, *Hellenists and Hebrews*, 117–38. Hill suggests that the first gentile converts had been proselytes who observed some Jewish practices. Disputes over table fellowship arose only when Gentiles without any ties to Judaism were received into the community. He suggests that the rationale for accepting such persons is accurately reflected in the argument of Acts 10:45–47: they had received the Spirit.
48.   Dietrich, *Das Petrusbild*, 288.
49.   Tannehill, *The Acts of the Apostles*, 133–36.
50.   *The Acts of the Apostles*, 137.
51.   *The Acts of the Apostles*, 183f.
52.   *The Acts of the Apostles*, 185f.
53.   All of the versions of this episode diverge. Mark contains the simple notice that someone drew a sword and cut off the man's ear. Matthew identifies the person as one of those with Jesus. He uses the occasion for Jesus to reject such armed revolt, to affirm that God could rescue him, and to remind the reader that the death of Jesus takes place as fulfillment of Scripture. Luke has shown that the disciples have swords (22:35–38). They ask if they are to resist before the deed. Jesus rejects resistance and heals the man. John identifies both Peter and the slave by name. The episode becomes grounds for identifying Peter as a follower of Jesus (18:26).
54.   Schnackenburg, *Commentary on Chapters 13–21*, 303–7, 344–47.
55.   Alan Culpepper, *Anatomy of the Fourth Gospel* (Philadelphia: Fortress Press, 1983), 174–79.
56.   Note the irony in this expression: Peter will die "for" Jesus not merely "with" him as in Luke 22:33. The reader of the Fourth Gospel knows that Jesus is the shepherd who lays down his life "for" the sheep (10:15).

57. If the author of John were familiar with a pre-Markan version of the story of Peter's confession, the episode might have concluded with "one of you is a devil" (v. 70). Mark identifies Peter as the "Satan" because Peter attempts to dissuade Jesus from the Passion (Mark 8:33). John interprets the referent as Judas (v. 71). Most scholars agree that this section of John bears some relationship to synoptic-like traditions. C. K. Barrett holds that John uses Mark; see *The Gospel According to St. John*, 2d ed. (London: SPCK, 1978), 271.

58. Raymond E. Brown et al. regard this scene as a confirmation of the tradition about Peter's impulsiveness. See *Peter in the New Testament* (New York: Paulist Press, 1973), 132f. However, the symbolic elements in the story as well as the dramatic shaping of character typical of the Fourth Gospel makes it unlikely that the episode preserves information about Peter's character.

59. Beasley-Murray, *John*, 233.

60. Raymond E. Brown et al., eds., *Peter*, 129–47. Brown has proposed that the "other sheep" of John 10:16 refers to churches of the Petrine tradition distinct from those of Johannine Christians; see *Community of the Beloved Disciple*, 81–88.

61. Schnackenburg, *Commentary on Chapters 13–21*, 348.

62. Arthur J. Droge, "The Status of Peter in the Fourth Gospel," *JBL* 109 (1990): 307–11.

63. D. H. Gee, "Why Did Peter Spring into the Sea (John 21:7)?" *JTS*, n.s., 40 (1989): 481–89.

64. Droge, "The Status of Peter," 311.

65. The Fourth Evangelist has the Beloved Disciple outrun Peter to reach the tomb in 20:4. If such a reaction were called for, he—not Peter— would have been first overboard.

66. Gee, "Why Did Peter?" 483.

67. See the discussion of ανεβη in verse 11 by Gee, "Why Did Peter?" 485– 87. The verse must refer to Peter's going up on the shore as in verse 9, not to his going back on board the boat (as translated in the RSV and NRSV).

68. Schnackenburg, *Commentary on Chapters 13–21*, 364–66.

69. Schnackenburg denies this reference, but he does so on the basis of a form-critical analysis of the saying itself, which he considers to be proverbial; see *Commentary on Chapters 13–21*, 366. The presence of a proverb may be an appropriate indication of the origins of the scene in the tradition. However, literary analysis of the text as it stands does suggest that the reader is intended to pick up on the parallelism.

70. Beasley-Murray, *John*, 404–5.

71. Schnackenburg, *Commentary on Chapters 13–21*, 364–66.

72.   *Commentary on Chapters 13–21*, 366.
73.   Haenchen, *Acts*, 164f.
74.   Fitzmyer, *Luke (I–IX)*, 253–54.
75.   Haenchen, *Acts*, 359.

CHAPTER 4

Peter in the New Testament Epistles

IN THE SHADOW OF PAUL

We have seen that the references to Peter in Paul's epistles have played a major role in shaping both the ecumenical and the historical debate about Peter's place in early Christianity. This concentration is not surprising, since Paul is the only witness who speaks about his own personal experiences with the apostle. The dispute between Peter and Paul reported in Galatians 2:11–14 has cast a long shadow over modern reconstructions of early church history. For many interpreters, the conflict appears to cancel out the harmonious agreement reported in Galatians 2:1–10. Even if the later opposition to Paul's mission came from persons more closely associated with James, some interpreters fault Peter for capitulating to their demands. If this view is rejected in favor of the centrist understanding of Peter's role advocated by many Roman Catholic exegetes, the conflict still leaves the impression that Christianity's two greatest apostles operated in a divided church.

Although we have dealt with the historical problems presented by these reports, we have not yet asked the question of Paul's Epistles that would be similar to the question put to the Gospels: what image of Peter is Paul presenting to his readers? The letters in which Paul refers to Peter were not written to report the past events to which they refer. Paul's references to Peter occur in polemical contexts where Paul's own authority as an apostle has been challenged. We have seen that earlier scholars magnified the poles of the rhetorical argument into conflicting wings of early Christianity. These alleged historical divisions served as first-century surrogates for disputes between Catholic and Protestant ecclesiology. Ancient readers, more attuned to the conventions of rhetoric that required sharp antitheses, might have been less quick to presume that Paul's relationship with Peter had been shattered.

In recent decades, scholars have used the categories of ancient rhetoric to analyze the Pauline letters. They have suggested that autobiographical references play a number of different roles in the argument. Biographical statements as well as claims about the "facts" of a case must used to elicit the good will of the audience. Rhetorical handbooks dictate the type of argument likely to accomplish this objective.[1] A speaker's integrity can be demonstrated by his single-handed struggle against deceitful opponents who are more powerful and might easily deceive his audience. Personal ambition or profit has been sacrificed on behalf of friendship or in the fulfillment of a mandate from the gods. Even a casual reading of Galatians 1:12–2:14 makes evident the rhetorical cast of its biographical statements about the apostle.[2] Paul's treatment of Peter belongs to his overall argument with the Galatians. The narrative of their dispute in Antioch (Gal. 2:11–14) concludes by making the issue to be determined by Peter identical with that to be determined by the Galatians: "should Gentiles be compelled to Judaize?"[3]

Studies of ancient letters and handbooks on letter-writing have also alerted scholars to the variety of set formulae that authors use in composition. Paul's expression of astonishment at defection from his teaching in Galatians 1:6, for example, does not imply that he has departed from his usual thanksgiving out of personal horror over the severity of the crisis. Such formulae beginning with "I am astonished that . . ." appear in common letters to indicate the recipient's aggravation or incredulity at the addressee's neglect.[4] Consequently, while the expression reflects unhappiness with a situation, it does not imply the danger that relationships between the two parties will be ruptured.

Peter stands in Paul's shadow in the New Testament in another way. Even when he is not being viewed through a lens created by Paul's later difficulties, Peter himself has been presented as like Paul. The principal vehicle for this understanding of Peter is the composition of letters in Peter's name. The language, the use of Pauline themes, and the construction of both Petrine Epistles make it evident that they were not the work of Peter himself. Most scholars agree that 1 and 2 Peter are stages in the emergence of the later Peter tradition.[5] 1 Peter indicates that Roman Christians had adopted the apostle as the model for its presbyter-shepherds by the last quarter of the first century. 2 Peter, from a later period, shows that Peter and Paul are guardians of the inherited teaching about Jesus' Second Coming and judgment. It joins apostolic authority with the emerging Christian canon to refute the opposition.

The circulation of Pauline letters in early Christianity quickly established expectations for the genre "apostolic letter." Both the pseudonymous composition of epistles bearing the names of apostles and the internal references in some of them to letters which the audience has already received (e.g., 2 Thess. 2:14, 2 Pet. 3:15–16) show that early Christians came to expect exhortation in the form of an epistle. 1 and 2 Peter both exhibit features which suggest familiarity with the Pauline type of letter.

If one must watch for rhetorical and epistolary conventions in evaluating claims about the writer of a letter, one must be equally cautious in treating its claims about others. The authors of pseudonymous letters may have greater freedom in constructing the fictive author and recipients, but they are also constrained by literary conventions and even established traditions. We are concerned with how the figure of Peter functions in the Epistles themselves, not with the historical accuracy of these references. Since 2 Peter refers its readers to the Transfiguration account, to a previous Petrine letter, and to the letters of Paul, we can see that several earlier treatments of the apostle have already fixed an image of Peter in the minds of its audience.

PETER IN PAUL'S EPISTLES: FELLOW APOSTLE
OR OPPONENT?

Paul's treatment of Peter has left interpreters divided over the question of whether or not Paul really intends the reader to consider Peter a "fellow apostle." On the one hand, Paul is anxious to associate his apostolic authority with that of Peter and the other witnesses to the Resurrection (1 Cor. 15:3–11). Paul is constrained to admit that he appears to be inferior to the Jerusalem apostles, since he had persecuted the church. On the other, even as he does so, Paul suggests that his ministry is superior to theirs (1 Cor. 15:10) because of the constant hardship he has endured to preach the gospel.

The Jerusalem apostles base their standing on relationships to the earthly Jesus (Gal. 2:6), a criterion which Paul seems to reject elsewhere when he comments that though he once know Jesus "according to the flesh," he no longer does so (2 Cor. 5:16).[6] The only apostles to whom Paul refers by name in listing witnesses to the Resurrection in 1 Corinthians 15:3–7 are Peter and James, the two with whom he says in

Galatians 1:18–19 he met on his first visit.[7] Although Paul refers to other apostles (1 Cor. 15:7), the Twelve (1 Cor. 15:5), and John (Gal. 2:9), this formulation suggests that Peter and James are the two with whom he expects readers to be familiar.

Schooled by lists of the Twelve in the Gospels as well as traditions which depict Jesus' family as outsiders to his ministry (e.g., Mark 3:21, 31–35; John 7:3–8), modern readers often assume that, like Paul, James has been converted from disbelief by his vision of the risen Lord.[8] Paul's parallel formulation—"he appeared to Cephas, then to the twelve. . . . he appeared to James, then to all the apostles" (1 Cor. 15:5, 7)—makes no distinction between the two. James may have been a follower of Jesus even before the Resurrection. When Paul denies having gone to Jerusalem upon his conversion to meet with "those who were apostles before me" (Gal. 1:17), he probably means Peter and James.

Paul uses the same construction to expand the list of Resurrection witnesses in 1 Corinthians 15:5–8 that he employs in Galatians 1:18–2:14, a series of clauses strung together with the adverbial "then," capped by a concluding clause that refers to Paul's experience.[9] Rhetorically, the series of "then" clauses assures the audience that nothing has been omitted.[10] Peter's presence at the head of the list stems from the kerygmatic tradition that the Lord appeared to him and then to the other disciples (e.g., Mark 16:7 and Luke 24:34).[11] While that temporal priority may have conferred some status on Peter in the early community, Paul's account does not conclude by affirming the superiority of Peter to the later apostolic witnesses. Though Paul seems to deprecate his own calling by speaking of his abortive emergence as an apostle after being a persecutor, Paul's calling is just as evidently an act of God as those of the initial apostles. Further, Paul's "last of all" implies that no further members will be added to this series. This indirect emphasis may be part of a rhetorical attack on a "downgrading" of Paul's apostolic authority among the Corinthians. The image of Paul as an "abortion" rather than a fully formed human being may have been lifted from the polemic against him.[12]

Further hints that such accusations have been made on the grounds of comparisons between Paul and other apostles like Peter appear in 1 Corinthians 9. Paul enlists the Corinthians on his side as witnesses to the reality of his apostleship (1 Cor. 9:1–2). He then turns to offer a defense to those who would sit in judgment on his conduct (1 Cor. 9:3).[13] The statement of the issue on which Paul is being tried moves from the general "right to food and drink" to the example of others, "the other apostles and the brothers of the Lord and Cephas" (v. 5). This list of persons who have a right to support for themselves and their families is a shorter version of that in 1 Corinthians 15:5–7. Scholars have investigated the socio-economic codes involved in the patronage relationships between a teacher and affluent pupils. Paul's failure to make such demands on the community would continue to be a source of suspicion among the Corinthians (2 Cor. 11:5–11; 12:13). The details of Paul's convoluted argument in 1 Corinthians 9 are not our concern here.[14] The rhetorical development of the passage begins with the suggestion that Paul's position with respect to the Corinthians should at least be equal to that of others. However, it concludes with the suggestion that the freedom Paul's apparently "slavish" behavior has given him in fact shows that Paul's apostleship is greater than that of those who depend upon the persons to whom they preach (1 Cor. 9:19–23). Thus both instances in which Paul appears to accept parity with other apostles including Peter are developed in such a way that Paul presents himself as equal to the core group of apostles recognized by all Christians as leaders in the church, Peter and James.

In 1 Corinthians 9:4 and 15:5, Peter's name is the most prominent in the list of apostles to whom Paul is compared. In ancient rhetoric, such comparisons are a standard means of establishing the character of the speaker. Is Paul responsible for creating these comparisons? Apparently not. 1 Corinthians opens with an appeal for unity. Paul has been told that there are quarrels among the Corinthians. He describes these quarrels as focused on the slogans by which groups claim to belong to Paul, Apollos, Cephas, and perhaps even Christ (1 Cor. 1:12). Apollos had worked in Corinth (3:5–9). Paul speaks of him as a "fellow worker" who watered what Paul had planted. Apollos himself is not in Corinth and has no immediate plans to return there (16:12). No concrete discussion of Peter's activity in Corinth appears alongside the references to Paul and Apollos. Consequently, many interpreters are not sure that Peter had ever been active in the city even though Paul's audience knows of Peter's missionary activity.[15]

After defending his own preaching of Christ crucified (1 Cor. 1:18–2:16), Paul returns to the slogans that are indicative of divisions in the community. Only Paul and Apollos are mentioned (3:4–5). Peter is mentioned in the list which Paul uses to expand the slogan "all things are yours": Paul, Apollos, Cephas, the world, life, death, present, future (3:22). Paul employs the stoic maxim "all things belong to the wise"[16] to reverse the Corinthians' partisan claims to individual apostles. If they reject human standards of evaluation (v. 21a), they will have all things because they are "of Christ" and, through him, of God.[17] Peter has been introduced into the discussion by some persons in Corinth, but the argument pursued in this section focuses on Apollos. The concluding description of how the Corinthians should consider the apostles begins as though Paul and Apollos are equals (1 Cor. 4:6). It suddenly shifts to the first person in a direct address to the community. There, Paul makes his own claim to superiority clear. Paul is their only "father" in the gospel. Though there are many guides in Christ, they should follow the exhortation of Paul's "beloved and faithful child," Timothy (4:17).

The concrete challenge to Paul's apostolic authority comes from within the Corinthian community, not from outside. Insofar as any outside missionary activity has contributed to the divisive behavior of the Corinthians, Apollos seems to be the one responsible. 1 Corinthians 9:1–5 suggests that those who are disposed to criticize Paul as an inferior or lesser apostle may have appealed to common knowledge about the "privileges" of other Christian missionaries to make their case. None of the references in 1 Corinthians suggest that Peter or persons associated with him are challenging Paul's authority. If the purpose of comparison with Peter is to elevate Paul's ministry in the eyes of persons who might have been swayed by the divisive criticism that has been going on, then these examples are evidence of the universal esteem in which Peter is held.

1 Corinthians never refers to any meeting between Peter and Paul. But its apparent use of Petrine authority to bolster Paul's own case suggests that the hostility in Galatians 2:11–14 may have been overemphasized. The construction of the creedal section in 1 Corinthians 15:5–7 parallels techniques that Paul follows in Galatians 2:1–14. This section of Galatians is divided by temporal clauses. Peter is clearly the central figure. James appears almost as an afterthought (Gal. 1:18–19).[18] His presence becomes critical in the final episode, since persons from James persuade Peter to withdraw from table fellowship with the gentile believers (2:12). The divine passive which acknowledges Peter's mission to Jews in Galatians 2:7 now appears as divine judgment against the apostle for a lack of faithfulness to the gospel (2:11).[19] Paul presents himself as the one who speaks the word of judgment against Peter. He hints that the charge has been made in a public assembly (v. 14). 1 Corinthians 5:1–5 calls upon the Corinthians to use such an

assembly to cast out a sinful brother against whom Paul has already pronounced sentence. But the judgment which Paul seems to elicit from his Galatian hearers has nothing to do with the earlier episode. He must persuade them to cast out those who have come into their community demanding circumcision (Gal. 4:28–29; 5:11–12).

Paul will use the allegory of Abraham's two wives to suggest that his audience take similar action against the Judaizers (4:21–31). Those who desire to be under the Law persecute and enslave the free children of Abraham. The word of Scripture itself pronounces the judgment against them (4:30). They are to be expelled from the community.[20] Paul has implied from the beginning of the letter that failure to accept or preach the gospel brings condemnation (Gal. 1:6–10). He first demonstrates the divine origins of the gospel he preaches by stressing his independence of human authorities. The dramatic shift in his own life from being the zealous Pharisee and persecutor of the church also demonstrates God's intervention (Gal. 1:11–17).[21] Paul knows from his own experience that zeal for the Law made him an enemy of the gospel. The narrative of facts which opens Paul's defense of the gospel juxtaposes Paul's character and faithfulness to the gospel with Peter's. Paul employs a set pattern in comparing himself with other apostles. He begins with a situation that appears to put him in an inferior position to others and argues for parity. He is as much an apostle as they are. Paul then moves from parity to argue for the superiority of his own apostolic ministry because of Paul's boldness in announcing the gospel. The sections on Peter are structured according to that principle. The Pharisee persecutor certainly appears to be inferior to those who were apostles before him. Whatever the original purpose of the first visit, Paul is in Jerusalem as Peter's guest (1:18–20). At the Jerusalem council, Paul and his entourage are engaged in an apostolate on the same level as Peter and the others (2:1–10). In the episode at Antioch, Paul is now Peter's judge and critic.[22] Though interpreters have often read this development as a condemnation of Peter, its rhetorical impact on those familiar with ancient rhetoric may have been somewhat different.

Ancient rhetoric developed the tradition of the true philosopher as a person who does not act out of regard for human opinion. Instead, the philosopher is like a physician whose only concern is to heal the soul of his audience. He may speak with harshness or gentleness as the occasion warranted. To show that he has this virtue, Paul needs an honorable opponent who will be in danger of falling into vice without his intervention. Paul supports his claim by describing Peter as a person without integrity who will be guided by the opinions or demands of others, even when the truth of the gospel is at stake (2:11–14). The language of spies who infiltrate in order to steal away the freedom of Christians used of the Jerusalem meeting (2:4–5) describes both the later Antioch episode[23] and the situation in Galatia for which it serves as a model. Paul casts Peter as the one whom he must oppose because Peter lacks the conviction to remain true to principles he accepts.[24] Vacillation and inconsistency are evidence of lack of character. Contrasted with Peter, Paul emerges as the only one who has the true interests of the audience at heart. Extra-textual interest in the extent of Petrine authority leads commentators to presume that the participation of Barnabas and the others in Peter's hypocrisy demonstrates the historical fact of Petrine authority.[25] From a rhetorical perspective, such a conclusion is unwarranted. Spying and deception with an intent to destroy the gospel were introduced in the reference to "false brothers" during the Jerusalem meeting (2:4–5). Now their deceit has overcome all who were party to the original agreement except Paul.

Thus this narrative follows the rhetorical convention of establishing that the speaker has demonstrated courage, integrity, and good will toward the audience by maintaining the truth against extraordinary odds. Of course, Paul tacitly acknowledges that the Antioch problem involves general participation in meals with Gentiles, not the question of circumcision. There is no historical evidence that Jews were prohibited from attending banquets given by Gentiles and otherwise socializing with Gentiles. Galatians 2:11 notes that Peter customarily does so.[26] Paul asserts that Peter gave up his customary practice "fearing those of circumcision" (v. 12). Interpreters have often taken "the circumcision" to refer to a Jewish Christian group allied with James. However, Paul's own usage in the previous section shows that "the circumcision" means "Jews." The Jerusalem agreement meant that Peter would evangelize among Jews; Paul, among Gentiles (vv. 7–8).[27] Fear of "the Jews" as a motive for hypocritical conformity to custom would remind the reader that Paul as a persecutor of the church was once the cause of such fear for the Christian community in Judea (Gal. 1:13, 23).

Paul has established his authority to judge conduct in the face of Jewish opposition by referring to his past as a persecutor. Galatians 1:10 encompasses that past under the negative rubric of currying favor with human beings. Anxious to discover historical information about the relationships between the parties involved, scholars commonly go outside the text. Those who identify the meeting in Galatians 2:1–10 with that in Acts 15:6–29 assume that Paul's argument fails and he breaks with Barnabas. Acts 15:36–41 reports such a break, though for different reasons.[28] Others argue that the meeting reported in Acts 15:6–29 concludes with agreements for minimal observance of kosher and marriage rules by gentile Christians that will resolve the conflict referred to in Galatians 2:11–14. Therefore, they locate some or all of the events in Galatians 2:1–14 prior to that time.[29] Both versions presume that the readers of Galatians have been told by Paul's opponents that Paul had been forced to concede to Peter.

From a rhetorical perspective, such a reading creates a dilemma. Paul usually moves from an example in which he appears to be subordinate to other apostles to asserting the divine foundation of his own apostolate. Other structural features in this passage such as the list of events and the changing verbal relationship between the two apostles make it appear that Galatians 2:11–14 would enhance Paul's position. Betz's rhetorical analysis of Galatians 1:12–2:14 points out that those defending themselves against a charge were exhorted to introduce subject matter on which they wish to be judged. Paul has done this with the contrast, according to human standards and according to God (Gal. 1:11, 12).[30] Yet the *narratio* is to end with the issue that is to be determined. Paul states it in the terms that apply to the Galatian situation: "compel Gentiles to adopt a Jewish manner of life" (2:14b). Though Paul's account never asserts that Peter actually made such a demand on Gentiles,[31] Paul leads the reader to infer that Peter's failure to defend the life he had adopted behalf of the gospel means that Peter could have done so.

Paul has constructed the whole account so that compelling (or even merely encouraging?) gentile Christians to adopt a Jewish way of life is nearly equivalent to Paul's former way of life "in Judaism," persecuting the church with the intent of destroying it. We do not know what extra-textual information Christians in Galatia brought to this passage. We have seen that earlier assumptions that there was an anti-Pauline campaign being conducted by Jewish Christian missionaries from Jerusalem are largely conjecture. If Paul construes the earlier Antioch episode as a victorious demonstration of the truth of his apostolate, he may be introducing it to the audience. The picture of Peter is deliberately unflattering because Paul wishes to demonstrate the probity of his own character by contrast. Paul has also constructed a persuasive rhetorical argument to support the two actions which he will ask his audience to take: to recognize that adopting a Jewish way of life is contrary to the gospel, and to expel those who are stirring up conflict in the community by advocating such a way of life.

In order to support Paul's own claims about his apostolate, the reader must be familiar with the importance of Peter in the early Church. The treatment of Peter in the Pauline letters might be compared to that in the Fourth Gospel. Peter's stature within the early Christian community cannot be denied by anyone. Even gentile converts in Galatia and Corinth who have had no contact with Peter or the Petrine mission recognize that he is one of the leading disciples of the Lord. However, both John and Paul contrast Peter with the apostle founders of non-Petrine churches. For John, this comparison takes place after the fact. Both men have died. For Paul, this comparison takes rhetorical form in the very real struggles which the apostle undertakes to preserve the gospel in the churches that he has founded. Peter's weaknesses are exploited to highlight God's presence in the Pauline mission.

EXCURSUS: THE JERUSALEM COUNCIL

Scholars continue to disagree over the relationship between Paul's account in Galatians 2:1–10 and the description of the Jerusalem council in Acts 15:1–30. Those who think that two different meetings are being described emphasize the fact that Paul refers to his meeting as a private one (Gal. 2:2). Acts 15:6 clearly envisages a public meeting. If the apostolic decree referred to at the conclusion of the Jerusalem meeting were in effect, it is difficult to see how the problems in Galatians 2:11–14 or even the conflict over eating idol meat in 1 Corinthians 8 could have arisen. Conservative scholars reject the identification of Galatians 2:1–10 and Acts 15:1–30. They propose various rearrangements in the actual historical order of events to harmonize the Pauline material with other accounts of his visits to Jerusalem in Acts. The usual result of such proposals is to locate all the events referred to in Galatians before the council of Acts 15.[32]

Other scholars insist that the Pauline account must take priority over Acts. Rhetorical criticism makes it particularly unlikely that Paul has deliberately reversed the order of the episode at Antioch and the Jerusalem meeting in Galatians 2. There is no sign that he has departed from the sequence in which the events actually occurred.[33] Acts 15 itself is problematic, since the account appears to conflate at least two different sources. Peter's speech in Acts 15:7–11 does not coincide with the proposal made by James in verses 14–23.[34] The introduction (Acts 15:2) agrees with Galatians 2:1–2 that Paul and Barnabas have come from Antioch to represent gentile Christians. Peter's speech presumes Peter has that role (Acts 15:7). As we have seen, the argument which Luke attributes to Peter is centered in the evidence for divine choice. God has chosen to include the Gentiles without requiring their conversion to Judaism.[35] This argument is as characteristic of Lukan theology as the christological argument of Galatians 2:15–21 is of Paul.

Luke's Peter has the virtues which Paul's account tries to show he lacks. Peter is loyal to Jewish dietary traditions and reluctant to associate with Gentiles until God gives him irrefutable evidence that Gentiles also receive the Spirit. Peter could never be deterred from preaching the truth of the gospel out of fear of some human authorities. Once he understands what God is asking of him, Peter never deviates from his mission. Luke will also insist that both Peter and Paul remain loyal to Jewish traditions even though their gentile converts are not required to Judaize. Even if Luke were familiar with a version of the Jerusalem council and the subsequent meeting between Peter and Paul in Antioch, he would not tell it as Paul does. He assumes that such a major change must begin with the Twelve and has interpreted the Cornelius episode as the key point even though Acts itself preserves evidence of different beginnings to the gentile mission.[36]

Since both Galatians 2:1–10 and Acts 15:1–30 have been addressed to very different concerns, they cannot be harmonized. Paul claims that Peter's missionary responsibilities were among Jews. The large Jewish community in Antioch would make Peter's visit there a natural expression of such concerns. At the same time, Paul's references to Peter's association with Gentiles (2:11, 14) show that the tradition behind the Cornelius episode is sound. Peter had been willing to baptize and eat with non-Jewish converts. We do not know what prompted James to advise that Peter desist. Perhaps increased persecution of Christians in Jerusalem led to concern over behavior which might appear to encourage apostasy from Judaism.[37] Peter appears to have agreed, more likely for pragmatic reasons than theological ones. Eventually, all three apostles will share a common fate, martyrdom.

None of them compromised the gospel in such a way that it really became pleasing to human beings.

1 PETER: THE APOSTLE AS FELLOW ELDER

1 Peter appears to have been composed along the lines of a Pauline letter[38] sometime after Peter's death. Its fictive setting is the apostle's imprisonment in Rome (5:1, 13). Its addressees are gentile Christians living in Asia Minor (1:1; 2:9–10). They are recognized by friends and associates as "different" and frequently find themselves maligned or persecuted simply because they are Christians (2:12, 20b; 3:14–17; 4:4, 12–16; 5:10). Most of the letter contains general exhortations to sustain the community against the danger that its members will go back to their old life-style.[39] Christians must recognize their unmerited suffering as an emulation of Christ's own suffering on our behalf. The figure of Christ focuses the problem faced by the addressees in terms of ancient Jewish understanding of the righteous martyr (see, e.g., 1 Pet. 3:13–22).[40] They are to understand suffering now as an eschatological trial which anticipates a future share in Christ's glory (4:12–13).[41]

How does a pseudonymous letter come to be addressed to Christians in Asia Minor (1 Pet. 5:12)? There is no historical hint of Peter's working in that region. Both Acts and Galatians agree that his missionary efforts were carried out in Syro-Palestine. Paul's reference to Peter in 1 Corinthians does not indicate that the apostle has actually been preaching in that city. They do indicate that he was well-known as a missionary and authority in the early community. Paul must show that his own apostolic ministry is equivalent to that of Peter and the other early disciples. Paul himself writes the Book of Romans to a church that he has neither founded nor visited. The fact that a Petrine letter is addressed to an area in which both Pauline and Johannine[42] traditions were strong suggests that Peter's importance for the church as a whole was acknowledged at a very early time. The conclusion of Matthew's Gospel indicates that the community founded on Peter, "the rock," is not limited to Palestine. The disciples have been commissioned to carry Jesus' teaching to "the nations." Therefore, 1 Peter should be seen as evidence for the universalizing of Peter as a leader for the whole church. The apostle's suffering and martyr's death will provide an example for the persecuted Christians in these Asia Minor churches.[43]

We have seen that John 21:15–19 combines a scene in which Peter is commissioned as shepherd of the flock with the prediction that he will undergo suffering. That tradition of a suffering shepherd has an analogue in the Pauline tradition of the suffering apostle (e.g., 1 Cor. 4:9–13; Gal. 6:14, 17). But the use of "shepherd" to designate church leaders does not appear in the Pauline letters. It does appear in the adaptation of the parable of the lost sheep to community leaders that we find in Matthew 18:10–14.[44] Acts 20:28 has Paul apply the terminology of an "overseer" (*episkopos*) of the flock to the elders of the church in Ephesus.

A similar development is evident in 1 Peter 5:1–4. Speaking to those who are elders in the churches of Asia Minor, Peter exhorts the shepherds of the post-apostolic generation to follow the example of those who had gone before them:[45] "So I exhort the elders among you, as a fellow elder and a witness of the sufferings of Christ as well as a partaker in the glory that is to be revealed. Tend the flock of God that is your charge, not by constraint but willingly, not for shameful gain but eagerly. Not as domineering over those in your charge but being examples to the flock. And when the chief Shepherd is manifested you will obtain the unfading crown of glory" (RSV). These verses form a final testament from the martyr-apostle Peter to his successors (cp. Acts 20:17–36; 2 Tim.).[46] The sufferings which they respectively endure are only the beginning of the messianic woes.[47] Such suffering anticipates the glory of the coming Christ.

Peter's exemplary suffering shows the post-apostolic generation what the exhortation to "tend the flock" requires. He identifies himself with those who will now inherit responsibility for the church from the apostolic generation.[48] The exhortation which constitutes the body of 1 Peter indicates what caring for the flock requires.[49] Ethical exhortation frequently requires the students to follow the example that they find in their teacher. A philosopher's doctrine can be read in his life. The Pauline letters make use of this motif frequently. Paul often exhorts his readers to imitate the example that he sets before them (e.g., 1 Cor. 4:16; 11:1). 1 Peter does not follow the Pauline model in this regard. Although both the author and readers are clearly familiar with some variant of the Petrine tradition, 1 Peter does not appeal to the example of Peter directly. Its example for the Christian who experiences persecution is always Christ. In the exhortation just quoted, Peter does not tell the elders to imitate him. Rather, he reminds them of both the suffering and later glory of Christ, who is the chief shepherd (1 Pet. 5:1–4).

For some interpreters, the lack of a developed image of the apostle Peter suggests a letter that was written close to the time of Peter's death. A major difference between 1 Peter and the Gospels and the Pauline treatments of Peter is its lack of ambiguity. The Peter who is presented as the author of this Epistle does not allude to weaknesses or failure. As is the case with Luke's portrayal of Peter in Acts, the reader is to assume that Peter is a true witness to Jesus.[50] Peter's name appears to have been used to invest the exhortation from the Roman church with apostolic authority in the communities of Asia Minor. The letter greeting employs a general list of churches in Asia Minor. The author may not have been familiar with any particular churches there.[51] Rather than being a letter written shortly after Peter's death to a particular community, 1 Peter appears to be a general exhortation to Christians in Asia Minor. The echoes of Pauline traditions in 1 Peter as well as the form of an apostolic letter, itself, suggest churches familiar with such letters as the basis for teaching and exhortation. Two associates of Paul's mission join in the final greetings, Silvanus and Mark (1 Pet. 5:12–13). They provide a link between the fictive author "Peter" and the churches in Asia Minor.[52] By the early second century, the reference to John Mark was understood to demonstrate that Mark had become Peter's disciple and interpreter in Rome. According to Papias, this Mark composed his Gospel based on what he had learned from Peter.[53]

2 PETER: GUARDIAN OF THE FAITH

2 Peter assumes that its readers are familiar with an extensive canon of authoritative texts including 1 Peter. Its author refers to "your apostles" as part of the heritage of the community (3:2) that is on the same level as the prophets and sayings of the Lord. 2 Peter 3:15–16 sets Paul and his letters on the same level as the Old Testament. Presumably, Paul forms part of the group referred to as "your apostles" along with Peter.[54] The testament form used in 1 Peter 5:1–4 as well as in Pauline pseudepigrapha (2 Tim.) is adopted by the author of 2 Peter for the entire letter.[55] As in the Pauline testaments (Acts 20:28–30; 2 Tim. 3:1–9), the apostle foresees the struggle with false teachers that will face his successors (3:3–4). The author has taken the apocalyptic prediction of the "scoffers" in the last days from Jude 17–18. But it has been changed to deal with the concrete teaching which the author's opponents are denying, the coming of Christ at the end-time.[56]

Interpreters disagree over the background to the opposing argument against the Second Coming. Some see the ontological promise of escape from the corruption of the passions to become sharers in divine nature (1:4) as evidence that 2 Peter has a Gnostic sect in view and may even have adopted some of the elements of Gnostic anthropology.[57] Others point to the extensive debate over the interpretation of the prophecies contained in Scripture as well as 2 Peter's adaptation of Jude and other apocalyptic traditions as evidence that prophecy forms the backbone of the argument.[58] Regardless of the origin of the opposing arguments, the fundamental outline of the dispute seems clear. Both sides accept a common Platonizing account of salvation which involves the divinizing of the soul as it progresses away from its attachment to corruptible material things and the passions. This process leads to stability as the soul comes to adhere to the divine world. Within the New Testament, Hebrews provides a striking example of how a Platonic anthropology was combined with the traditional language of Christian eschatology.[59]

2 Peter opens with an exhortation by the dying apostle addressed to those he leaves behind (1:3–15). It is to serve as a reminder to them of his teaching (v. 15).[60] The testament genre requires that the dying patriarch exemplify the virtues which he exhorts his children to follow. 2 Peter 1:3–11 implies that Peter has obtained the divine glory and excellence which comes from putting aside the corruption of the world. Therefore, he is about to enter the eternal kingdom of Jesus Christ.[61] The genre itself provides additional authority to the argument against the opponents which follows. The words of a dying patriarch were themselves felt to have the character of divine revelation.[62]

Unlike 1 Peter, which draws on common forms of early Christian paraenesis, 2 Peter exploits very different traditions. The opening section has Hellenized its treatment of virtue to the point that it has no connection to earlier Petrine exhortation.[63] However, the first argument against those who deny the Parousia is taken from a specifically Petrine Gospel tradition, the Transfiguration (1:16–18). The wording suggests that the author of 2 Peter is summarizing a Gospel account. The author insists that he can confirm as an eyewitness the glory which God bestowed on Jesus. The unstated premise is that this glory is a sign of Christ's Parousia rather than the glory of his Resurrection and return to the Father.[64] The second argument which 2 Peter puts forward against its author's opponents is the certainty of prophecy, which is grounded not in human invention but in the activity of the Holy Spirit

(1:19–21). The two arguments are connected, since the Transfiguration demonstrates that the prophetic teaching about Jesus' status is true.[65]

After an extended set of proofs for eschatological teaching taken largely from Jude in which the current false teachers are likened to false prophets of the past, the Petrine voice reappears in 2 Peter 3:1. Although 2 Peter makes no use of any material from 1 Peter, this reference to the earlier letter reminds the reader to pay attention to the apostolic teaching.[66] The final appeal to apostolic authority takes an unusual turn. The opponents apparently appeal to the letters of Paul. 2 Peter 3:15–16 admits that some collection of Pauline writings has come to function as Scripture. However, they are easily misunderstood. Consequently, the eschatological tradition that has been defended in 2 Peter should be the key to determining what Paul intended to teach. The language in which this appeal to the Pauline writings is cast associates Peter with Paul. Paul's writings are even given the status of inspired Scripture which should remind the readers of apostolic teaching.[67] The ignorance and instability of the opponents are contrasted with the stability and knowledge that 2 Peter attributes to its addressees (1:2–6, 12, 20; 2:20–21; 3:8, 18). The accusation against the opponents has been sharpened. They not only teach destructive heresies (2:1); they pervert inspired Scripture to their own destruction (3:16).[68]

The conclusion of 2 Peter shows that the Pauline letter collection shaped the early Christian image of an inspired, apostolic letter. Both 1 and 2 Peter are indebted to the authority of the Pauline model for their effectiveness as vehicles of Christian teaching. The Hellenistic language and Asiatic style of 2 Peter as well as much of its content make 2 Peter unlike other Epistles in the Pauline tradition. Though the author intends the reader to recognize this letter as the second letter from Peter, no verbal connections are made between 2 Peter and the earlier 1 Peter. The unusual rendering of the fictive author's name in 2 Peter 1:1, "Sumeōn Petros," departs from the "Petros" in 1 Peter and the common "Simon Petros" in most of the New Testament. Peter is referred to as "Sumeōn" by James when he renders the decision at the Jerusalem council in Acts 15:14. Since this form, a transliteration of the Hebrew, is used of Simon Maccabeus once in 1 Maccabees 2:65 (by his father), it appears to be the Semitic version of the name which Jews more commonly used in its Greek form. In Acts, Luke uses it to emphasize the Jewish origins of James. 2 Peter might be deliberately archaizing, or the form may have been common in the Jewish Christian circles from which the author draws the apocryphal material that he uses for much of the content of the work.[69]

The author of 2 Peter may not have even possessed a copy of 1 Peter. The fact of its existence was sufficient to justify a second letter in Peter's name to defend the traditional eschatological hope of the Parousia against those who deny its truth. If the Pauline letters have become weapons used by the false teachers, then the author of 2 Peter will invoke an even stronger apostolic authority. Peter, the eyewitness to Jesus' own glorious Transfiguration, provides the definitive interpretation of Christian hope.

Galatians and 2 Peter may be chronologically separated by over a half century. In the interim, the apostolic authority which Paul struggled to maintain in the churches he had founded by writing letters has come to reside in a collection of those letters themselves. The success of the apostolic letter as a vehicle for exhortation and unity between far distant teachers and churches spawned other letter traditions. 1 Peter not only adopts a form and traditional paraenesis that could have been at home among Paul's churches; it even invokes the authority of known associates of Paul, Silvanus and Mark. When 2 Peter refers to the fact that his addressees possess an earlier letter from Peter, it suggests the founding of a normative Petrine collection to match the Pauline collection that has come to be a source of Christian teaching.

The development in the image of Peter reflected in 2 Peter continues the process by which Peter is once again remade in the image of Paul. Peter can become the universal shepherd in the larger church if his letters provide the basis for a resolution of the controversy over the interpretation of Paul's letters. 1 Peter has led the way for such a development by summarizing the paraenesis of Roman Christians for their persecuted fellow Christians in Asia Minor. The Petrine tradition can make an appeal which Paul could never invoke, the link between the apostle and the historical Jesus. For 1 Peter, that association is represented in the combination of witness to the sufferings of Jesus and the tradition of Peter as a shepherd who follows in the footsteps of the glorious shepherd, Jesus. For 2 Peter, the association is claimed by reference to a Gospel tradition about the Transfiguration of Jesus.

Paul's letters show that Peter's prestige and authority had already been recognized by Christians well beyond the area of Syro-Palestine in which Peter worked. We do not know what the Galatians or the Corinthians had been told about Peter by others. But the rhetoric of

Paul's letters makes it clear that Paul cannot affirm his own authority as apostle even in churches that he has founded without accounting for his relationship to other apostles, especially Peter. Since Peter is being used as an authoritative figure in an argument to validate Paul's mission, Peter may appear in a Pauline mold even in Paul's letters. The comparisons are always drawn to show that Paul is "just like" Peter. Even when the two are said to disagree in Galatians 2:11–14, Paul presents himself as fearlessly calling Peter back to a practice of table fellowship in which he and Paul had been "just alike." The difference over the means of apostolic support referred to in 1 Corinthians 9:1–6 admits that Peter and the others act under the authority of Scripture and even of the Lord's own command. Paul defends his practice as the act of freely renouncing his right to seek support from those to whom he preaches.

As we turn to trace the developments of the Peter traditions in the next two centuries of early Christianity, we will see all the variants suggested by the canonical traditions played out. For some, Peter and Paul are heroic missionary martyrs united in their testimony to the gospel just as they had been in their preaching. We have already seen that by the end of the second century, Dionysius of Corinth treats the two apostles as parallel figures. For others, the divisions between the two are highlighted. In some Jewish Christian circles, Paul is the arch-heretic. In some Gnostic circles, Peter is the representative of an authoritative leadership that rejects the spiritual testimony of Gnostic teachers and seeks to drive them out of the community. Legends fill in gaps in Peter's life by providing stories of his encounters with the risen Lord and of his further adventures as the missionary leader of the Twelve, scenes with a daughter, and accounts of his martyrdom and that of his wife.

NOTES

1. See Duane Frederick Watson, *Invention, Arrangement, and Style: Rhetorical Criticism of Jude and 2 Peter*, SBLDS 104 (Atlanta: Scholars Press, 1988), 37–39.
2. For a detailed analysis of this section as the *narratio* in an apologetic speech, see Hans Dieter Betz, *Galatians* (Philadelphia: Fortress Press, 1979), 58–62.
3. Betz, *Galatians*, 62.
4. See the description of letter conventions which John L. White has derived from his analysis of documentary letters in *Light from Ancient*

Letters (Philadelphia: Fortress Press, 1986), 193–220. Richard Longenecker makes extensive use of epistolary conventions and formulae in analyzing the structure of Galatians; see *Galatians*, WBC 41 (Dallas: Word Books, 1990), cv–cix.

5.   This is the position taken in the Lutheran-Roman Catholic study *Peter in the New Testament*. The combination of apostolic authority and canonical Scripture leads the authors to agree that regarding the latest of the New Testament writings, 2 Peter, one might even speak of a Petrine magesterium. See Raymond E. Brown, Karl P. Donfried, and John Reumann, eds., *Peter in the New Testament* (New York: Paulist Press, 1973), 155f.

6.   Longenecker, *Galatians*, 54.

7.   Ronald Y. K. Fung, *The Epistle to the Galatians* (Grand Rapids: Wm. B. Eerdmans, 1988), 74.

8.   Betz, *Galatians*, 78f.

9.   Paul has altered the creedal formula that concluded with a reference to the appearance to Cephas (and the Twelve) by introducing "then," before the list of witnesses; see Gordon Fee, *1 Corinthians* (Grand Rapids: Wm. B. Eerdmans, 1987), 723 n. 52.

10. Longenecker, *Galatians*, 45.

11. Fee, *1 Corinthians*, 728.

12. See, e.g., Fee, *1 Corinthians*, 732–36.

13. Fee, *1 Corinthians*, 392–401.

14. See, e.g., Fee, *1 Corinthians*, 403–33.

15. *1 Corinthians*, 57.

16. Diogenes Laertius, *Lives* 7.125; Hans Conzelmann, *1 Corinthians*, trans. J. W. Leitch (Philadelphia: Fortress Press, 1975), 80.

17. The use of the expression "of Christ" in 1 Corinthians 3:23 in contrast to the list "Paul or Apollos or Cephas" (3:22) supports the suggestion that the "of Christ" slogan in 1:12 is Paul's rhetorical expansion; see Fee, *1 Corinthians*, 58–59.

18. Fung, *The Epistle to the Galatians*, 75.

19. Martin Karrer, "Petrus im paulinischen Gemeindekreis," *ZNW* 80 (1989): 217.

20. Betz, *Galatians*, 250f.

21. Martin Karrer, "Petrus," 217.

22. Fung, *The Epistle to the Galatians*, 105.

23. F. F. Bruce, *Galatians* (Grand Rapids: Wm. B. Eerdmans, 1982), 115.

24. Fung, *The Epistle to the Galatians*, 110.

25. See Longenecker, *Galatians*, 75–76.

26. E. P. Sanders, "Jewish Associations with Gentiles and Galatians 2:11–14," *The Conversation Continues: Studies in Paul and John*, ed. R. T. Fortna and B. Gaventa (Nashville: Abingdon Press, 1990), 170–88.

27. Longenecker, *Galatians*, 73. Other examples of Paul's use of the expression "the circumcision" to mean "Jews" occur in Romans 3:30; 4:9, 12; and 15:8.

28. Raymond E. Brown and John P. Meier, *Antioch and Rome: New Testament Cradles of Catholic Christianity* (Ramsey, NJ: Paulist Press, 1983), 38–39.

29. E.g., Bruce, *Galatians*, 128f.; Longenecker, *Galatians*, lxxx–lxxxi.

30. Betz, *Galatians*, 59.

31. Against those who have assumed that Paul's statement means Peter did require circumcision—e.g., George Howard, *Crisis in Galatia*, SNTSMS 35 (Cambridge: Cambridge University Press, 1979), 24–25; and David R. Catchpole, "Paul, James and the Apostolic Decree," *NTS* 23 (1977): 441—see Charles H. Cosgrove, *The Cross and the Spirit: A Study in the Theology of Galatians* (Macon: Mercer University Press, 1988), 129–30. Cosgrove's interest in historical consequences leads him to conclude that Paul uses the verb "compel" because the result of the events in Antioch was that gentile Christians sought to live like Jews.

32. See Bruce, *Galatians*, 106–27; Longenecker, *Galatians*, lxxx–lxxxi; Fung, *The Epistle to the Galatians*, 86–88.

33. Betz, *Galatians*, 61.

34. Joseph A. Fitzmyer, *Paul and His Theology*, 2d ed. (Englewood Cliffs: Prentice Hall, 1989), 16.

35. See the discussion of the possible sources behind this account in Wofgang Dietrich, *Das Petrusbild der Lukanischen Schriften* (Stuttgart: W. Kohlhammer, 1972), 308–19. The sudden shift to a christological perspective in verse 11 may be a sign of Lukan editing (*Das Petrusbild*, 319).

36. See Paul J. Achtemeier, *The Quest for Unity in the New Testament Church* (Philadelphia: Fortress Press, 1987), 36–43. Actemeier proposes yet another historical rearrangement of the events in question which challenges the assumption that Paul was in fact present at the meeting in Acts 15. He thinks that the decree from that meeting was the cause of the conflict referred to in Galatians 2:11–14. See *The Quest for Unity*, 58.

37. Betz, *Galatians*, 82.

38. For a discussion of the letter formulae used in 1 Peter, see Troy W. Martin, *Metaphor and Composition in 1 Peter*, SBLDS 131 (Atlanta: Scholars Press, 1992), 41–79.

39. *Metaphor*, 139, 155–60.

40. *Metaphor*, 215–26.

41. See J. Ramsey Michaels, *1 Peter*, WBC 49 (Waco, TX: Word Books, 1988), 259–63.

42. The letters to the seven churches in Asia Minor which open Revelation

and the later traditions that link the apostle John with Ephesus both testify to the strength of Johannine Christianity in the area.

43. See Leonhard Goppelt, *Der Erste Petrusbrief*, Meyer Kom XII/1 (Göttingen: Vandenhoeck and Ruprecht, 1978), 30–37.

44. 1 Peter 2:25 applies the "straying sheep" image to the addressees. Christ is the "shepherd" and overseer (Greek, *episkopos*) of their souls to whom they have returned. For a discussion of the use of the "shepherd" and "overseer" imagery, see Goppelt, *Der Erste Petrusbrief*, 324f.

45. See Michaels, *1 Peter*, 278–80. Michaels notes the similarity between this exhortation and Paul's address to the Ephesian elders in Acts 20:17–38.

46. Martin, *Metaphor*, 257.

47. *Metaphor*, 244–50.

48. Michaels, *1 Peter*, 281.

49. Rudolf Pesch, *Simon Petrus*, Geschichte und geschichtliche Bedeutung des ersten Jüngers Jesu Christi. Päpste und Papstum Bd. 15 (Stuttgart: Anton Hiersemann, 1980), 151.

50. Michaels, *1 Peter*, lxi.

51. *1 Peter*, xlv.

52. Goppelt, *Der Erste Petrusbrief*, 348–49.

53. *Der Erste Petrusbrief*, 353.

54. Richard J. Bauckham, *Jude, 2 Peter*, WBC 50 (Waco, TX: Word Books, 1983), 287–88.

55. Michaels, *1 Peter*, 278.

56. Ernst Kaesemann, "An Apologia for Primitive Christian Eschatology," *Essays on New Testament Themes*, SBT 41, trans. W. J. Montague (London: SCM, 1964), 169–95. See also Bauckham, *Jude, 2 Peter*, 282–83. 2 Peter has used Old Testament models to formulate the denial of the Lord's coming taken from the skeptical denials of God's coming judgment encountered in the prophets—e.g., Malachi 2:17 and Jeremiah 17:15 (*Jude, 2 Peter*, 289).

57. E.g., Pesch, *Simon Petrus*, 143; T. V. Smith, *Petrine Controversies in Early Christianity: Attitudes Towards Peter in Christian Writings of the First Two Centuries*, WUNT 2 Reihe 5 (Tübingen: J. C. B. Mohr, 1985), 90–95. Smith argues that 2 Peter has adopted Gnostic motifs so that the issue is not simply orthodoxy vs. heresy.

58. See Jerome Neyrey, "The Form and Background of the Polemic in 2 Peter," *JBL* 99 (1980): 407–31.

59. E.g., Hebrews 10:19–11:3. On the mixed background to Hebrews, see Harold Attridge, *Hebrews* (Philadelphia: Fortress Press, 1989), 27–29.

60. For a detailed rhetorical analysis of this section as a single enthymeme, see Watson, *Invention*, 96–101.

61. *Invention*, 90.

62. *Invention*, 91; Bauckham, *Jude, 2 Peter*, 199.
63. Bauckham rescues 2 Peter from some of the charges of theological irrelevance that have resulted from this adaptation by stressing the inclusion of specifically Christian topoi such as love and baptismal cleansing from sin in the process outlined by the opening sermon; see *Jude, 2 Peter*, 182–84.
64. *Jude, 2 Peter*, 205–12.
65. *Jude, 2 Peter*, 223.
66. Watson, *Invention*, 125.
67. *Invention*, 137.
68. *Invention*, 138.
69. Though I agree that the form came from Jewish Christian circles with which the author of 2 Peter was associated, I see no reason to infer that the form implies the author knew Jewish Christian leaders in Rome with ties to Palestinian Judaism, as Bauckham proposes (*Jude, 2 Peter*, 166f.).

CHAPTER 5

Peter, Witness and Martyr

COMPLETING THE STORY

We have seen that the New Testament information about Peter leaves a number of gaps in the account. Later Christian traditions fills out many of the missing details. In this chapter, we will survey examples which retell the story of the apostle. These stories show us how the earliest Christians pictured Peter's life. The New Testament contains several hints about the direction that such fuller stories could take. The allusions to Peter's death in John 21:18–19 and the Petrine Epistles remind us of the untold story of the apostle's death. Peter disappears from the account in Acts after the Jerusalem council. Hints in Paul's letters as well as in the Petrine correspondence suggest a wider area of missionary activity in Asia Minor. Luke ends Acts with Paul, under house arrest, preaching the gospel in Rome. What about Peter? Did he also preach in Rome before he was martyred?

Another piece of "missing tradition" concerns the visionary experience of the risen Lord that is attributed to Peter. Modern scholars sometimes attempt to fill the gap by suggesting that the Transfiguration was originally a post-Resurrection story. We have seen that 2 Peter 1:16–18 understands the Transfiguration as evidence for the Second Coming of the Lord in glory. If Paul can receive his "gospel" through a revelation of the risen Lord (Gal. 1:15–17), then what has the Lord revealed to Peter, who is the first among the apostles?

A third element in the Petrine tradition, the commission to shepherd the flock (John 21:15–17), also raises questions. Did this charge apply only to the activities of Peter in the early Jerusalem community such as we find in Acts? Or did Peter become "shepherd" of other churches after he was forced to leave Jerusalem? We have also seen that this passage has traditionally generated questions about the relationship between Peter's activity and that of the other apostles. The early chapters of Acts depict Peter as the spokesperson for the Twelve. To what extent is their teaching Petrine? 2 Peter 3:15–16 suggests that Petrine teaching should become the norm for evaluating interpretations of the letters of Paul, for example. By the second century, Papias exploits the link between Peter and Mark (1 Pet. 5:13) to defend the authority of Mark's Gospel against suspicion that the account was not in adequate order. Conceding the difficulties, Papias insists that Mark reflects the anecdotal teaching of Peter (see Eusebius, *Historia Ecclesiastica* 3.39.15).[1]

Several traditions about Peter which emerged in the second and third centuries in narrative form—a Gospel, several Acts, and the non-Gnostic *Apocalypse of Peter*—respond to the natural curiosity generated by the canonical portraits of Peter. The Gnostic *Apocalypse of Peter* will be treated in the next chapter, which surveys the treatments of Peter as the defender of true Christian teaching. In some Gnostic examples, Peter becomes the defender of Jesus' true (= Gnostic) teaching against the corruption of that teaching by orthodox church authorities.

EXPANDING ON GOSPEL TRADITIONS

Second-century Christians produced several Petrine pseudepigrapha which other early Christian writers frequently cited and treated as authoritative. 1 and 2 Peter could be seen as the beginning of this process. 2 Peter is often assigned to the early second century on the basis of its elaborate vocabulary and Asiatic style as well as its assumption that a collection of Pauline letters has the same status as the Old Testament. 2 Peter combines the Transfiguration with Jewish apocalyptic material taken from Jude in its defense of early Christian teaching concerning the Parousia. 1 Peter 3:19 expands the tradition of Jesus' Passion and Resurrection with the descent to preach to the spirits in prison. These features are combined in an *Apocalypse of Peter* which survives primarily in an Ethiopic translation, a fairly extensive Greek fragment, and some smaller Greek fragments.[2] In the discussion which follows here, the distinction between this *Apocalypse* and the Gnostic *Apocalypse of Peter* found in a Coptic translation among the Nag Hammadi writings will be made after the title, with the language of the particular work in parentheses: *Apocalypse of Peter* (Ethiopic) and *Apocalypse of Peter* (Greek) refer to this writing; *Apocalypse of Peter* (Coptic), to the third-century Gnostic text.

The *Apocalypse of Peter* (Eth.) opens as a revelation dialogue between Jesus and Peter in which Jesus reveals the events of the Parousia and the judgment that comes on those who are not faithful. The disciples approach Jesus on the Mount of Olives with the request that he teach them about the Parousia so that those who hear the apostles preaching will remain on guard for the time of the Lord's return (chaps. 1–2). Echoes of the synoptic discourse in Mark 13 are evident in the setting. Jesus, seated on the Mount of Olives, is approached by the three disciples in his inner circle, who ask about the sign of Jesus' return and the close of the age (Mark 13:3).[3] The discourse opens with a warning about false prophets (Matt. 24:4). The opening sections continue with variations of apocalyptic sayings from the synoptic apocalypse or elsewhere in the Jesus tradition.

The proximity to well-known Gospel material might well make the *Apocalypse of Peter* (Eth.) indistinguishable from the canonical traditions for those whose familiarity with both depends upon their hearing them rather than their having read an analysis of the texts. Just as Peter asks about the withered fig tree in Mark 11:21, here he demands that Jesus explain his reference to learning the time from the fig tree (chap. 2, 1; cf. Matt. 24:32–33). Further exchanges which draw on apocalyptic images from the Gospels take a strong anti-Israel tone. The Jews crucified the Messiah and are making martyrs of his followers, who are not willing to follow the false prophets—*Apocalypse of Peter* (Eth.) 2.9–13. Since Clement of Alexandria refers to the *Apocalypse of Peter* (Gk.) as written by the apostle Peter,[4] that work was probably in circulation by the middle of the second century A.D. Some interpreters have proposed that the "false messiahs" whom many Christians rejected at the cost of their lives represent the Jewish rebels of the Bar Cochba period.[5] The martyrs appear to have followed the false messiah, Bar Cochba, in the beginning but later rejected him. Through the intervention of Enoch and Elijah, they were able to unmask the deceiver.[6] Whether or not one thinks that references to the Bar Cochba rebellion are behind the text, the *Apocalypse of Peter* (Eth.) has expanded the synoptic scenario. Its false messiahs are still persons who lead the people astray with false claims about the historical events of the end-time. They are not the skeptics who claim that teaching the end of the world is a myth from 2 Peter.

Another question from Peter elicits an extended description of the torments which await sinners (chaps. 7–12). The punishments accorded various types of sins create an Inferno ordered around standard catalogues of vices.[7] Although the *Apocalypse of Peter* (Eth./Gk.) is our earliest witness for this Inferno tradition, the author appears to have made use of Jewish apocalyptic sources.[8] The visions of reward for the righteous which follow the tour of hell combine the tradition of the opening of Paradise with the Transfiguration (chaps. 15–17). Between the two, the Lord sends Peter to Rome, where he will undergo martyrdom (chap. 14, 3–6).[9] This mission requires that Peter preach the message throughout the world. As a result of Peter's preaching and death, the power of Satan over the world will be broken.[10]

With the Transfiguration scene, the echoes of the synoptic tradition that are so frequent in the opening sections return. The text expands the description of the figures who appear with Jesus. A question from Peter leads Jesus to identify the heavenly figures as Moses and Elijah. Peter then asks where the patriarchs and other righteous ancestors are and is shown a vision of Paradise. He is told that Paradise will soon be opened to the martyrs (chaps. 15–16, 6). Peter's next request for permission to build three booths echoes the Matthean version of the Transfiguration story (Matt. 17:4). It brings an expected rebuke in which Satan is said to have gotten hold of Peter and infected his heart with a love for material things. The rebuke is apparently a transposition of the episode which occurs before the Transfiguration in Mark 8:32–33.[11] Peter may be resisting his own entry into Paradise as a martyr. Jesus shows the disciples the heavenly tabernacle. A divine voice identifies Jesus as the Beloved Son.

As the apostles watch, Jesus, Moses, and Elijah all ascend into the heavens where they are greeted by a host of human beings. When the heavens close, the apostles pray and descend from the mountain. There is considerable disagreement about the significance of the final vision.[12] It appears to mark the Transfiguration as part of a post-Resurrection revelation on the Mount of Olives that culminates with the Ascension rather than an episode from the life of Jesus. If the canonical traditions of Christ's preaching among the dead (1 Pet. 3:19–20; 4:6 and Eph. 4:8–10) are behind this passage, then the hosts of human beings are the righteous, who had waited in a lower paradise until Christ's triumphal ascent opened the heavens to them.

The heavenly tabernacle and the heavenly ascent of the final vision underline a significant difference between the eschatology of *Apocalypse of Peter* (Eth.) and 2 Peter. We have seen that 2 Peter adopts a Platonized understanding of the divinization of the soul and its union with God in the divine world. The *Apocalypse of Peter* (Eth.) constantly speaks of the bodily existence of both the sinners and the righteous. Resurrection of sinners and the righteous precedes the judgment. The animals are required to return every bit of flesh they may have consumed so that the bodies of humans can be reconstituted (chap. 4, 4–5). The *Apocalypse of Peter* (Eth.) has developed the eschatological and visionary traditions associated with Peter by incorporating Jewish apocalyptic traditions of the punishment of sinners in hell and the paradise of the righteous. It has also continued the ancient tradition of historical apocalyptic, reading the sign of God's impending judgment in the political distress of the times.

2 Peter 1:16 introduces its reference to the Transfiguration with the assertion that its teaching concerning the coming of the Lord is not a "cleverly devised myth." By insisting upon the concrete understanding of the judgment, the *Apocalypse of Peter* (Eth./Gk.) provides ammunition for just such charges. The paraenesis evident in the association of sins with appropriate punishments in the Inferno section demonstrates that, like 2 Peter, *Apocalypse of Peter* (Eth./Gk.) uses this material to warn the righteous. If the traditional material found in the *Apocalypse of Peter* (Eth./Gk.) was already circulating as Petrine teaching in the early second century, then it may have generated the accusations about eschatology that 2 Peter seeks to answer. We have seen that 2 Peter constantly insists upon the truth of prophecy. The *Apocalypse of Peter* (Eth.) suggests that the end-time judgment should follow the collapse of the Bar Cochba rebellion. Such a concrete and contemporary example of failed prophecy may have been a stronger impetus to reject the established tradition than the temporal gap which separated believers from the Resurrection of Jesus.

Although we do not have sufficient evidence to secure a second-century date for 2 Peter, associating the dispute over Christian eschatology with the *Apocalypse of Peter* (Eth.) provides a context for insisting on Petrine teaching as the guarantee of traditional, apocalyptic eschatology, and the certainty of prophecy. The Transfiguration scene is not the only evidence for the truth of Jesus' teaching about the Parousia. Peter, James, John, and Andrew receive the Lord's teaching about the end-time on the Mount of Olives (Mark 13:3–4). The *Apocalypse of Peter* (Eth.) depicts the preaching and martyrdom of Peter as breaking the power of Satan. We have already seen that John 21:18–23 contrasts the martyrdom of Peter with the death of the Beloved Disciple. The narrator's comment that some have misunderstood Jesus' prophecy about the Beloved Disciple seems to imply that the latter would remain alive until the Parousia (John 21:23). Clearly, the deaths of those who provided the community's link to its founder created uncertainty, especially if subsequent events appeared to contradict prophetic words attributed to Jesus. The Bar Cochba rebellion demonstrated that Rome's power remained as secure as ever. The deaths of the apostles had not brought the end-time any closer. Those who responded by treating such speculations as "myths" sought to preserve the tradition by attributing an alternate explanation to Paul. By defending the traditional teaching in a pseudepigraphical letter which also presented itself as the last testament of the martyr-apostle Peter, 2 Peter also responds to the uncertainty about the significance of Peter's death.

While Petrine authority was attached to the Gospel of Mark, Mark was not the only account of Jesus traced to the apostle in the second century. A *Gospel of Peter* was in circulation by the end of the century. Eusebius preserves an excerpt from a treatise concerning the *Gospel of Peter* by Serapion, bishop of Antioch (*Hist. Eccl.* 6.12.3–6). Finding this gospel in use among Christians at Rhossus during a pastoral visit, Serapion initially thought it harmless. He subsequently was informed that it was the source of heretical teaching including that of some persons called Docetists. Having made an investigation, the bishop concluded that the *Gospel of Peter* contained heretical additions even though most of it corresponded with true teaching. None of the other references to this work in antiquity contains quotations from it or information about its contents.[13] The same manuscript that contained fragments of the *Apocalypse of Peter* (Gk.) also contained fragments of the *Gospel of Peter*. A few smaller fragments have since been published.[14]

The large fragment concerns the trial, Crucifixion, burial and Resurrection of Jesus. Unlike the docetic Crucifixion account that forms the basis of the revelation in the *Apocalypse of Peter* (Cop.), the Passion account—a mix of traditions familiar from the synoptics—makes no attempt to negate the death of Jesus. Indeed, the narrative suggests that Jesus felt pain and torment even though he may have appeared not to (*Gos. Pet.* 4). Some scholars have claimed that the epiphany of the risen Christ as well as some details of the Passion preserved in the *Gospel of Peter* are more primitive than the accounts of the canonical Gospels.[15] However, the surviving text shows extensive relationships to the canonical Gospels, especially Matthew's version of the passage. The second-century *Gospel of Peter* knows those traditions[16] and may even expect that the reader or hearer is already familiar with the general outlines of the story. The dramatic expansion of the story of the guards at the tomb who see the risen Christ emerge between two angels that is found in the *Gospel of Peter* fills in the gaps in that story. Rather than redacting the Gospel of Matthew as Matthew and Luke reworked that of Mark, the *Gospel of Peter* reflects oral expansion and development of the story.[17] Expansion is so common in oral story-telling that one can hardly fault Serapion for asserting that the *Gospel of Peter* was acceptable for public use. Only the unusual procedure of investigating the text revealed departures from commonly held teaching. Since we only have fragments of the *Gospel*, we cannot identify which elements in the story were in dispute.[18]

The fragment begins with Pilate's washing his hands, a rite the Jews refuse to perform. In order to explain how Jesus was crucified if the procurator had decided to have nothing to do with the case, the *Gospel of Peter* has Herod present in the court with Pilate. Herod gives the order to execute Jesus. When Joseph, said to be a friend of both the Lord and Pilate, asks for the body, Pilate must request the body from Herod. No Romans are involved in the Crucifixion itself. Jesus dies at the hands of a Jewish mob. Since we later learn that Peter is the narrator, we must presume that he was presented as the witness to the trial proceedings as well. The *Gospel of Peter* contains no reference to Peter's denial. Indeed, all of the disciples remain in the vicinity. The *Gospel of Peter* tells its readers that the sorrowing disciples are forced into hiding because the authorities are looking for them as persons who might torch the temple. They spend their time in hiding, fasting and mourning (sec. 7). The final surviving section (sec. 14) explains that at the end of the Passover festival the Twelve, still in mourning, return home to Galilee. Peter, Andrew, and Levi go out in their boat to fish. Presumably, this notice will be followed by an appearance similar to that in John 21:1–14. The *Gospel of Peter* departs from the canonical traditions which have Jesus appear to his disciples on Easter Sunday. The Galilean appearance traditions do not occur until the disciples have journeyed home with the other pilgrims. For the *Gospel of Peter*, the Jerusalem appearance becomes an actual vision of the risen One emerging from the tomb. However, only those hostile to Jesus see this vision. Both the Roman guards and Pilate agree that the vision proves Jesus is Son of God. In order to avoid being stoned by their own people, the Jewish leaders ask Pilate to silence the centurion and his soldiers. How Peter, the narrator, comes to know of these events is never clarified. Perhaps, the centurion, identified as Petronius, was believed to have become a Christian.

The apologetic function of having the risen Christ overwhelm his enemies forms the primary focus of this narrative. Since the *Gospel of Peter* alludes to elements of the story familiar in different canonical Gospels, its brief account of the disciples may not be a deliberate correction of the earlier, more ambiguous versions of their behavior during the Passion. Knowing that the disciples were not present at the Crucifixion or burial and that they later saw Jesus in Galilee, the author may have created the brief notices in which Peter describes their behavior as transitional passages to harmonize the elements in the Passion and Resurrection account known to him. What survives of the *Gospel of Peter* does not expand the Peter tradition as it is known from other early Christian sources. It merely explains the apostle's movements during the Passover week and his return to Galilee.

EARLY TESTIMONY CONCERNING PETER'S MARTYRDOM

Both the *Apocalypse of Peter* (Eth.) and the *Gospel of Peter* follow the lead of the canonical Gospels. Their picture of the apostle remains based on what is stated in, or may be inferred from, those accounts. Early second-century writings generally remain surprisingly silent concerning Peter's life at points where the canonical traditions provide no clues. Writers consistently maintain that Peter died as a martyr, but narrative details concerning the circumstances, time, and place are scanty. Jesus' command to go to the city in the West in the *Apocalypse of Peter* (Eth./Gk.) may have been modeled on the picture of Paul in Acts. The other hints that Peter died at Rome remain limited to the fictive origin of 1 Peter, assuming that Babylon symbolizes Rome (1 Pet. 5:13), and on the statement in Clement's letter to the Corinthians (*1 Clement* 5.4). Clement is equally reticent. The governing rubric of the section is that jealousy and division lead the wicked to persecute the good. Clement hopes that the Corinthians will pass the same negative judgment on those who have usurped the authority of the elders in their community (1 Clement 44.6; 47.6).[19]

Clement does not directly identify the place or manner of Peter's death. He only comments that Peter suffered many trials as a result of jealousy and that after giving his final witness, he went to the place of honor which was his due. Peter is first in a series which continues with Paul and then the multitude who have recently given Christians an example of endurance (1 Clem. 6.1). Clement gives considerably more space to the testimony, trials, and death of Paul than to Peter, though no details are provided in any of the examples. This paucity of evidence continues to lead some scholars to wonder whether or not Peter was actually martyred in Rome or died at some other place.[20] Further evidence for knowledge of Peter's activity in Rome at the beginning of the second century is sometimes found in Ignatius of Antioch. In his letter to the Roman Christians, requesting them not to take steps to have him freed, Ignatius comments in *To the Romans*: "I am not commanding you as Peter and Paul did, they were apostles . . ." (4.3).[21] However, Ignatius may not be referring to the martyrdom of Peter and Paul but to their respective Epistles. Ignatius employs the topos of his own unworthiness to give orders in his other epistles, *To the Trallians* (3.3) and *To the Ephesians* (3.1).

Another short notice which might refer to the martyrdom of Peter appears in the *Martyrdom and Ascension of Isaiah* (4.3). The end-time incarnation of Beliar, apparently to be identified with Nero (4.2),[22] is said to have attacked the plant sown by the twelve apostles. One of the Twelve is delivered "into his hand." With echoes of the account of the beast in Revelation 13, the *Ascension of Isaiah* says that this lawless king leads the peoples of the world to worship him as god. Most of the faithful will be deceived. The few who remain servants of Christ will flee to the desert until the Second Coming (4.4–13). Many interpreters think that the member of the Twelve handed over to Beliar refers to a prominent martyr, either Peter or Paul.[23] However, a reference to handing a person over to Satan might not indicate martyrdom at all. Paul uses the expression in the context of the immoral brother whom the Corinthians are to expel (1 Cor. 5:5). If the *Ascension of Isaiah* has slipped from Beliar as Nero back to Beliar as the power of evil which has ruled the world from the beginning (4.2), then the one member of the Twelve who is handed over to Satan is Judas.[24] In either case, this allusion is prior to the reference to Nero's general persecution (4.13) in the narrative chronology. It represents the same ambiguity we find in the sequence of events in *1 Clement*.

EXCURSUS: NERO, THE FIRE, AND THE CHRISTIANS

The early tradition associates the martyrdom of Peter and Paul with Rome and with Nero's persecution indirectly rather than explicitly. Even Justin Martyr, who was later martyred at Rome (ca. 165), never

refers specifically to the death of Peter there.[25] Yet Eusebius cites a
letter of Dionysius of Corinth written a few years later (ca. 170) to
show that Peter and Paul had both taught in Rome and then died there
under Nero (*Hist. Eccl.* 2.25.8). Later, Eusebius gives a summary of
Peter's mission in Asia Minor. When Peter was martyred at Rome,
Eusebius tells us, he was crucified head down (*Hist. Eccl.* 3.1.2).
Eusebius claims to have taken from Origen the traditions about the
deaths of Peter and Paul under Nero.

The persecution conducted by Nero, to which this tradition had
become attached, is referred to by Roman historians as well as later
Christian authors. A major fire levelled large sections of Rome during
July of A.D. 64. Nero's visionary plans for rebuilding the city involved
considerable personal aggrandizement. The colossal statue he intended
to set up outside his new golden palace is testimony to the megaloma-
nia which is emphasized in Christian sources, where he is accused of
demanding worship of his image (Rev. 13:14; *Ascen. Isa.* 4.11). Yet the
emperor's character was no less offensive to many members of the
Roman upper classes, who began to turn against him. Nero's response
to the plots against him, coupled with his pressing financial needs,
would lead to his persecution of members of this class as well—by
executing them and confiscating their property.[26]

Though probably not true, the rumor that Nero was responsible for
the devastating fire had continued to circulate around the city. Roman
historians report that he attempted to deflect criticism among the
populace by blaming the unpopular sect of the Christians.[27] To demonstrate their culpability, Nero used Christians as human torches to
light the way to his games. There is no recoverable evidence of why
the emperor chose this sect. Some scholars think that the pro-Jewish
sympathies of Nero's wife, Poppaea, contributed to the choice.[28]
Whatever the reasons, the strategy failed to stem the growing tide of
disaffection with the emperor. As the list of prominent Roman victims
grew—a number that included the Stoic philosopher Seneca—Christians might indeed have gained apologetic points from the deaths of
some of their own most prominent leaders.

THE APOCRYPHAL *ACTS OF PETER*

From the late second century into the third century, apocryphal
Acts of the apostles begin to provide expanded narrative traditions
about the apostles themselves.[29] The genre of the apocryphal Acts is

frequently described as a Christian adaptation of the popular novel. An encratite rejection of marriage creates the anticipated tension between female converts and the males who pursue them. Miraculous events, dangerous journeys, and conflicts between the apostle heroes and the enemies of Christianity provide the necessary elements of entertainment as well as instruction.[30] However, other features of these writings are not based on the novel. As propaganda, the apocryphal Acts often emphasize the miracles of the apostles. Their exhortation and propaganda pick up elements of the lives of philosophers. Therefore, the apocryphal Acts cannot be assigned to a single literary genre.[31]

The Samaritan magician Simon, over whom Peter wins victory in Acts 8:9–24, provides the primary opponent for Peter in the *Acts of Peter*. Though this conflict would be expanded in other Petrine literature to advocate Jewish Christian orthodoxy against Paulinism,[32] that sort of polemic is not evident in this writing. Nor is Peter presented as the opponent of some form of Gnosticizing heresy.[33] The work seems primarily directed toward entertainment and exhortation. Miraculous healings, resurrections, and visions form the primary content of the *Acts of Peter*.[34] Since this work is used in the *Acts of Paul*, which can be dated to the end of the second century, the *Acts of Peter* probably stems from 180–190 A.D. The martyrdom scene which appears in *Acts of Peter* includes both the elements of death under Nero and of crucifixion head down that we find emerging at this time.

The martyrdom is introduced by a final contest between Peter, whose miracles are worked by God, and Simon the magician. Simon Magus announces to the whole city of Rome that he will ascend to God, thus demonstrating his divine nature as "He-who-standeth" or "the standing one."[35] Simon astonishes the crowds by flying over the city until Peter's prayer brings him crashing to the ground; having broken his leg in three places, he is smuggled out of the city by sympathizers to die elsewhere. Meanwhile, Peter's popularity results in the conversion of several prominent and beautiful women. As is typical of the "romance genre" of the apocryphal Acts, the women are converted to lives of celibacy. Their enraged suitors or husbands then launch a persecution against the responsible apostle, in this case Peter.

Informed of the conspiracy against Peter, the Christians persuade him to withdraw from the city. As he is departing, Peter sees the Lord entering Rome and recognizes that it is now time for him to be crucified (chap. 35). An enthusiastic martyr, Peter preaches a lengthy sermon. For half of the sermon, he is hanging upside down on the cross explaining why he has chosen to be crucified in that fashion: (a) it represents the perversion caused by the sin of the first Adam, which Christ came to set right; (b) in allegorical form, it represents the process of conversion or salvation—the Word is the upright piece, human nature the cross bar, and the nail holding the two together is conversion or repentance (chap. 38).[36] Peter concludes his homily with a thanksgiving prayer which is said to represent the inner words of the Spirit working in the heart, not the ambiguous and deceitful words of human speech:

> Jesus Christ, I thank thee with silence of the voice with which the spirit within me that loves thee and speaks to thee and sees thee makes intercession. Thou art known to the Spirit only. Thou art my Father, thou art my Mother, thou my Brother, thou my Friend, thou art Servant, thou art House-keeper; thou art All, and the All is in thee; thou art Being, and there is nothing that is except Thou. With him then do you also take refuge, brethren, and learning that in him alone is your real being, you shall obtain those things of which he says to you, "*What eye has not seen nor ear heard nor has it entered the human heart*" (1 Cor. 2:9). We ask then for what thou has promised to give us, O Jesus, undefiled; we praise thee, we give thanks to thee and confess thee, and being yet men without strength we glorify thee; for thou art God alone and no other, to whom be glory both now and for all eternity, Amen. (chap. 39)

As the crowd roars its "Amen" to his prayer, Peter dies. This account of Peter's martyrdom departs from the usual version of events under Nero—in which Peter is executed by the enraged husband of one of his converts. Angered at being deprived the opportunity of torturing Peter for having made converts within the imperial household, Nero launches a general persecution against those converts themselves. But a dream vision shortly before Nero's death causes the emperor to cease his persecution of Christians (chap. 41). *Acts of Peter* concludes with a ringing affirmation of the joy and unity of the "brethren" at Rome, a theme taken from Acts 2:46. By concluding with the martyrdom account, the author of *Acts of Peter* has presented a schema in which the controversies stirred up by Simon Magus' false preaching have been overcome. The church has been strengthened by the death of its martyr hero and his companions.

The conflict between Peter and Simon in *Acts of Peter* provides the opportunity for a dramatization of Christianity's superiority over its pagan rivals. The two square off in a number of "contests" of magical power. Peter is consistently able to raise the dead when Simon is not. These episodes permit the author to describe the process of conversion which requires renunciation of idolatry, rejection of uncleanness and lust, and fellowship with Christ (chaps. 26–28). Those who have been following Simon are only chasing a miracle-monger. Their conversion does not entail a genuine transformation of their lives.[37]

The tales in *Acts of Peter* also point to a complex social history in which the competition between Peter and Simon is depicted as a contest to secure the favor of a wealthy patron.[38] The first person Peter raises from the dead is the son of a poor widow (chaps. 25–27). However, the next request comes from a wealthy mother whose dead son is of senatorial rank. The woman's Christian slaves have brought her to Peter and Simon. Simon can only get the corpse to gesture. Before he revives the boy, Peter wins concessions from his mother. He negotiates over the status of the slaves. Then the woman and her son provide the Christian community with considerable material donations (chap. 28).[39] Another powerful figure, Marcellus, temporarily sides with Simon. But when Marcellus repents, he recognizes that money does not buy "salvation," power, or influence with God (chap. 10). Eventually, he learns to use his money to assist the orphans and widows of the community because they are "servants of Christ" and not to serve his worldly pleasures (chap. 19).

Acts of Peter appears to use the dispute between Peter and Simon Magus as an opportunity to defend the Christian vision of salvation against competing claims by other cults as well as the demands of wealthy patrons. Whenever such a person changes sides, his or her household follows suit. The noble death of its hero enhances the image of Christianity. The unusual twist of a martyrdom which outwits the desires of Nero echoes the conventions of the Stoic upper classes, who would chose suicide rather than permit the emperor to have them executed. Throughout *Acts of Peter*, the apostle serves as the "broker" of Christ's benefits, concretely displayed as healing. We never learn how this power is passed on after the apostle's death. Perhaps, the apostle himself continues to inspire particular individuals to guide the community—in much the same way that he appears to Marcellus in a vision, protesting the expensive burial Marcellus has given his body (chap. 40).

The encratite cast of the second- and third-century apocryphal Acts might seem to conflict with an apostle hero who was known to be married. Two fragmentary traditions provide evidence for how the tradition about Peter's family was incorporated into the legends of the apocryphal Acts and martyrdom. A codex which otherwise contains Gnostic texts, the Berlin Codex, includes a fragment of an *Acts of Peter* in Coptic.[40] The crowds who have witnessed Peter's healings challenge him to heal his own very beautiful virgin daughter of the paralysis on one side of her body. To prove that God is not powerless, Peter commands her to walk but then requires her to return to being paralyzed. He explains that her beauty has been a severe temptation to men from the time she was ten years old. A rich man, Ptolemaeus, kept demanding to marry her even though the girl's mother objected. The paralysis preserved her virginity. As a distraught Ptolemaeus is about to commit suicide, a revelation of Jesus tells him that it is wrong to defile Christ's virgin, whom he should treat as a sister. As in the other miracles, Ptolemaeus begins to convert others and to do good. The land he leaves to Peter's daughter on his death is sold and given to the poor. Thus, Peter instructs his audience that God does good for all the faithful. This story combines the common motif of virginity with echoes of the shared property of Acts 4:32–37.

Clement of Alexandria uses a legend about the martyrdom of Peter's wife to demonstrate that the true Christian despises all the pleasures of the world. When Peter sees his wife being led off to martyrdom, he shouts encouragement to her. Thus, Clement concludes Peter is the perfect example of a Christian husband. He follows Paul's advice and exercises self-control within marriage (1 Cor. 7:29, 35). Peter also exhorts his wife to true love of the Lord (*Stromateis* 7.11.63–64). These examples indicate that Peter's family had been transformed into the model family for second- and third-century Christians. Clement uses the martyrdom legend to argue that Peter's marriage demonstrates the detachment called for in 1 Corinthians 7. The Berlin Codex fragment of *Acts of Peter* also depicts the apostle's daughter as a Christian virgin. God's intervention rescues her from a rich, Christian husband.

The Coptic Gnostic codices found near Nag Hammadi contain an unusual tale that is titled *Acts of Peter and the Twelve Apostles*.[41] Obeying the Lord's command to preach to the nations, the Twelve have set out to sea and have come to a city on an island in the middle of the ocean. Peter meets a fellow stranger who is going about the city offering pearls even though he does not have the merchant's pouch, only a book in one hand and a staff in the other. Seeing no merchandise, the wealthy refuse to listen. The poor ask to see the pearl, since they know that people do not give pearls to beggars. Challenged to come to the man's city, Peter asks about the way there, so that he and the others can preach in that city.

Warned that the route requires total renunciation, Peter goes to get the others and journeys to the city. Because they have carried out the renunciation required, they arrive in front of the city and meet a stranger who appears to be a doctor. He reveals that he was also the pearl merchant and is actually the risen Christ. Christ gives the apostles the physician's box. They are sent back to the city in the ocean to preach the name of Jesus and heal the sick. John protests that they are not physicians. Jesus replies by instructing them to be physicians of the soul. Physical healings are only a method for winning faith so that souls can be healed. Jesus also tells his disciples to avoid the rich and not to accept invitations to their houses. Partiality toward the rich has ruined many churches. People can be influenced by the rich to follow their sinful ways.

Its allegorical treatment of the soul and the image of the pearl merchant probably made this unusual text popular in ascetic Gnostic circles. However, the allegory itself contains no peculiarly Gnostic features. Disciples are encouraged to renounce everything that belongs to the world. The author is particularly critical of the wealthy. They are unable to recognize Christ in the strange pearl merchant with the book and staff, a common enough representation of a sage to be intelligible. The influence wielded by the rich within the churches has led to partiality and neglect of the poor. This desire to counteract the effects of such a bias in favor of affluence, coupled with a series of allegorical visions, has led some interpreters to compare *Acts of Peter and the Twelve Apostles* to the *Shepherd of Hermas*.[42] *Hermas* was frequently considered canonical. The Muratorian Canon (ca. A.D. 200) claims that its recent origins, in mid-second century Rome, make *Hermas* unacceptable as part of the canon thought it might be profitable private reading. *Acts of Peter and the Twelve Apostles* may reflect this trend in mid-second century Roman Christianity. Unlike the more elaborate Acts of later in the century, this work is more concerned with the teachings of the mysterious stranger Christ than with the apostles themselves. Its conclusion also demonstrates some reticence about faith and miracles. Unless a person goes beyond what appears to the outward senses, he or she will never recognize Jesus.

Based on the surviving evidence, narrative traditions concerning Peter undergo a major development in the last third of the second century. Earlier writings such as the *Apocalypse of Peter* (Eth./Gk.) or the *Gospel of Peter* remain close to the first-century material. Expansions may be added from other traditions such as the Jewish apocalyptic found in 2 Peter or in the *Apocalypse of Peter* (Eth./Gk). Such additions do not alter the basic versions of the Peter traditions found in the first century. Where the early tradition is largely silent, the early second-century material remains silent as well. Consequently, we do not hear of Peter's preaching and healing in Asia Minor or Rome. We know that Peter was martyred but have only vague hints that he died at Rome. No account is given of the event or even of circumstances surrounding Peter's death. Indeed, the identification of time and place are so vague in the sources that some have questioned whether or not Peter died at Rome. However, the later tradition quite strongly favors the fact of Peter's martyrdom under Nero, so we may assume that the earlier hints do point to that event as a fact as well.

With the traditions which make up the apocryphal Acts, the restraint vanishes. Dramatic accounts of Peter's martyrdom are incorporated into *Acts of Peter*. Peter's preaching centers in the city of Rome. There he defeats the arch-heretic Simon Magus. The contests with Simon as well as the legend of Peter's daughter have been cast as stories which compel the crowds who witness them to praise the Lord and to convert.[43] The tradition that Peter was able to work miracles takes a prominent place in this appeal for conversion. Some of the changes in the later tradition depict a Christianity that is dependent upon its wealthy patrons. They must be enjoined to sacrifice the normal power and patronage relationships of ancient society. The unusual variant of the Acts tradition, *Acts of Peter and the Twelve Apostles*, takes a harsher line than other versions of the tradition. It suggests that true Christianity cannot exist as long as disciples and churches are locked into patronage relationships with the rich.

Finally, we have seen that the early period's hints concerning the martyrdom of Peter at Rome were developed into full-fledged martyr accounts. Nero had been known for the vicious executions of members of the upper orders of Roman society as well as his own mother. Even the Roman historians who report that Nero executed Christians to deflect suspicion away from himself do not believe that Christians deserved that fate. Some interpreters have seen the reason which is given in the *Gospel of Peter* for the disciples' hiding—that the Jews were looking for them as persons who might burn the temple—as an indirect allusion to the spurious charges made by Nero. By the later second century, the Christian apostle belongs among the upper orders of society. Peter's martyrdom can thus be viewed as comparable to the fate of other prominent persons under Nero.

If we possessed more information about the social context of the communities from which the second- and third-century Peter stories come, we might discover better connections between the changes in the depiction of Peter and the circumstances in which Christians found themselves. In any event, the ambiguities in the character of Peter the disciple, which are so prominent in the Gospels, have disappeared. As martyr and apostle, Peter testifies boldly to the truth about Jesus. We have also seen that the social inferiority of his Galilean, fisherman origins have all but disappeared. By the end of the second century, the apostle can take his place as an equal among the educated elite. Such narrative developments provide a glimpse of the popular view of Peter during this period. This picture provides a basis for the use of the figure of Peter to ground the true teaching of the church which we shall investigate in the next chapter.

NOTES

1. T. V. Smith, *Petrine Controversies in Early Christianity: Attitudes Towards Peter in Christian Writings of the First Two Centuries*, WUNT 2 Reihe 5 (Tübingen: J. C. B. Mohr, 1985), 36.
2. See Ch. Maurer and H. Duensing, "Apocalypse of Peter," in *New Testament Apocrypha*, ed. Edgar Hennecke and Wilhelm Schneemelcher, trans. R. McL. Wilson (Philadelphia: Westminster Press, 1965), 2:653–83; Dennis D. Buchholz, *Your Eyes Will Be Opened: A Study of the Greek (Ethiopic) Apocalypse of Peter*, SBLDS 97 (Atlanta: Scholars Press, 1988); Martha Himmelfarb, *Tours of Hell: An Apocalyptic Form in Jewish and Christian Literature* (Philadelphia: University of Pennsylvania Press, 1983), 127–39.
3. Mark 13:3 speaks only of the sign of the end-time destruction of the temple. *Apocalypse of Peter* (Eth.) is closer to Matthew 23:3–4.
4. See Eusebius, *Historia Ecclesiastica* 6.14.1. Though Eusebius is careful to list *Apocalypse of Peter* (Gk.) as among the disputed books, Clement

may have considered it authoritative. The Mauritorian canon appears to count *Apocalypse of Peter* (Gk.) along with Revelation as canonical or at least acceptable for reading in church. However, the Mauritorian canon includes a note that some reject its being read in church (ll. 71–73).

5. Maurer and Duensing, "Apocalypse of Peter," *HSNTA* 2:664.

6. Buchholz, *Your Eyes*, 278–79.

7. *Your Eyes*, 306–38; Himmelfarb, *Tours of Hell*, 85–121.

8. Himmelfarb, *Tours of Hell*, 127–39.

9. The Ethiopic text is garbled. For a restoration based on one of the surviving Greek fragments, see Buchholz, *Your Eyes*, 353–38.

10. *Your Eyes*, 362.

11. *Your Eyes*, 370–71.

12. See *Your Eyes*, 374–75.

13. Arguing that the memoirs of Peter referred to in *Dialogue with Trypho* 106.3 indicates that Justin considered the *Gospel of Peter* a written gospel distinct from Mark, P. Pilhofer then attempts to find references to *Gospel of Peter* in Justin's writings. Pilhofer would place the composition of *Gospel of Peter* in the first third of the second century A.D. See "Justin und das Petrusevangelium," *ZNW* 81 (1990): 60–78.

14. See Wilhelm Schneemelcher, "Gospel of Peter," in *New Testament Apocrypha*, 2d ed., ed. Wilhelm Schneemelcher, trans. R. McL. Wilson (Louisville: Westminster/John Knox Press, 1991), 1:216–22.

15. See J. D. Crossan, *Four Other Gospels* (New York: Winston, 1985), 125–81; and H. Koester, *Ancient Christian Gospels* (Philadelphia: Trinity Press International, 1990), 216–40.

16. Cf. the parallels laid out in Koester, *Ancient Christian Gospels*, 222–39. John P. Meier provides a careful summary of the argument against the claim that *Gospel of Peter* is based on an early Passion narrative that forms the basis for the development of the canonical traditions; see *A Marginal Jew, Rethinking the Historical Jesus 1: The Roots of the Problem and the Person* (Garden City: Doubleday, 1991), 116–18.

17. See Susan E. Schaffer, "The Guard at the Tomb (*Gos. Pet.* 8:28–11:49 and Matt. 27:62–66; 28:2–4, 11–16): A Case of Intertextuality?" *Society of Biblical Literature. 1991 Seminar Papers* (Atlanta: Scholars Press, 1991), 499–507.

18. Schneemelcher rightly challenges those scholars who have based elaborate theories concerning the traditions behind *Gospel of Peter* on the few surviving fragments; see "Gospel of Peter," 218–20.

19. Raymond E. Brown and John P. Meier, *Antioch and Rome: New Testament Cradles of Catholic Christianity* (Ramsey, NJ: Paulist Press, 1983), 159–68.

20. See, e.g., Smith, *Petrine Controversies*, 33f.

21. William Schoedel, *Ignatius of Antioch* (Philadelphia: Fortress Press, 1985), 176; Rudolf Pesch, *Simon Petrus, Geschichte und geschichtliche Bedeutung des ersten Jüngers Jesu Christi. Päpste und Papstum Bd. 15* (Stuttgart: Anton Hiersemann, 1980), 118f.

22. Beliar's incarnation is described as "a lawless king, slayer of his mother." The earliest historians of the Flavian period despised Nero. Pliny the Elder speaks of him as "the destroyer of the human race," "the poison of the world" (*Natural History* 7.45, 22.92). Though Nero's mother was alleged to have murdered Claudius to put her son on the throne, Nero was said to have murdered his mother, his wife, and many other members of the aristocracy on charges of conspiracy (Josephus, *Antiquities of the Jews* 20.153; Tacitus, *Annals of Rome* 14.1–13).

23. Pesch, *Simon Petrus*, 120; M. A. Knibb, "Martyrdom and Ascension of Isaiah," in *The Old Testament Pseudepigrapha*, ed. J. Charlesworth (Garden City: Doubleday, 1985), 2:161.

24. As we have seen, Luke has Satan enter Judas' heart at the beginning of the Passion (22:3) and Jesus pray that Satan's testing will not cause Simon's faith to fail (22:31–32).

25. Daniel Wm. O'Connor, *Peter in Rome: The Literary, Liturgical and Archaeological Evidence* (New York: Columbia University Press, 1969), 26.

26. See Miriam T. Griffin, *Nero: The End of a Dynasty* (New Haven: Yale University Press, 1984), 129–33, 166.

27. Tacitus, *Annals* 15.44f.; Suetonius, "Nero," *Lives of the Caesars* vi, 16.2; Pesch, *Simon Petrus*, 123f., 128.

28. Griffin, *Nero*, 133.

29. See F. Bovon et al., *Les Actes apocryphes des Apôtres* (Geneva: Labor et Fides, 1981).

30. See Jean-Daniel Kaestli, "Les principales orientations de la recherche sur les Actes apocryphes des Apôtres," in *Les Actes apocryphes des Apôtres* (Geneva: Labor et Fides, 1981), 57–67.

31. "Les principales orientations de la recherche," 65–67.

32. See Simon Légasse, "La polémique antipaulinienne dans le judéo-christianisme hétérodoxe," *BLE* 90 (1989): 85–93.

33. Smith, *Petrine Controversies*, 55.

34. Schneemelcher, "Acts of Peter," *HSNTA* 2:273.

35. "He-who-standeth" or "the standing one" was an established epithet for God in Platonic piety; see Michael Williams, *The Immovable Race*, Nag Hammadi Studies 29 (Leiden: E. J. Brill, 1985), 37–57.

36. For a general study of conversion in the apocryphal Acts, see Eugene V. Gallagher, "Conversion and Salvation in the Apocryphal Acts of the Apostles," *Second Century* 8 (1991): 13–29. This brief allegory in the *Acts of Peter* typifies the significance which the authors of the apocryphal

Acts give to conversion as the miraculous transformation of a person's way of life. The miracles which figure so prominently in these works must be understood within that framework.

37.   Gallagher, "Conversion and Salvation," 22.
38.   See Robert F. Stoops, Jr., "Patronage in the *Acts of Peter*," *Semeia* 38 (1986): 91–100.
39.   Stoops emphasizes the fact that these patrons do not acquire a dependent clientele among the Christians. Nor do they become persons of influence in the community. They must act solely to honor God. See "Patronage," 94–96.
40.   See "Acts of Peter," *HSNTA* 2:276–78; or James M. Robinson, ed., *The Nag Hammadi Library in English*, 3rd ed. (San Francisco: Harper and Row, 1988), 529–31.
41.   See Robinson, ed., *Nag Hammadi Library*, 289–94.
42.   See Douglas M. Parrott, "The Acts of Peter and the Twelve Apostles," *Nag Hammadi Library*, 288–89.
43.   Gallagher, "Conversion and Salvation," 14–17.

CHAPTER 6

Peter and Authentic Tradition

PETER'S TEACHING AS TRUE TRADITION

Second-century writings explore the traditions of Peter as a witness to the gospel in his preaching and martyrdom at Rome. The dramatic confrontations between Peter and the heretic Simon Magus in these writings demonstrate the apostle's divine authority. In disputes over Christian teaching, Peter defends communal orthodoxy against views held to be deviant or heretical. We have seen that Matthew's Gospel depicts Peter as the disciple who was able to interpret Jesus' tradition for the later community. One of the problems faced by that community was balancing its Jewish Christian heritage with the influx of gentile Christianity. By the later second century, the open Jewish Christianity of Matthew would be marginalized by developments in mainstream Christianity. This development led to Jewish Christian appropriation of the figure of Peter as the defender of its tradition. His conflict with Paul is disguised as an encounter with Simon Magus.

Sometime in the early second century, 2 Peter invoked the apostle's authority to address a particular crisis over authentic Christian teaching. His visionary witness to Jesus' glory provides one argument in the case. Another argument presents Peter as the person who is able to determine the meaning of other apostolic writings. This claim shows that the idea of a canon of authoritative writings had begun to develop. 2 Peter acknowledges the importance of the Pauline letter canon. At the same time, the author insists that Paul's true meaning had to be consistent with Petrine teaching. False teachers who claim to discover some teaching in Paul's writings which contradicts common Christian tradition cannot claim apostolic authority for their views. From this perspective, any teaching which contradicts Petrine tradition is to be rejected as heretical.

A number of Gnostic writings in which Peter is the leading figure confirm the significance of Peter as an authority for true Christian teaching. In some examples, Peter represents hostile church authorities who seek to wipe out the Gnostic sect. But other examples turn Peter into the teacher of Gnostic doctrine. Clearly, these authors feel the best way to demonstrate that a particular teaching represents the teaching of Jesus is to make Peter its guarantor.

PETER OPPOSES THE HERETIC, SIMON MAGUS

We have seen that the Simon Magus episode in Acts 8:9–24 is transposed to Rome in the *Acts of Peter*. Contests with the magician provide Peter with the opportunity to demonstrate the power of the gospel. This development follows the picture of Simon Magus in Acts as a magician who attempts to buy the power of the Spirit. The development from Simon the Samaritan magician to Simon the archheretic is not altogether clear. A Samaritan figure called Simon was said to have founded a Gnostic sect early in the second century A.D.[1] Justin Martyr writes in his *First Apology* that Simon was active in Rome under Claudius. Along with his consort Helena, Simon Magus claimed to represent the divine dyad of a Gnostic system, the divine Father and his Thought (26.1–3). Although Justin treats Simon Magus as the forefather of all the Gnostic sects, he does not describe Peter as the ancestor of the orthodox. Some scholars have suggested that the traditions concerning Peter's activity and those about Simon Magus the heretic had not been combined when Justin was writing at the middle of the second century.[2]

Justin establishes a pattern that would be repeated by Christian heresiologists after him. Just as philosophical schools had doctrines which were transmitted in the line of successive heads of the school, so Gnostic heresies derived from the founder Simon Magus. The followers of a particular school often defended the purity of their teaching by contrasting the unity of their beliefs with the many divisions that had been generated in the other philosophical schools. Though Acts limits the encounter between Simon and Peter to Samaria, Justin claims that Simon had spread his heresy to Rome as well. Reading the inscription on an ancient monument as though it referred to Simon,[3] Justin is able to argue that he was venerated by the Romans. Justin even asserts that the senate had been led astray and erected the statue to Simon (*1 Apol.* 46). Justin's *Second Apology* is cast as an appeal to the senate to recognize the truth of Christianity on the evidence of the courageous death of its martyrs. Its conclusion promises that accepting the appeal will put an end to deceitful doctrines like that of Simon Magus (*2 Apol.* 15).

Neither Peter's authority nor his martyrdom figures in Justin's defense of Christianity. We have seen that the popular *Acts of Peter* tradition was exploiting the dramatic possibilities of encounters between the Peter and Simon in Rome by the end of the second century. Justin's argument provided the framework for the Christian apologists who followed him to combine the two traditions. Irenaeus wishes to demonstrate that the true apostolic teaching contained in Scripture proves that Christ never taught Gnostic doctrines as his opponents allege. In *Adversus Haereses*, he adopts Justin's account of the origin of all Gnostic teaching with Simon Magus (Book 3, preface).[4] When he introduces the genealogy of heresies, Irenaeus cites the sections from Acts. Acts follows Peter's description of Simon's heart, which implies Simon's bondage to Satan, with a plea by the magician that the curse not come to pass (Acts 8:23–24). The reader was not told whether Peter interceded for Simon. Irenaeus omits the plea.

Before giving a lengthy account of the teaching of Simonian Gnostics, Irenaeus fills in the narrative between the end of Acts and the emergence of the sect. In doing so, he has merely put the traditional material that we find in Justin and *Acts of Peter* into a brief biographical note. The love of money and "gall of bitterness" that Peter detects in Simon's heart leads to Simon's increased effort to contend against the apostles. Simon devotes himself even more intensely to learning the magic arts. As a result, he is able to deceive the Roman people into dedicating the statue to him. Simon also makes himself the subject of the Christian gospel by claiming to be the incarnation of the divine Trinity: Son among the Jews, Father among the Samaritans, and Holy Spirit among the nations. Thus the designation "great," *magus*, no longer refers to Simon's magical powers but to his alleged identification with the supreme God (*Adv. Haer.* 1.23.1). The fictive setting of Justin's *Second Apology* promises that its acceptance by the Roman senate will rid the city of the pollution of deceitful teaching and religious cults.[5] Irenaeus, the heresiologist bishop, has transformed the promise of his own writing by assimilating Justin's model of the pedigree of Gnostic sects to the image of the satanic opposition to apostolic teaching. Just as Peter has defeated Simon, so the bishop's exposition of the heart of the false teaching will drive these new, many-headed descendants of Simon out of the churches (*Adv. Haer.* 3, preface).

Hippolytus also developed the genealogy of his Roman predecessor Justin by incorporating in his *Refutation of All Heresies* an excerpt from a Simonian Gnostic work and expanding the account of Simon's career with traditional material (6.9–17). The confrontations with Peter culminate in Simon's most daring attempt to imitate the Christian story. He promises that if his followers bury him alive, he will rise on the third day. According to those version of the legend, Simon still remains buried in the grave that was dug for him (*Ref.* 6.20.2–3).

The popularity of encounters between Peter and Simon led to yet another geographical migration. The Pseudo-Clementine *Recognitions* situates an encounter between Peter and Simon Magus at Caesarea. When he is defeated, Simon flees for Rome, where he is acknowledged as a god (3.29–58; *HSNTA* 2:549–52); Peter's own departure is motivated by the need to make sure that Simon's lies do not become accepted everywhere (3.59; *HSNTA* 2:553). Eusebius, who depends upon Justin and Irenaeus for his report, gives a similar description of Simon's motivations for journeying to Rome: he thinks that in the capital, he can distort the gospel. However, God's providence delivers to Rome the apostle chosen to be spokesperson for all the rest in bringing the good news from East to West (*Historica Ecclesiastica* 2.14).

The sermons of Peter in the Pseudo-Clementine writings appear to be derived from a Jewish Christian source which saw the Paulinism of mainstream Christianity as a false gospel.[6] The figure of Simon stands for the apostle Paul in this literature. Under his influence, non-Jewish Christians have misused Old Testament prophecies and Christian writings in order to justify abandoning the Law of God. An opening epistle in the Pseudo-Clementines addressed to James requests that he convey these teachings only to those who have been properly tested. Paul's account of the Antioch episode (Gal. 2:11–14) was a false claim to know Peter's true teaching:[7] "For some from among the Gentiles have rejected my lawful preaching and have preferred a lawless and absurd doctrine of the man who is my enemy (Mt. 13:28). And indeed some have attempted while I am still alive to distort my words by interpretations of many sorts, as if I taught the dissolution of the Law and, although I was of this opinion, did not express it openly" (1.2.3–4; *HSNTA* 2:112). The author sets Peter's authority as an eyewitness of the Lord against Paul's claim to have received the gospel through a visionary experience of the risen Lord (Pseudo-Clementine Homily 17.13.1–19.6).[8] Christ encountered Paul as an enemy to be converted, not as someone who was instructed in his teaching. If Paul had really known the teaching of Christ, he would not have slandered and reviled Peter but would have learned true doctrine from him. When Marcion used Pauline authority to establish a sectarian version of Christianity that rejected the Old Testament and its God, he appealed to Paul. Consequently, some interpreters think that the name "Simon" in *Kerygmata Petrou* really stands for the Paul of Marcion's preaching.[9] In arguing against the authenticity of Marcion's gospel, Irenaeus and Tertullian emphasize the primacy of Peter over Paul as well as the unity of true apostolic preaching. The Marcionites alleged that Paul's revelation gave him the truth about God, which was not possessed by the other apostles. Irenaeus counters this interpretation by pointing to the passages in the Pauline letters (especially 1 Cor. 15:1–11) in which Paul insists that he preaches the same message as the other apostles. Paul's visits to Jerusalem show that his ministry was subordinate to the authority of the apostles there (*Adv. Haer.* 3.13).[10]

These developments in the Petrine tradition emphasize the role of the apostle as the source of orthodox Christian teaching. The *Kerygmata Petrou* recognizes that claims to visionary experience and prophetic inspiration could be used by heretical groups as well as the orthodox. True apostolic tradition must be fixed by criteria which cannot be twisted by anyone who is inspired to claim divine authority. By the time the Pseudo-Clementines were composed, Jewish Christianity was so marginalized that most Christians would have considered its demands to follow the Law and its purity regulations as an heretical denial of Jesus' divinity. The time for a mediating incorporation of Jewish Christianity suggested by the original Jerusalem council had passed.[11] Eusebius links the Papias claim that Mark represents written Peter traditions to the end of the Peter/Simon conflict. After witnessing the apostle's defeat of the heretic, Roman Christians recognized that they could not rely on oral testimony. They pressed Mark to provide a written record of Peter's teaching. Eusebius claims that Clement of Alexandria's *Outlines* also reported that Peter himself authorized the public reading of the Gospel of Mark in the churches (*Hist. Eccl.* 2.15).

According to Eusebius, Papias pointed to the mention of a Christian named Mark in 1 Peter 5:13 as evidence for the Petrine source of Mark's Gospel as well as its Roman origin. The quotations from Papias preserved in Eusebius suggest an opposition to the persons who followed commandments that differed from the teaching of the Lord. On the one hand, Papias alleges to have interviewed as many persons who had known original disciples of Jesus as possible. He asserts that living voices are superior to books. On the other, he defends the written Gospels of Mark and Matthew as evidence for authentic oral teaching. Ever since F. C. Baur, some scholars have suggested that this emphasis on tradition which can be traced back to the sayings of Jesus represents suspicion about the growing influence of Pauline Epistles in the churches of Asia Minor.[12] While 2 Peter 3:15–16 suggests the assimilation of Pauline tradition under Petrine authority, Papias and the *Kerygmata Petrou* indicate that other Christians found the canonizing of the Pauline letter corpus a threat to the true teaching of the apostles.[13]

PETER AS SPOKESPERSON FOR CONVENTIONAL CHRISTIANITY

The traditions we have been investigating depict Peter as the spokesperson for an author's view of orthodox Christian teaching. In the apologists, orthodoxy implies adherence to the commonly accepted creed and traditional interpretations of the Gospels and Epistles of Paul. The Gnostic claims that Jesus had transmitted an esoteric teaching to some or all of the apostles were rejected. The dramatic conflict between Peter and the arch-heretic Simon provided the example for later Christian teachers in their conflict with Gnostic opponents. The effectiveness of this strategy may be gauged by the revisionist treatments of Peter in Gnostic writings. Petrine authority for traditions claiming to stem from the historical Jesus could not be ignored.[14]

The imperfections attributed to Peter and Jesus' other disciples in the Gospels provided Gnostic teachers with evidence that Peter and the others did not know Jesus' full teaching. Thus, where other Christian traditions in the second and third centuries omitted these failings from their narratives, Gnostics picked up those details. Gnostic hermeneutics distinguished those who interpreted the sayings of Jesus literally—the majority of Christians and their bishops—from persons of true insight. Jesus' rebukes addressed to his apostles in the Gospels show that they had not achieved higher understanding.[15] The ignorant disciples are the models of the equally ignorant church leaders.

This Gnostic polemic forced Christian apologists to defend the picture of the apostles presented in the canonical writings. Irenaeus cites Peter's sermon from the Cornelius episode in Acts 10:34–44 to show that the disciples could not have had the imperfect understanding of Jesus' teaching that Gnostics attribute to them (*Adv. Haer.* 3.12.7). The God whom Peter and the others preach to the Gentiles must be identified as the God of the Jews. Gnostic traditions encapsulated the conflict between the imperfect understanding of Peter and that of the true Gnostic in scenes which pit Peter against Mary Magdalene. Mary's close relationship with the Savior makes her an ideal source for authentic Jesus tradition (e.g., *Gospel of Philip*, C.G. III 59.7–10; *Nag Hammadi Library* 145;63.33–64.9; *NHL* 148).[16] She demonstrates the superiority of her insight to that of various members of the Twelve during dialogues with the risen Lord. Her questions show that she perceives the inner meaning of the Savior's words (e.g., *Dialogue of the Savior* C.G. III 139.9–13; 140.14–17; *NHL* 252).[17]

Scenes in which Peter protests Mary's place among the disciples only to be rebuked by the Lord or by other disciples demonstrate that for these authors Peter represents the orthodox Christian opposition. The conventions of polemical rhetoric against philosophical or religious opponents often generate the charge that the opposing view appeals only to women. This tactic appears in the pastoral Epistles (e.g., 2 Tim. 3:6–7). The exaltation of Mary Magdalene as the source of the true teaching of Jesus to challenge Petrine authority does not mean that Gnostic sects pitted women teachers against the male presbyters and bishops of the orthodox churches.[18] The concluding saying in the *Gospel of Thomas* (Logion 114; *NHL* 138) has Peter attempt to expel Mary from the company of the disciples because women are unworthy of life.[19] Jesus' rebuke promises to "make her male" so that she too can become a living spirit.[20] Whatever Gnostic significance the phrase "make her male" had, the rebuke demonstrates that Peter has attempted to limit the circle of disciples. Unlike the Peter of Acts 10:44–48 and 11:17, the Peter of the *Gospel of Thomas* does not recognize the power of the Spirit to make disciples.

Other sayings in the *Gospel of Thomas* are also aimed at subordinating Petrine authority. *Gospel of Thomas*, Logion 13, presents a variant of "Peter's Confession" (*NHL* 127). Asked to state a suitable comparison for the Savior, Peter responds first with "righteous angel." Thomas is the one who really recognizes the Savior's glory. He is unable to say what Jesus is like. This recognition is followed by a variation of the tradition that the true confession is followed by a beatitude (as in, e.g., Matt. 16:17). Thomas no longer requires Jesus as master. He has drunk from the bubbling spring of the Spirit that Jesus measures out (cf. John 4:14, 7:37–39). Thomas then receives a private revelation from the Savior which he refuses to divulge to the others lest they stone him.

The most dramatic demonstration of Peter's lack of insight and hostility toward those to whom the Savior has given wisdom occurs in the *Gospel of Mary*.[21] The disciples are too frightened by the thought of suffering like Jesus to engage in the mission of preaching entrusted to them. Mary must remind them of the words of Jesus and the divine power of protection (BG 8.6–24; *NHL* 525).[22] After she has shared with the apostles a private revelation concerning the soul's ascent, Andrew and Peter are offended. The Savior cannot have taught the "strange things." Jesus could not have chosen to reveal to her what he would not tell his other disciples (BG 17.10–22; *NHL* 526). Mary protests against Peter's suggestion that she is lying about the Savior and has made the whole thing up. Levi charges Peter with the character flaw of a hot temper which has led him to treat Mary as though she were an adversary. He enunciates the principle that disciples have no right to overrule the Savior's choice. Jesus' love for Mary is evidence of the truth of her character, since the Lord knows human nature. Instead, the disciples should become perfect and set out on the mission Jesus has entrusted to them without adding to the commands given by Jesus (BG 18.1–21; *NHL* 527).

As in the *Dialogue of the Savior*, Mary is allied with Levi (= Matthew) against Peter and Andrew. Though she is favored, she is not the only one able to perceive that Jesus' true teaching is represented in the hidden wisdom of the Gnostics. Contrary to the claims of the heresiologists like Irenaeus, true Christian teaching is not limited to the public, commonly known tradition. The dispute over esoteric and public teaching formed a major point of conflict between Gnostic teachers and their orthodox opponents. *Gospel of Thomas* 13 concludes with Thomas' refusing to reveal his knowledge to Peter and Matthew, whose answers show that they do not possess the Spirit.[23] Levi's exhortation echoes the concluding saying in the *Gospel of Thomas*. But, to the shame of the disciples, Mary is the only "true male" in the group. The others must be transformed before they can carry out the mission that Jesus has given them.[24]

Levi attributes Peter's refusal to accept Gnostic teaching to anger. This comment stems from a common catalogue of vices, not a particular observation about Peter in particular. Anger is a clear sign that a person does not possess the control over the passions which comes with wisdom (e.g., James 1:19–21). *1 Clement* initiates its attack on the conflict at Corinth with a catalogue of vices: "jealousy, envy, strife, sedition, persecution, disorder, war and captivity" (3.2). One Gnostic text describes the hostility of those who persecute the Savior's envoys in the name of Christ as "hating" the Gnostics and "serving two masters" (*Second Treatise of the Great Seth* C.G. VII 59.19–60.3; *NHL* 366f.).

Further examples of Peter's ignorance occur in a later, diffuse compilation of Gnostic traditions, *Pistis Sophia*.[25] Mary is the chief questioner during this revelation. Peter sometimes demands that Jesus silence her so that he can speak. While the request is granted, Mary's superior wisdom is always affirmed (chaps. 36 and 146). In another episode, Mary initially declines to provide an interpretation because she fears Peter (chap. 72). Given the negative descriptions of Peter as hostile, angry, and prone to make rules that are not in accord with the Lord's will that we find elsewhere, one of the Peter episodes comes as a surprise. Jesus challenges Peter to demonstrate mercy by asking him to cut off a woman who has done nothing worthy of the mysteries after three baptisms. Peter's refusal demonstrates that he is merciful (chap. 122). The massive compilation of material in *Pistis Sophia* makes it difficult to determine whether or not the sudden appearance of a merciful Peter indicates a modification of the earlier picture. It may simply be another variant of the Peter/Mary story that was in circulation. The rest of the instances fit the picture of Peter as ignorant and jealous of the superior wisdom possessed by others.

These Gnostic accounts of Peter have clearly been shaped by the conflict between Gnostic and orthodox Christians. Both sides agree that Peter is the spokesperson for the understanding of Christian truth held by the majority of Christians. They also agree that Peter provides the model for those who seek to defend that tradition. We have seen that the picture of the conflict in the *Gospel of Mary* appears to be related to the tradition behind some of the sayings in the *Gospel of Thomas*. The strong anti-Petrine cast of this particular tradition suggests that Gnostic teachers were sensitive to the polemic of orthodox authorities.[26] Petrine authority must have been a significant element in the persuasiveness of the orthodox case.

PETER AS A GNOSTIC APOSTLE

At the conclusion of the *Gospel of Mary*, the apostles go forth to preach (B.G. 19.1–2; *NHL* 527). The reader must conclude that this apostolic preaching included the Gnostic teaching provided by the revelations in the text. Thus, the text grants another of the topoi developed by the heresiologists: apostolic tradition must be known to all the apostles. In this case, esoteric tradition and common, public tradition are combined with the revelations which the disciples receive prior to their actual departure to preach. Another variant of this combination of exoteric and esoteric revelation designed to support the Gnostic claim that truly apostolic tradition is Gnostic appears in the *Apocryphon of James*. The opening scene describes the various apostles writing down what the Lord had told them, whether publicly or privately (C.G. 1.2.1–16; *NHL* 30).[27] Here we see the growing influence of the written canon understood as the repository of apostolic tradition.

However, the text continues to insist that the apostles do not all have the same ability to understand the true teaching. The Lord appears and takes James and Peter apart for a revelation, which the ending of the work suggests is to be the last. Though the *Apocryphon of James* does not exhibit the hostility to Peter that we find in other writings, James is the only one who really receives the tradition from Jesus. He is also the one to determine who can receive esoteric writings (C.G. 1.1.8–35; *NHL* 30). At the conclusion, he alone returns to Jerusalem. The other apostles are sent elsewhere by James because they have become distressed about the salvation which the Gnostic race is to receive (15.34–16,11; *NHL* 37).

Peter has the peculiar role of being a witness to the fact that Jesus has given the revelation contained in the dialogue. Yet Peter is not truly enlightened. Donald Rouleau has pointed out that James asks the questions which lead to actual developments in the dialogue. Peter merely makes exclamations at various points. James represents the later Gnostic Christians. Like the conventional Christians, Peter thinks that he is "full," when actually he needs to be filled with the Spirit (*Ap.Jas*.4.3–19; *NHL* 31).[28] Unlike the more polemical writings, the *Apocryphon of James* seeks to demonstrate that Gnostic revelation is in fact coherent with the publicly known teachings of Jesus. It refers to lists of parables and to other sayings of Jesus throughout.[29] Gnostics interpret the same canonical texts as other Christians do. Peter provides evidence for the authenticity of that interpretation, even if he is not completely enlightened.[30]

Gnostic attempts to appropriate the prestige of Peter as custodian of apostolic tradition did not end with the picture of Peter as witness to a

Gnostic tradition that he did not fully understand. The two Nag Hammadi texts in which Peter is the apostolic foundation for Gnostic tradition[31] have clearly been influenced by the orthodox use of canonical traditions about Peter in anti-Gnostic polemic. The *Epistle of Peter to Philip* has Peter summon all the apostles to gather on the Mount of Olives so that they can organize their effort before undertaking their separate preaching missions. As the apostles, fearful of those who seek to kill them, pray to the Father and the Son for strength, the risen Jesus appears in a great vision of light (CG VIII 133.17–134.18; *NHL* 434). The revelation that Jesus imparts constitutes a short catechism of Gnostic teaching (134.19–138.3; *NHL* 434–36). After they return to the temple area in Jerusalem, Peter delivers a "Pentecost" sermon in which the Spirit inspires him to provide a docetic interpretation of the Passion story. Jesus was a stranger to the suffering he underwent (139.9–30; *NHL* 436). The story concludes with the apostles' healing, preaching, and rejoicing in the permanent presence of the Lord among them. With the exception of the references to Gnostic mythology and doctrine in the content of the revelations themselves, the rest of this writing echoes themes from the Acts of the Apostles.[32]

References to suffering and persecution as well as the necessity for the apostles to preach in the world in order to counteract the power of the liars suggest some form of controversy with orthodox Christians. However, the text provides us with little to use in reconstructing the issues at stake. Its construction appears to be a direct answer to the common orthodox argument that the Acts of the Apostles prove that the early catechesis derived from a common apostolic faith. The *Epistle of Peter to Philip* concurs but traces that faith to a Gnostic revelation.

The Crucifixion also forms the setting for the Gnostic *Apocalypse of Peter* (Coptic).[33] In a series of brief visions and interpretations, Jesus shows Peter the events of the Passion from a Gnostic perspective. He sees the spiritual, immortal Christ separate from the physical body that his enemies nail to the cross. Jesus warns Peter that most will not believe the true teaching. Instead, they will place false hopes in one who is crucified:

> For many will accept our teaching in the beginning. And they will turn from them again by the will of the Father of their error, because they have done what he wanted. And he will reveal them in his judgment, i.e. the servants of the

Word. But those who became mingled with these shall become their prisoners, since they are without perception. And the guileless, good, pure one they push to the worker of death and to the kingdom of those who praise Christ in a restoration. And they praise the men of the propagation of falsehood, those who will come after you. And they will cleave to the name of a dead man, thinking that they will become pure. But they will become greatly defiled and they will fall into the name of a great error, and into the hand of an evil, cunning man and a manifold dogma, and they will be ruled heretically. (CG VII 73.23–74.22; *NHL* 374)

Their false confidence in a "dead man" also leads the orthodox Christians to think that martyrdom will gain them perfection rather than true fellowship with those who have received enlightenment from Christ (78.32–79.6; *NHL* 376). The *Apocalypse of Peter* (Cop.) refers to those who claim authority from God as bishops and deacons (79.22–27; *NHL* 376) but rule over the "little ones" who belong to Christ (80.8–11; *NHL* 376). Consequently, the author appears to address his exhortation to Gnostic Christians who remain within congregations subject to orthodox church authorities.

Peter is the "foundation" for this hidden, persecuted group of Christian Gnostics. The *Apocalypse of Peter* (Cop.) opens with allusions to the twin foundations: Jesus' word of revelation (70.20–27; *NHL* 373) and the apostle Peter, whose name shows that Jesus has chosen him to be the foundation for the elect remnant (71.15–21; *NHL* 373). The docetic vision of the Crucifixion is introduced to alleviate Peter's fear when he sees the authorities coming against them (72.4–17; *NHL* 373). Even after Peter has been assured that his enemies are blind and cannot harm Jesus, he suggests that he and Jesus flee (81.25–27; *NHL* 377). Jesus reveals the inner Savior to the apostle and again tells him to "be strong," knowing that what hangs on the cross is merely the body that belongs to the demonic rulers (81.29–82.26; *NHL* 377). Peter has a vision of the inner spiritual nature of Jesus united to the fullness of the heavenly light world and the Holy Spirit (81.4–16; 82.7–15, interpretation of the vision). As a result of this revelation, Peter is the custodian of the "mysteries" which he will reveal only to the elect of the immortal race. A final exhortation to "be strong" along with the conventional promise of Jesus' eternal presence and peace wish brings the work to its conclusion. Ecclesiology, soteriology, and

Christology are all implicated in the conflict with orthodox Christianity. Since the author uses a phrase from 2 Peter's description of heretical opponents, "waterless canals" to describe church leaders (79.30–31; 2 Pet. 2:17), these ecclesiastical authorities probably appealed to Petrine authority in support of their own position.[34] The *Apocalypse of Peter* (Cop.) indirectly acknowledges the strength of Petrine authority when it takes such pains to recast the traditional picture of the apostle.

Though the heresiologists used the stories of Simon Magus to demonstrate that Peter himself had defeated the father of all Gnostic heresies, the Gnostic appropriation of Petrine tradition does not turn to those stories. Gnostics must have been aware of the popularity of stories about Peter among orthodox Christians. Probably any association with magic was too likely to evoke suspicion. We do find that tradition turned against Christians in the later anti-Christian polemic of the philosopher Porphyry (ca. 260). According to St. Augustine, Porphyry's early work *On the Return of the Soul* considered the life of Christ exemplary. Jesus' disciples, especially Peter, were responsible for the later corruption of Christianity. Porphyry supported his charges against Christianity by depicting Peter as a person who dabbled in the black arts (Augustine, *De Civitate Dei* 18.53).[35] They allege that Peter used magic to enchant the world to believe in Christ. Augustine fixes on the disparity between the "innocent" Jesus and the magician disciple. Peter could not have learned the art of enchantment from Jesus. Though Augustine ridicules Porphyry's argument, the use of the contests between Peter and Simon Magus as propaganda for Christianity in the *Acts of Peter* during the third century provides a basis for that conclusion. Augustine also reports that Porphyry challenged Christian claims that the world will come to an end. To prove Porphyry's inconsistency, Augustine notes that Porphyry praises the wisdom of the Hebrew God. However, the Psalms speak of the heavens' perishing. In fact, Christian teaching is correct. Only the world and the lower heavens perish; the highest heaven remains forever. Augustine employs 2 Peter as evidence for apostolic teaching. Logically, his opponents should also use 2 Peter to defend the Hebrew piety which they praise. However, they would never cite the words of Peter, "whom they vehemently detest" (*Civ. Dei* 20.24).

The figure of Peter came to play a significant role in Christian disputes about authentic teaching. *1 Clement* was able to invoke Paul's authority in writing to a divided Corinthian church because the apostle had written letters to that church. But the figure of Peter as leader and spokesperson for the Twelve had a more universal appeal. We have seen that when writing the bishop of Rome, Dionysius of Corinth (ca. A.D. 170) underlined the fact that both Peter and Paul had sowed the seed of the gospel in Corinth (*Hist. Eccl.* 2.25). Although the Pauline letters came to have scriptural authority, they could not be alleged to embody the teaching transmitted by Jesus to the apostles as a group.

We have also seen that by the second half of the second century, the picture of Peter and the early church in Acts shaped the general understanding of Peter's mission. Peter's encounter with the magician Simon Magus became the core of the popular tradition about the apostle. Irenaeus' refutation of Gnostic teachers makes use of more of Acts. The Cornelius episode serves as evidence that Peter did possess full insight into the teaching of Jesus. Another significant image from Acts was the sending of the apostles to preach throughout the world. Even Gnostic writers were forced to adopt a version of that tradition if they were to maintain the claim that their teaching reflected the true meaning of Jesus' words.

Orthodox polemics from Justin onward focused on the Simon Magus episode as evidence for the diabolical origins of the Gnostic heresies. Gnostics responded to the attack by rewriting the Peter traditions. They either exploited the weakness of the apostle or insisted that he had indeed possessed gnosis. Perhaps the most striking example of Gnostic rewriting occurs in the *Apocalypse of Peter* (Cop.). There the author turns the polemic of 2 Peter back against the bishops of the orthodox communities. They are the ones who are "waterless canals" because they have rejected the apostle's teaching concerning the spiritual, living Christ for faith in a dead man.

Whether it is the Gnostic writers of the late second and third centuries A.D. or Porphyry in the middle of the third century, the picture is the same. Peter represents orthodox or authentic Christian teaching. To refute Christian teaching, one need only show that its primary spokesperson was either ignorant of the truth or morally suspect.

NOTES

1. For a brief account of this group, see Kurt Rudolph, *Gnosis*, trans. R. McL. Wilson (San Francisco: Harper and Row, 1983), 294–98.

2. Daniel Wm. O'Connor, *Peter in Rome*: The Literary, Liturgical and Archaeological Evidence (New York: Columbia University Press, 1969), 26.

3. See the illustration and discussion of this monument in Rudolph, *Gnosis*, 295; see also Raymond E. Brown and John P. Meier, *Antioch and Rome: New Testament Cradles of Catholic Christianity* (Ramsey, NJ: Paulist Press, 1983), 206.

4. See Pheme Perkins, "Irenaeus and the Gnostics," *VigChr* 30 (1976): 193–200.

5. The contamination of the city by foreign cults and the imperial bans against astrologers, magicians, and the like reflect a long history of Roman claims to purify the city in order to restore its true, originating greatness; see Ramsey MacMullen, *Enemies of the Roman Order: Treason, Unrest and Alienation in the Empire* (Cambridge: Harvard University Press, 1966), 103, 125–26.

6. See T. V. Smith, *Petrine Controversies in Early Christianity: Attitudes Towards Peter in Christian Writings of the First Two Centuries*, WUNT 2 Reihe 5 (Tübingen: J. C. B. Mohr, 1985), 59–60; and Strecker, "The Kerygmata Petrou," *HSNTA* 2:102–13.

7. See Simon Légasse, "La polémique antipaulinienne dans le judéo-christianisme hétérodoxe," *BLE* 90 (1989): 85f.

8. See "La polémique antipaulinienne," 87f.

9. Smith, *Petrine Controversies*, 60. Smith concludes that Paul is more likely the referent because of the extended dispute over visions.

10. Also see Tertullian, *Adv. Marc.* 5.3.3.

11. Brown and Meier, *Antioch and Rome*, 207f.

12. See Charles M. Nielsen, "Papias: Polemicist against Whom?" *TS* 35 (1974): 529–35.

13. Nielsen points to changing patterns of ecclesial authority in Asia Minor as a cause for the simmering conflicts. Polycarp insists upon the canonical status of Paul's writings. The Roman presbyter Clement invokes Pauline authority to support his intervention in the conflict at Corinth. See Nielsen, "Papias," 533–35.

14. See Pheme Perkins, *The Gnostic Dialogue* (New York: Paulist Press, 1980), 113–30.

15. See, e.g., Heracleon on John 4:33 in Origen, *In Joh.* 13.35.

16. Smith, *Petrine Controversies*, 104.

17. In this scene, Jesus has selected an inner group of disciples, Jude, Matthew, and Mary—apparently a deliberate attempt to counter the authority of the "Peter, James, and John" group. This new group, as Mary recognizes, is commissioned to spread true teaching to others. See Stephen Emmel, Helmut Koester, and Elaine Pagels, *Nag Hammadi Codex III, 5: The Dialogue of the Savior*, NHS 26 (Leiden: E. J. Brill, 1984), 13–15.

18. All of the named Gnostic teachers and founders of sects are men, though the founder of the Simonian sect is said to have been accompanied by a former prostitute, Helena, as his consort. On the problems of determining the social facts of women's participation in ancient religious groups, see the ground-breaking study of Ross Shepard Kraemer, *Her Share of the Blessings: Women's Religions Among Pagans, Jews and Christians in the Greco-Roman World* (New York: Oxford University Press, 1992). The emphasis on inspired prophecy in Montanism appears to have led to the prominent position of a number of women prophets (*Her Share of the Blessings*, 157–73).

19. Cf. 2 Timothy 3:7, where it is said that women "can never come to knowledge of truth."

20. The meaning of the promise to "make her male" is hotly disputed. It may refer to an ascetic rejection of all the marks of gender by the Gnostic solitary ones, or to a return to the androgynous asexuality of Adam with the spiritual Eve before the hostile creator god separated them, or to a ritual through which women passed before they could be members of a Gnostic sect. See J. J. Buckley, "An Interpretation of Logion 114 in *The Gospel of Thomas*," *NovT* 27 (1985): 245–72.

21. See Perkins, *Gnostic Dialogue*, 133–37.

22. In this context Mary Magdalene speaks of the Savior's having "prepared us and made us into men." The expression apparently refers to the process of attaining spiritual insight regardless of the gender of the recipient of revelation.

23. See Anne Pasquier, *L'Évangile selon Marie*, BCNH 10 (Québec: L'Université Laval, 1983), 99.

24. *L'Évangile*, 100.

25. See Perkins, *Gnostic Dialogue*, 137–41.

26. See Smith, *Petrine Controversies*, 112–16.

27. See Perkins, *Gnostic Dialogue*, 145–56; Smith, *Petrine Controversies*, 110–11; Donald Rouleau, *L'Épître de Jacques (NH I,2)*, BCNH 18 (Québec: L'Université Laval, 1987).

28. See Rouleau, *L'Épître*, 15–17.

29. *L'Épître*, 17–20.

30. *L'Épître*, 96.

31. Peter also appears with James in the *Apocryphon of James*, though James is the true teacher of Gnostic doctrine in that text and in an apocryphal Acts, the *Acts of Peter and the Twelve Apostles*, where he and the other apostles meet Christ in the mysterious guise of a pearl merchant. This fanciful story does not engage in doctrinal polemic. In addition, the three Gnostic writings in the Berlin Codex are followed by a fragment of an *Acts of Peter* which recounts another of the "chastity" stories common to the genre. The crowd challenges Peter to heal his

own paralyzed daughter, since he is able to heal others. Peter demonstrates that Jesus can make the paralyzed girl walk again. However, he refuses to ask that her healing be permanent because her striking beauty led a wealthy man to attempt to rape her when she was ten years old. Her continued paralysis will protect her chastity.

32. And possibly Luke 24; see, e.g., Smith, *Petrine Controversies*, 119–25.
33. The Gnostic *Apocalypse of Peter* (Coptic) is not to be confused with the second-century Christian work of the same title, which survives in an Ethiopic version. Though some interpreters have tried to argue that the Gnostic *Apocalypse of Peter* was a response to this popular Christian writing, the evidence is not convincing. Also see Dennis D. Buchholz, *Your Eyes Will Be Opened*, SBLDS 97 (Atlanta: Scholars Press, 1988), 6–19.
34. See Perkins, *Gnostic Dialogue*, 118–20.
35. W. H. C. Frend, *The Rise of Christianity* (Philadelphia: Fortress Press, 1984), 442.

CHAPTER 7

Peter, Bishop of Rome

FROM MARTYR TO BISHOP

We have seen that the earliest traditions about Peter's death hint that he was martyred in Rome. They also allude to his role as shepherd of Jesus' flock. However, that activity is not necessarily linked to missionary or pastoral activity in the Roman churches. His earlier career in Jerusalem and the surrounding regions provides an adequate context for that affirmation. We have also seen that although the earliest tomb monument to Peter has been discovered under St. Peter's in the Vatican, there are no first-century inscriptions concerning the apostle. If his bones are among those unearthed near the monument, archaeologists have not been able to make a certain identification of them.

Since we have no evidence of when Peter arrived in Rome or of the circumstances that led to his execution, later claims that he was bishop in a Roman community must rest on the traditions about the apostle which emerged in the second century. For the first century of its existence, there was probably not a single bishop in the Roman church. Ignatius of Antioch never refers to a bishop in his letter to the church at Rome. Instead, he speaks of the church itself "presiding" in the district of the Romans and "presiding over love" (*To the Romans*, Salutation).[1] Ignatius also asks the Roman church to pray for the church in Syria (= Antioch), which his martyrdom will leave without its shepherd (*Rom.* 9.1). All of the churches in Asia Minor are addressed by Ignatius in the person of their bishops.[2]

Eusebius begins his account of the bishops of Rome after the death of Paul and Peter with Linus (*Historia Ecclesiastica* 3.2.1). The tradition that Peter died as a martyr there appears to be considerably older than the accounts of Peter preaching in the city. As we have seen, the earliest traditions tend to remain silent on those points where they have no clues in the New Testament material. The responsibility for shepherding the flock was delegated to the presbyter bishops of local churches, as we have seen (Acts 20:28; 1 Pet. 5:2-3).[3] However, the designation of Peter as shepherd over Jesus' flock was not originally attached to the episcopal overseeing of a particular church. Peter will follow Jesus, the chief Shepherd of the whole flock (1 Pet. 5:4), in teaching and in death (John 21:15-19).

By the second half of the second century, the situation changes. A tradition of Peter's preaching at Rome is established in the popular legends about the apostle. The New Testament exemplar for that activity was found in the confrontations with Simon Magus. Extended explanations of the ongoing conflict between the two were given to demonstrate that Peter went to Rome to protect apostolic teaching against the heretic Simon (see Eusebius, *Hist. Eccl.* 2.14). *1 Clement*'s insistence on a model of authority and hierarchical office derived from Roman civic life came to shape the community. Whereas those mentioned as bishops prior to the middle of the second century A.D. in Rome probably presided over particular house churches, Bishop Anicetus (154-165 A.D.) appears to have been the first bishop of the whole city.[4] As the Roman church came to play an important role in second-century disputes over authentic Christian practice and teaching, the Petrine tradition gave the Roman episcopacy a universal voice.

FOUNDING MARTYR OF THE ROMAN CHURCH

1 Clement supports its intervention in the disputes among Christians at Corinth primarily on the ground of a common Pauline heritage.[5] The heritage of the apostle's teaching was strengthened by the example of his martyrdom in Rome. Though not explicitly stating the fact, *1 Clement* hints that Rome had the glory of two martyr-apostles, Paul and Peter. When Dionysius of Corinth wrote the bishop of Rome, he suggested a certain equality between the two sees based on the common activity of Peter and Paul in both cities. However, their martyrdom in Rome gave a certain prominence to that city.

The tradition that Peter and Paul were both martyred in Rome under Nero also played a role in the second-century argument for the unity of apostolic tradition. Marcion appealed to Paul's revelation (Gal. 1:18) and his rebuke of Peter (Gal. 2:11-14) as evidence for the superiority of his gospel to the teaching of James, John and Peter.[6] Tertullian replies that Peter could as easily have charged Paul with inconsistent behavior. The revelation Paul received could not have taught a different "gospel," especially since 2 Corinthians 12:4 affirms that they were not in human words. Both John and Peter are on the same level through the glory of the martyrdom they received (*De Praescriptione Haereticorum* 24.4). Irenaeus insists on the unity of apostolic preaching against heretics. His account of their unity brings the composition of the four Gospels as close to the apostles as possible. Matthew writes in Hebrew while Peter and Paul are preaching at Rome. The joint preaching of Peter and Paul was the foundation of the Roman church. After their deaths, Mark recorded Peter's teaching, and Luke recorded Paul's. Sometime later, the Beloved Disciple published his Gospel in Ephesus (*Adversus Haereses* 3.1.1).

Eusebius reports the martyrdom of Peter and Paul under Nero based on another anti-heretical debate (*Hist. Eccl.* 2.25). Writing against the Montanists, who based their claim to apostolic origins on the tomb of John, the Roman presbyter Gaius (ca. A.D. 200) points to the tomb monuments of Peter, on the Vatican hill and of Paul on the Ostian Way. Thus, Gaius argues, the Roman church has two apostolic founders. The two founders make this church superior to those who have only one. Tertullian provides evidence of a more formal expansion of this principle in his defense of apostolic teaching. The tradition of apostolic churches with martyr founders as well as apostolic written traditions circle the Roman world from Greece through Asia, Italy, and even Carthage, in North Africa. Rome's double witness provides a special sign of unity since Peter's death was like the Lord's, and Paul's was like that of John the Baptist (*Praescrip.* 36.3).[7]

The motif of a unified apostolic tradition expressed by the dual martyrs evoked another important theme in late-Roman times. The concern for concord and solidarity is frequently expressed in civic as well as religious discourse. Though Christians in other periods were content with a single patron saint or martyr, the churches in the later Roman period show a distinct preference for pairs.[8] The deep divisions in the city of Rome in later times would make the Feast of Sts. Peter and Paul a reminder of the ideal of harmony.[9] By the fourth century, the shrine of Peter on the Vatican hill symbolized the new patronage systems of the church. Gifts to the poor at the shrine shifted almsgiving away from its traditional political base. What had been a male activity enlisted the support of wealthy Christian women. Such women not only gave alms and supported the martyrs' shrines; they also participated in the ceremony surrounding the cult of the saints.[10]

Late antique Rome revised the tradition of Peter's daughter to serve as the patron saint and model for such Christian women. In a painting from A.D. 396, a Roman noblewoman is depicted in her burial chamber behind a martyr shrine. Another elegant Roman lady, identified as Peter's daughter, Petronilla, stands beside her.[11] Clearly, the older *Acts of Peter* story of the paralyzed, virgin daughter of the apostle has given way to imagery more appropriate to the wealthy Christian patroness.

SUCCESSION LISTS AND PETRINE AUTHORITY

Possession of a martyr's shrine provided the faithful with the presence of the divine in their midst. It also gave the bishop of the see control over access to the saint. A young Justinian attempted to get fragments of Peter's body for Constantinople. He was roundly refused and was instead sent one of the handkerchiefs that pilgrims used to insert through a window into the shrine.[12] During the fourth century, pilgrimages to the Vatican shrine on the Feast of Sts. Peter and Paul were celebrated with magnificence. The alleged date of their martyrdom coincided with the old pagan celebration of the founding of Rome. The founding of the city has been replaced by the founding of the Roman church by her martyr-apostles.[13]

The physical presence of the apostle Peter through the shrine and its associated rituals provided tangible evidence for the antiquity and primacy of the Roman see. In that sense, the martyr-apostle needs no successor, since his presence remains with the community. However, we have seen that the second- and third-century disputes over authoritative teaching relied upon another model of authority, the succession of teachers in a philosophical school or the disciples of a famous rabbi. A continuous list of authorized teachers guaranteed the fidelity of a particular school to its founder's teaching. Justin established the pattern of using the argument from succession against heretics by providing a genealogy of heretical teachers.

Gnostic writings attempted to provide alternate apostolic origins for their writings by establishing different groups among Jesus' disciples.[14] Levi, Jude, Thomas, Philip, and Mary Magdalene figure in a number of Gnostic writings. We have seen that in some cases, the Gnostic authors single out one disciple—James, John, Thomas, Mary Magdalene, or even Peter—as the sole recipient of Jesus' wisdom. They may even admit a temporal gap between Jesus' immediate disciples and the coming of the Gnostic elite. Thus in the *Apocryphon of James* (C.G.

I.16.7–30; *NHL* 37), James dismisses the others from Jerusalem, while he waits there for the appearance of the Gnostic race. In the conclusion to this work, we find a Gnostic version of the handing on of the tradition: from James to the anonymous recipient of the letter with its apocryphal revelation and to those "beloved ones" who constitute the true heirs of the Kingdom.[15]

The tradition of a Roman primacy based on the heritage of Petrine teaching antedates the establishment of a list of Roman bishops beginning with the apostle. The earliest lists are not consistent. In the mid-second century, Hegesippus drew up a list to guarantee transmission of true doctrine amid the claims of rival Gnostic groups (see Eusebius, *Hist. Eccl.* 4.22).[16] Eusebius quotes a section of Hegesippus which indicates that he also catalogued Gnostic sects and Jewish sects opposed to Christianity. The principle of such catalogues was to show where they had deviated from the true faith. Eusebius has not preserved Hegesippus' list in complete form. His references to the succession of Roman bishops begin with Linus (*Hist. Eccl.* 3.13), not Peter. Other scholars prefer to reconstruct Hegesippus from a list in Epiphanius that ends with Anicetus (*Panarion* 27.6). Epiphanius' list refers to Peter and Paul jointly as the first bishops of Rome.[17] However, the designation of both as "bishops" seems suspect. Irenaeus is more careful to designate Peter and Paul founders of the Roman church. Epiphanius may have adapted the list to the later conviction that the founders had been the first bishops.

Irenaeus' list (*Adv. Haer.* 3.3.3) gives the first bishop, Linus, apostolic credentials by asserting that he is the Linus who appears among those sending greetings in 2 Timothy 4:21. The succession of twelve Roman bishops from Linus until Irenaeus' time guarantees the transmission of authentic tradition. Irenaeus then gives shorter notices for two other churches. Smyrna, where he had grown up, could look to Polycarp. Polycarp was instructed by the apostles and other eyewitnesses. Irenaeus claims that he saw Polycarp as a young man. Polycarp's activities in combating the heresies of Valentinus and Marcion were preceded by those of John and are taken up by Irenaeus himself. Paul and John are linked to the church at Ephesus. In these cases, Irenaeus has no list beyond the first two generations (*Adv. Haer.* 3.3.4). Since both Polycarp and John the Evangelist lived to be very old, the reader is not to be troubled by the gap between the last-mentioned authority and the present. With its dual founders, Rome can lay some claim to Pauline tradition. The reader may conclude that the Roman list alone guarantees the security of Christian teaching. One can always see that what is taught as "apostolic" elsewhere conforms to the rule of faith in the Roman church. Irenaeus insists that the rule of faith is universal. It applies to the intellectual as well as the simple believer. It applies to converts among the diverse languages and cultures of the world (*Adv. Haer.* 1.10.1–2).

The list of Roman bishops with their periods of rule drawn up early in the third century by Hippolytus has been lost. Scholars who think the heresiological work quoted by Eusebius in the *Historia Ecclesiastica* 5.28 was by Hippolytus conclude that counting Victor thirteenth after Peter implies that Peter was counted as the first bishop in the list.[18] The rest of Eusebius' references consistently treat Peter and Paul together as founders of the Roman church. As we have seen, this interest in paired founders stems from the effort to make the church a prominent example of concord. The picture of Peter as the first bishop of Rome apparently develops in third-century contexts which envisage succession as a legal handing-over of authority from one person to the next. Tertullian's account of the authentic tradition which guarantees the faith of the churches claims that Peter ordained Clement. Similar processes obtain in the other apostolic churches (Tertullian, *Praescrip.* 32). Heretical teachers cannot prove the apostolic truth of their doctrine or of their office. This view may be dependent upon the legends of Clement and Peter reflected in the Pseudo-Clementines. Peter formally installs Clement as his successor before the assembled faithful (Pseudo-Clementines, *Epitome* 2.145–47; *HSNTA* 2:569). In this scene, he confers on Clement the formal power to bind and loose, lays hands on Clement, and installs him in the episcopal chair.

PETER AND EPISCOPAL AUTHORITY

The installation scene in the Pseudo-Clementines points to a formal, juridical tradition. The powers of the apostle to teach and govern the community are transferred to each successor in office. The opening letter of the *Kerygmata Petrou* provides a narrative basis for the transfer of office from Peter to his successor, the Old Testament image of Moses. Peter asks James to take care to transmit his writings only to those who are worthy, just as Moses had given authority to seventy elders (*Keryg. Pet.* 1.2, 2.1–2, 3.1–2; *HSNTA* 2:111f.). The divisions within the church of the mid-third century over discipline, penance, and membership would make this dimension of the Petrine office prominent. Two North African theologians, Tertullian and Cyprian, provide examples of the transition.

Our earliest evidence for the veneration of the tombs of Peter and Paul at Rome was elicited by the need to argue for apostolic founders against the Montanists. The Montanist schism highlighted a more practical crisis as well, the disciplinary problem of deciding whether and on what conditions persons who had committed serious sins could be readmitted to the church. The need to judge individual cases which were by no means unambiguous required that a juridical power of forgiveness be vested in the bishop.[19] Tertullian as a Montanist saw the readmittance of sinners as defiling the holiness of the church. When the bishop of Carthage, Agrippinus, permitted those guilty of adultery and other sexual sins to rejoin the community, Tertullian replied with the angry treatise *De Pudicitia*. The discussion about the power of the keys in this work is aimed at the local bishop, not the bishop of Rome.[20]

The Catholic position which Tertullian opposes holds that the local bishop possesses the "chair of Peter" and thus the power bestowed on Peter to retain or forgive sin (Matt. 16:17–19; *Pud.* 21.9). Most of the argument has been structured to show the logical absurdity of the bishop's position. Even if the power of the keys meant the power to forgive such sins, Tertullian argues, it was given to Peter alone. Peter did not have the authority to transmit such authority to the present-day bishops (*Pud.* 21.11–15). Tertullian holds that spiritual power resides in individuals, not in the office. Peter had such spiritual power (*Pud.* 21.10). For any other persons to have such status, the Spirit must be working directly through those persons (*Pud.* 21.16ff.).[21] For rhetorical purposes, Tertullian grants that Matthew 16:19 refers to a power to forgive sin. However, he appears to favor a different interpretation of the passage. The keys refer to the saving confession of the church and the witness born by her martyrs (*Scorpiace* 10). This reading combines the two most common understandings of Petrine authority, true teaching and martyrdom.

Although Tertullian does not address the issues at Rome directly, a parallel development did occur there. Its bishop, Callistus, was reputed to have relaxed penitential discipline (see, e.g., Hippolytus, *Refutation of All Heresies* 9.12.20f.). This new juridical use of the "power of the keys" in the early third century added considerable strength to the office of bishop.[22] The formal definition of the powers which attached to the episcopal office in contrast to the other positions in the church would be even more sharply defined by the bishop of Carthage in the mid-third century A.D., Cyprian. The crises facing the church were much more severe than those at the beginning of the century. Severe persecutions aimed at destroying the church had created large numbers of *lapsi*. They had denied their faith under threat of arrest, confiscation of property, and martyrdom. When the persecutions ended, they sought to return. Those who had risked death for the faith often claimed that they possessed the power to forgive such sins.[23] Later the Novatianist schism raised the question of the validity of baptism by the sectarians. Novatian and his followers rejected the readmission of *lapsi* to the church. Cyprian held that even if the Novatianist clergy used the same form as Catholic Christians, their converts would have to be rebaptized in order to be admitted to the Catholic church. This view, which consistent with the practice elsewhere in North Africa, brought Cyprian into conflict with the bishop of Rome, Stephen.[24]

This controversy provoked Cyprian's reflections on the unity of the church. Without unity, there can be no church (*Letter* 55.8). The bishop is the focus of this unity (*Letter* 66.8).[25] We are not well informed about the arguments of Stephen. Cyprian's comments suggest that Stephen appealed to the Peter tradition as evidence that his authority was superior to that of other bishops (*Letter* 74.1, 8, 10; 71.3).[26] Cyprian's treatise *On the Unity of the Catholic Church* survives in two editions of the critical discussion of episcopal authority in chapter 4.[27] The authority which Jesus gave to Peter was conferred on all the apostles as well. The reference to an individual points to the unity of the church. The "primacy" which is attached to Peter does not reside in an authority different from that of the other apostles but in the temporal priority which is a symbol of unity.[28] Peter received the authority of the keys before the Resurrection of Jesus. After the Resurrection, all the apostles receive this power as well.

The first edition of Cyprian's treatise uses the one church, one chair of Peter, and one flock as evidence that no one can separate himself from the "chair of Peter" and still claim to belong to the church. The expression "chair of Peter" is ambiguous. When Cyprian is writing about the bishop of Rome, the expression "chair of Peter" refers to him. In Letter 55.8, Cyprian defends the legitimate appointment of Cornelius as bishop of Rome. However, the term may also refer to the episcopal office, wherever it is embodied in a legitimate bishop.[29] In the second edition, the reference to unity with the "chair of Peter" has been deleted. Instead, Cyprian has substituted Scripture quotations to confirm his argument. The first edition refers only to the saying to Peter in John 21:15–17. The second edition drops that quotation and demonstrates that a "like authority" to forgive was conferred on all the apostles (John 20:21–22). Additional citations from the Song of Songs (Song 6:9) and Paul (Eph. 4:4ff.) have been added to the conclusion of the second edition to prove the unity of the church.

Elsewhere "Peter's confession" from John 6:67–69 is used to demonstrate the response which Christians should make to the threat posed by the schismatics (Letter 59.7). Peter answers for the whole group of the apostles. Cyprian remarks that Peter is the one "on whom the Lord had already built the church." In this context, believing and adhering to Jesus appears to be what Cyprian means by Peter as the one upon whom the church was built.

In order to respond to these various crises, Cyprian uses the Petrine texts to enhance the authority of the bishop who is heir to the "chair of Peter." However, individual bishops cannot exercise this authority in isolation form one another, or the unity of the church might be broken by schismatics or by the disputes between individual bishops. Therefore, the tradition of the unity of the apostolic testimony appears in the mutual harmony and love of the episcopate as a group.[30] Cyprian defends Cornelius' position as bishop of Rome by appealing to the unanimous assent of all bishops to his consecration. He cannot be replaced by a schismatic bishop because there is no ordination outside the church.

The third century required a juridical understanding of episcopal authority to meet the crises that arose over membership in the church. Peter as martyr and teacher becomes Peter as shepherd bishop. Though we have hints that Roman bishops may have seen Matthew 16:17–19 as evidence for the special status of their see, a more universalized understanding of Petrine authority prevailed in other communities.

EXCURSUS: INTERPRETING MATTHEW 16:17–19

Cyprian begins chapter 4 of the treatise *On the Unity of the Catholic Church* with Matthew 16:17–19. The first edition combines this text with John 21:17; the second, with John 20:21. For the mid-third century A.D., these passages refer to the episcopal office. The bishops are shepherds of the one flock. They also exercise the power to forgive and remit sins. For most interpreters, the successors of Peter in the Roman see share this authority with other bishops. Claims of Roman primacy may have been advanced by Stephen during his dispute with

Cyprian, but that is not the common use of the passage.[31] Even the third century, juridical use reflects a late and relatively minor tradition. Its importance in redefining the role of the episcopacy in the mid-third century may be the reason Cyprian assumes that the juridical interpretation is clear and manifest (*Letter* 75.17).

The more common interpretations of this passage in early Christianity follow the models established by Origen and Tertullian.[32] For Origen, the passage as a whole must refer to any Christian who has achieved spiritual insight. Peter's confession is one which every Christian makes. Therefore, the revelation of God is what makes confession possible, and the subsequent beatitude must also refer to any Christian who has attained spiritual insight (*Contra Celsum* 6.77; *Commentary on Matthew* 12.10).[33] This description of the spiritual person as the subject of the Matthean saying could be a reply to the Gnostic tradition. In the *Apocalypse of Peter* (Coptic) (C.G. VII.70.20–71,21; *NHL* 373), the beatitude on the "spiritual ones," the future Gnostics, opens the revelation to Peter. Spiritual persons belong to the Father, who reveals life to them. The author gives his variant of Matthew 16:17–19. God has given Peter his name so that he will be a foundation for the remnant that the Savior has summoned to knowledge.

The *Apocalypse of Peter* (Cop.) combines this tradition with a special revelation experience. Origen combines the Matthean passage with the Transfiguration scene (*C. Cels.* 6.77.10). Responding to Celsus' mockery, Origen distinguishes between the Word as it appears to persons who are not enlightened and the spiritual truth that those who can follow him up the Mount of Transfiguration will perceive. Peter is the type of any person who has the ability to perceive the Word. The Word builds an indestructible church on such people.

The same typological interpretation appears in Origen's *Commentary on Matthew* without emphasizing the distinction between the masses and the spiritually enlightened based on the Transfiguration. Instead, Origen emphasizes the fact that all are called to be like Peter. As evidence that the rock refers to every disciple, Origen points to 1 Corinthians 10:4. Christ is the spiritual rock from which all are to drink. The church is built on the rock—on each Christian who becomes perfect (*In Matt.* 12.10). The church is not built on Peter alone, but on all the apostles and the perfect. They are the ones whom the gates of hell cannot conquer. To prove that the words to Peter apply to all the apostles, Origen cites John 20:22 (*In Matt.* 12.11).[34]

We have seen that Peter became the evidence that true apostolic tradition was preserved in a community. Tertullian invokes Matthew 16:17–19 to refute heretical claims that the understanding of Jesus' disciples was deficient. Tertullian collects all the passages in which Jesus teaches his disciples, keeps them close to him, reveals his glory on the mountain, teaches them after the Resurrection, and sends the Spirit (*Praescrip*. 22). The heretics falsely claim that Peter was ignorant of Jesus' teaching because he was rebuked by Paul, an interpretation that requires them to reject the testimony of Acts (*Praescrip*. 23). Tertullian uses the changing of Peter's name as part of his demonstration that Christ cannot be understood apart from Old Testament prophecies and types. Marcion's rejection of the Old Testament God is inconsistent (*Adv. Marcion* 4.13).[35] Divine name changes are prefigured in the Old Testament. By giving the name "rock" to Peter, Jesus has shared one of his own designations. He also indicated the strength of Peter's faith.

The options for interpretation of Matthew 16:17–19 do not exclude one another. Spiritual interpretation is inherently polyvalent. The context of the argument and word associations with other texts provide for numerous variations in detail. An author may focus on the christological significance of Christ as the rock, on Peter as the model for the believer, or on the security of apostolic faith. Matthew 16:17–19 applies to episcopal authority only in instances where that authority needs to be strengthened. The suggestions that it also implied Roman primacy were clearly resisted by Tertullian and Cyprian. The emergence of Roman primacy as the primary meaning of the passage for Catholic theologians resulted from the schism that has permanently divided Western Christendom, the Protestant Reformation.[36]

In the New Testament depiction of Peter, the apostle does not have a successor. Through the second century, this distinction appears in the treatment of Peter and Paul as founders. The unity of their teaching along with that of the other apostles guarantees the truth of apostolic tradition. Founding is not merely a claim about continuity in teaching. It also involves powerful evidence of divine presence in the cult of the saints that begins to appear in the second century. With the conversion of the emperor, the ritual surrounding the cult becomes more elaborate. Martyrs' shrines are places of pilgrimage and the source of considerable authority for the bishop in whose see they are found.

Double martyrs Peter and Paul secured an even more prominent place for the Roman church. Heretics like Marcion who attempted to separate the two were running against a deep-seated Roman desire for concord. Theological or exegetical arguments aside, the believers who saw Peter and Paul united in martyrdom would not believe that they had been divided in teaching. Although Paul was the more prominent figure in the earlier period, by the third century, Peter precedes Paul in the order of death. The Simon Magus/Peter legends suggested that Peter had arrived in Rome earlier than Paul. Eventually, the stories of how each died led to further symbolic relationships. Paul was beheaded like John the Baptist. Peter was crucified like the Lord, though upside down. This symbolic correlation reverses their status. However, the most dramatic claim to the concord of the dual founders will emerge in the liturgical tradition which situates their martyrdom on June 29, the founding of the city of Rome. This tradition is already attested in A.D. 310.[37] A sermon on the feast by Leo the Great would make the point of the contrast directly: "the Apostles have better protected the city than those who built its walls and soiled it by fratricide."[38]

The issues which surround Peter's role as founder, teacher, and martyr in Rome constantly return to the problems of unity. Against the heretics who seek to divide the apostles in order to claim authorization for their teaching, Peter with the other apostles represents true teaching. On the more popular level, against the tensions, divisions, and evils by which Satan attempts to destroy the church, Peter wields the power of the Spirit. Against the schismatics, who would divide the church in the name of preserving her holiness, Peter represents the power of the local bishop to forgive sin and restore such persons to the community. Against those who might appropriate the episcopal authority of Peter to the Roman see alone, Peter as spokesperson for the apostles was the first to receive the power granted to them all, which requires that they act in collegial unity and love. For all believers, Peter is the rock of faith which is Jesus.

NOTES

1. Elsewhere in Ignatius, "presiding" refers to the exercise of authority over other churches—e.g., *To the Magnesians* 6.1–2. See also William Schoedel, *Ignatius of Antioch* (Philadelphia: Fortress Press, 1985), 165–66.

2. See Ignatius, *To the Ephesians* 2.1; *To the Magnesians* 2.1; *To the Philadelphians*, Salutation; *To the Smyrneans* 8.1; *To the Trallians* 1.1, as well as the letter to Polycarp, bishop of Smyrna.

3. The Christians in Rome gathered in local house churches, which appear

to have had differing individual characteristics. Jeffers distinguishes two very different groups in Rome at the end of the first century. A house church of freedmen who prided themselves on their ties to noble Rome families was associated with the Clement of *1 Clement*. A very different congregation, made up of urban poor and ex-slaves, is addressed in the *Shepherd of Hermes*. See James S. Jeffers, *Conflict at Rome: Social Order and Hierarchy in Early Christianity* (Minneapolis: Fortress Press, 1991), 90–120.

4.   Jeffers, *Conflict*, 190–93.

5.   Hans von Campenhausen, *Ecclesiastical Authority and Spiritual Power in the Church of the First Three Centuries*, trans. J. A. Baker (Stanford: Stanford University Press, 1969), 87.

6.   Jaroslav Pelikan, *The Emergence of the Catholic Tradition (100–600)* (Chicago: University of Chicago Press, 1971), 112–14.

7.   Rudolf Pesch, *Simon Petrus*, Geschichte und geschichtliche Bedeutung des ersten Jüngers Jesu Christi. Päpste und Papstum Bd. 15 (Stuttgart: Anton Hiersemann, 1980), 122.

8.   See Peter Brown, *The Cult of the Saints: Its Rise and Function in Latin Christianity* (Chicago: University of Chicago Press, 1981), 96f.

9.   Brown, *Cult*, 97. Another symbol of the ideal unity was Peter portrayed as Moses in a rebellious community (*Cult*, 166 n. 64).

10.   *Cult*, 46.

11.   *Cult*, 58f.

12.   *Cult*, 87f.

13.   Daniel Wm. O'Connor, *Peter in Rome*: The Literary, Liturgical and Archaeological Evidence (New York: Columbia University Press, 1969), 117.

14.   See Parrott, "Gnostic and Orthodox Disciples in the Second and Third Centuries," in *Nag Hammadi, Gnosticism and Early Christianity*, ed. C. Hedrick and R. Hodgson (Peabody, MA: Hendrickson, 1986), 193–219.

15.   Donald Rouleau, *L'Épître de Jacques (NH I,2)*, BCNH 18 (Québec: L'Université Laval, 1987), 137.

16.   Von Campenhausen, *Ecclesiastical Authority*, 159–65.

17.   D. W. O'Connor, *Peter in Rome*, 28.

18.   *Peter in Rome*, 31.

19.   Von Campenhausen, *Ecclesiastical Authority*, 234.

20.   *Ecclesiastical Authority*, 235.

21.   *Ecclesiastical Authority*, 230.

22.   *Ecclesiastical Authority*, 236.

23.   Michael M. Sage, *Cyprian* (Cambridge, MA: Philadelphia Patristic Foundation, 1975), 177–221.

24.   Sage, *Cyprian*, 303–35.

25. See Von Campenhausen, *Ecclesiastical Authority*, 268f.

26. *Ecclesiastical Authority*, 276.

27. See the discussion in Maurice Bévenot, *Cyprian: De Lapsis and De Ecclesiae Catholicae Unitate* (Oxford: Oxford University Press, 1971), xi–xiii.

28. Bévenot, *Cyprian*, xiv.

29. Bévenot, *Cyprian*, 63 n. 5.

30. Von Campenhausen, *Ecclesiastical Authority*, 278.

31. Pesch, *Simon Petrus*, 166; Ulrich Luz, "Das Primatwort Matthäus 16.17–19 aus wirkungsgeschichtlicher Sicht," *NTS* 37 (1991): 418.

32. Luz, "Das Primatwort," 419.

33. "Das Primatwort," 419.

34. The same combination occurs in the second version of Cyprian's *De Unitate* 4.

35. Luz, "Das Primatwort," 419–20.

36. "Das Primatwort," 419.

37. The tradition which situates the martyrdom of Peter and Paul with the founding of Rome may go back to the mid-third century A.D.; see D. W. O'Connor, *Peter in Rome*, 116.

38. Letter 82; cited in D. W. O'Connor, *Peter in Rome*, 117.

Conclusion
Peter for the Whole Church?

Simon, a Galilean fisherman, was transformed into Peter, a foundation rock and shepherd by Christian communities that had nothing to do with his native Galilee. Soon persecution drove Peter from Jerusalem. Whatever Peter's acquiescence to the demands of representatives from James meant, finally there was no road back from "living in the manner of the nations" (Gal. 2:14). As the stream of pilgrims made their way to Peter's tomb on the Feast of Sts. Peter and Paul in fourth-century Rome, the Vatican door opened to display a tub of boxwood leaves.[1] The fisherman, shepherd, founder, and martyr could still be found watching over the newly Christian empire.

Today as we celebrate the Feast of Sts. Peter and Paul, Christian churches are looking toward a post-imperial future. The legacy of Western cultural hegemony that shaped much of Christian history cannot speak for Christians of Arab, Eastern European, Asian, or African descent. Even those Christians whose heritage is Northern European feel uncomfortable with the church of the imperial elite, the ministry of the privileged to the privileged with an occasional dole to the masses. The story of the wealthy imperial nobleman Paulinus of Nola, who abandoned wealth and family to embrace a life of monastic poverty during the celebration of this feast in 394, seems suspect. Within a few years, he was pressed into church service as a bishop (A.D. 409). We have seen that even the women of Peter's family were transformed into the models of the wealthy Christian women, patronesses, and ascetics. The question about Peter is really a question about the church, not about the historical conditions of Galilean fishermen two millennia ago. The foundation of that church in the earliest Peter traditions remains Jesus.[2] Peter, as Tertullian and Origen insist, reflects discipleship for all those who belong to the community.

Peter's pastoral commission flows out of his own fragile discipleship. He must repent, return to his love for the Lord, and then strengthen and feed others (Luke 22:32; John 21:15–17). The New Testament authors also remind us that discipleship will mean his suffering like Jesus did. Both Peter's resistance to the message of the cross (Mark 8:31–33) and his boast that he would lay down his life for Jesus (John 13:37) describe partial truths about Peter's life. Peter is both "rock" (Matt. 16:18) and "stumbling block" (Matt. 16:23).[3] Thus, Peter as disciple in the New Testament exhibits the ambiguities that many Christians feel in today's church.

Though Galatians 1:18–2:14 gives the impression that Peter's ministry as a "pillar" in the Jerusalem church allied him with Jewish Christians in Judea, the rest of the New Testament suggests otherwise. Paul depicts himself as "apostle" and father to those churches he has founded (1 Cor. 4:15, 9:2). Peter is not depicted as the founder of any particular churches. Rather, Peter is the universal "foundation" for all the churches. The canon itself might be viewed from this Petrine perspective. With the attribution of Mark to Peter's oral tradition and the addition of Peter as shepherd in John 21:15–17, all four Gospels as well as Acts have some connection to Petrine tradition. 1 Peter directs exhortation much like that found in Pauline letters to churches in Asia Minor.[4] 2 Peter even brings the Pauline letter collection into the Petrine fold.

Many Christians find it difficult to appreciate Peter as exemplary disciple and universal apostle founder because they think that unity in the apostolic church meant that all the apostolic traditions were uniform. Diversity in the earliest Christian communities still comes as a surprise to many people. Yet there is no figure who encompasses more of that diversity than Peter. Because of the diversity in first- and second-century Rome, its churches remained without uniform episcopal leadership or even uniform liturgical practice well into the second century A.D. Closer to the historical Peter, one finds that the complex diversity of Judaism and Jewish Christianity at Jerusalem and in Syrian Antioch created rough waters which were not always easy to negotiate.

Many others have learned to treat Peter and Paul as initiators of distinctive and conflicting patterns of faith. Some may suspect that Petrine tradition sold out the radical freedom of the Gospel that Paul had sought to preserve. Scholars are coming to recognize that this perception has been generated by historians who imposed categories of ideological conflict on the New Testament. We are increasingly aware that the diversity of first-century Judaism implied a similar diversity in early Christianity. When an unprecedented number of Gentiles came to be absorbed into the churches, the issues raised could not be neatly resolved. Nor were the relationships between the various parties involved easily defined.[5] Peter represents a policy of accommodation and adaptation to the changing circumstances of the community.

Peter's faith makes him the source of unity in the apostolic testimony. Ulrich Luz has observed that Matthew's picture of Peter as the one who is able to interpret the teaching of Jesus for Christian conduct in different circumstances is too narrow. Peter is more than the disciple of a rabbi. As Papias' account of how the Gospel of Mark came to be written shows, Peter was felt to be a living link to the words and deeds of Jesus. Neither Paul nor James, the brother of the Lord, could claim such a relationship with the Lord.[6] The same Papias story reminds us that our faith is mediated through the canonical traditions. It is shaped by the ongoing process of preaching and interpreting those traditions in the churches. We cannot step outside the community into some immediate experience of the Lord.

Having observed that Peter is always Peter interpreted by the Christian community at a particular time and place, Luz argues that the interpretation of a text cannot be divorced from the question of application to new situations. While some exegetes have adopted a liberationist criterion for determining what a text ought to mean, Luz suggests returning to the norm proposed by St. Augustine. All Scripture aims at charity. Can the twin criteria of charity and universality make the papalist development of the Peter tradition viable in the future church? Its justification would depend upon whether or not it can be seen to serve the truth which comes to us through the Gospel narratives of Jesus. The question cannot be resolved once and for all, since it is intertwined with the institutional situation of the churches.[7]

Since Vatican II, the bishops of Rome have redefined the role of the papacy in more global terms. Pope John XXIII demonstrated that the office could be a ministry to the universal human community. The pope's presence is not geographically confined to Rome. His concern for world affairs is not narrowly focused on religious issues that affect Catholics. More than any other religious leader, the pope is in a position to provide a personal center for Christianity.[8] However complex the problems of greater institutional unity between Christian churches may be, many non-Roman Catholics have come to appreciate the need for a Christian religious figure who stands on a par with political leaders around the globe.

A Petrine ministry for the Christian churches of the twenty-first century certainly cannot be limited to the historical form that it has taken in the bishop of Rome. In Peter, the ship of faith has had to cross political, cultural, and religious boundaries in order to serve the gospel. The canonical picture of Peter lacks the certainty of Paul's dramatic conversion and conscious apostleship. Instead, Peter consistently has to learn "on the job." Often, he learns that his own initial reactions are at cross purposes with what the Lord will require of him. The Cornelius episode in Acts 10 provides a dramatic image of the divine interventions required to reform Peter's convictions about the Gentiles. The Fourth Gospel provides the epigraph which summarized Peter's career as disciple, apostle, and martyr: "When you were young, you dressed yourself and went wherever you wished; but when you are old, you will stretch out your hands and another will bind you, and take you where you do not wish to go" (John 21:18; RSV).

NOTES

1. Daniel Wm. O'Connor, *Peter in Rome*: The Literary, Liturgical and Archaeological Evidence (New York: Columbia University Press, 1969), 117.
2. John Bigane has shown that until the strong anti-Lutheran reaction of the mid-sixteenth century, most Catholic exegetes held that "rock" referred to faith or to Christ, not to Peter as the foundation of the papacy; see *Faith, Christ or Peter: Matthew 16:18 in Sixteenth-Century Roman Catholic Exegesis* (Washington: University Press of America, 1981).
3. Ulrich Luz, "Das Primatwort Matthäus 16.17–19 aus wirkungsgeschichtlicher Sicht," *NTS* 37 (1991): 423.
4. "Das Primatwort," 425f.
5. Craig C. Hill supports the claim that Peter's accommodations at Antioch are more representative of Greek-speaking Christianity than Paul's resistance to limiting table fellowship between Gentiles and Jews; see *Hellenists and Hebrews: Reappraising Division within the Earliest Church* (Minneapolis: Fortress Press, 1992), 103–47.
6. Luz, "Das Primatwort," 426.
7. "Das Primatwort," 430f.
8. John de Satgé, *Peter and the Single Church* (London: SPCK, 1981), 150–52.

Selected Bibliography

Achtemeier, Paul J. *The Quest for Unity in the New Testament Church*. Philadelphia: Fortress Press, 1987.

Anonymous. *Catéchisme de l'église catholique*. Paris: Mame/Plon, 1992.

Attridge, Harold. *Hebrews*. Philadelphia: Fortress Press, 1989.

Augustine, Aurelius [= *Civ. Dei*]. *Der Gottesstaat. De Civitate Dei*. Trans. Carl Johann Perl. 2 vols. Paderborn: Ferdinand Schöningh, 1979.

Barrett, C. K. *The Gospel According to St. John*. 2d ed. London: SPCK, 1978.

Bauckham, Richard J. *Jude, 2 Peter*. Word Biblical Commentary 50. Waco, TX: Word Books, 1983.

Beasley-Murray, George R. *John*. Word Biblical Commentary 36. Waco, TX: Word Books, 1987.

Best, Ernest. *Mark: The Gospel as Story*. Edinburgh: T. and T. Clark, 1983.

Betz, Hans Dieter. *Galatians*. Philadelphia: Fortress Press, 1979.

Bévenot, Maurice. *Cyprian: De Lapsis and De Ecclesiae Catholicae Unitate*. Oxford: Oxford University Press, 1971.

Bigane, John E. *Faith, Christ or Peter: Matthew 16:18 in Sixteenth-Century Roman Catholic Exegesis*. Washington: University Press of America, 1981.

Black, C. Clifton. *The Disciples According to Mark: Markan Redaction in Current Debate*. Journal for the Study of the New Testament, Supplement Series 27. Sheffield: JSOT Press, 1989.

Bovon, F., et al. *Les Actes apocryphes des Apôtres*. Geneva: Labor et Fides, 1981.

Brown, Peter. *The Cult of the Saints: Its Rise and Function in Latin Christianity*. Chicago: University of Chicago Press, 1981.

Brown, Raymond E. *The Gospel According to John (XIII–XXI)*. Anchor Bible 29A. Garden City: Doubleday, 1970.

———. *Community of the Beloved Disciple*. New York: Paulist Press, 1979.

Brown, Raymond E., Karl P. Donfried, and John Reumann, eds. *Peter in the New Testament*. New York: Paulist Press, 1973.

Brown, Raymond E., and John P. Meier. *Antioch and Rome: New Testament Cradles of Catholic Christianity*. Ramsey, N.J.: Paulist Press, 1983.

Bruce, F. F. *Galatians*. Grand Rapids: Wm. B. Eerdmans, 1982.

Buchholz, Dennis D. *Your Eyes Will Be Opened: A Study of the Greek (Ethiopic) Apocalypse of Peter*. Society of Biblical Literature Dissertation Series 97. Atlanta: Scholars Press, 1988.

Buckley, J. J. "An Interpretation of Logion 114 in *The Gospel of Thomas*." *Novum Testamentum* 27 (1985): 245–72.

Bultmann, Rudolf. *The History of the Synoptic Tradition*. 2d ed. Translated by John Marsh. New York: Harper and Row, 1968.

Campenhausen, Hans von. *Ecclesiastical Authority and Spiritual Power in the Church of the First Three Centuries*. Translated by J. A. Baker. Stanford: Stanford University Press, 1969.

Caragounis, Chrys C. *Peter and the Rock*. Beihefte zur Zeitschrift für die neutestamentliche Wissenschaft 58. New York: Walter de Gruyter, 1990.

Catchpole, David R. "Paul, James and the Apostolic Decree." *New Testament Studies* 23 (1977): 428–44.

Claudel, Gérard. "Review of Chrys C. Caragounis *Peter and the Rock*," *Biblica* 71 (1990) 570–76.

Clement of Alexandria [= *Strom.*]. *Clemens Alexandrinus Stromata Buch VII und VIII. Excepta Ex Theodoto. Ecklogai Propheticae. Quis Dives Salvetur. Fragmente*. Ed. Otto Stälin Griechischen Christlichen Schriftsteller 17. Leipzig: J. C. Hinrichs, 1909.

Clement of Rome [= *1 Clem.*]. "Der Klemensbrief," *Die Apostolischen Väter*. Erster Teil. Ed. Karl Bihlmeyer. Tübingen: J. C. B. Mohr (Paul Siebeck), 1956, 35–70.

Conzelmann, Hans. *1 Corinthians*. Translated by J. W. Leitch. Philadelphia: Fortress Press, 1975.

Cosgrove, Charles H. *The Cross and the Spirit: A Study in the Theology of Galatians*. Macon: Mercer University Press, 1988.

Crossan, J. D. *Four Other Gospels*. New York: Winston, 1985.

————. *The Historical Jesus: The Life of a Mediterranean Jewish Peasant*. San Francisco: Harper Collins, 1991.

Cullmann, Oscar. *Peter: Disciple—Apostle—Martyr*. 2d ed. Translated by Floyd V. Filson. London: SCM, 1962.

Culpepper, Alan. *Anatomy of the Fourth Gospel*. Philadelphia: Fortress Press, 1983.

Darr, John A. *On Character Building: The Reader and the Rhetoric of Characterization in Luke-Acts*. Louisville: Westminster/John Knox Press, 1992.

Davies, W. D., and Dale C. Allison. *Commentary on Matthew VIII–XVIII*. Vol. 2 of *The Gospel According to St. Matthew*. International Critical Commentary. Edinburgh: T. and T. Clark, 1991.

Dietrich, Wofgang. *Das Petrusbild der Lukanischen Schriften*. Stuttgart: W. Kolhammer, 1972.

Diogenes Laertius, *Lives of Eminent Philosophers*. Trans. R. D. Hicks. Loeb Classical Library. 2 vols. Cambridge: Harvard University Press, 1925.

Dowd, Sharyn Echols. *Prayer, Power and the Problem of Suffering: Mark 11:22–25 in the Context of Markan Theology*. Society of Biblical Literature Dissertation Series 105. Atlanta: Scholars Press, 1988.

Droge, Arthur J. "The Status of Peter in the Fourth Gospel." *Journal of Biblical Literature* 109 (1990): 307–11.

Dunn, James D. G. *Unity and Diversity in the New Testament: An Inquiry into the Character of Earliest Christianity*. Philadelphia: Westminster Press, 1977.

Edwards, Douglas R. "First Century Urban/Rural Relations in Lower Galilee: Exploring the Archaeological and Literary Evidence." In *Society of Biblical Literature Seminar Papers 1988*, edited by D. Lull, 169–82. Atlanta: Scholars Press, 1988.

Emmel, Stephen, Helmut Koester, and Elaine Pagels. *Nag Hammadi Codex III,5: The Dialogue of the Savior*. Nag Hammadi Studies 26. Leiden: E. J. Brill, 1984.

Epiphanius [= *Pan.*]. *Ancoratus und Panarion*. Ed. Karl Holl. Griechischen Christlichen Schriftsteller 25. Leipzig: J. C. Hinrichs, 1915.

Eusebius [= *Hist. Eccl.*]. *Eusebius Werke zweiter band. Die Kirchengeschicte*. Ed. D. Eduard Schwartz. Griechischen Christlichen Scriftsteller 9. Leipzig: J. C. Hinrichs, 1903.

Fee, Gordon. *1 Corinthians*. Grand Rapids: Wm. B. Eerdmans, 1987.

Fenn, Richard. *The Death of Herod: An Essay in the Sociology of Religion*. Cambridge: Cambridge University Press, 1992.

Fitzmyer, Joseph A. "Aramaic *Kephā'* and Peter's Name in the New Testament." In *To Advance the Gospel*, 112–24. New York: Crossroad, 1981.

————. *The Gospel According to Luke (I–IX)*. Anchor Bible 28. Garden City: Doubleday, 1981.

————. *The Gospel According to Luke (X–XXIV)*. Anchor Bible 28A. Garden City: Doubleday, 1985.

————. *Paul and His Theology*. 2d ed. Englewood Cliffs: Prentice Hall, 1989.

Fowler, Robert. *Let the Reader Understand: Reader-Response Criticism and the Gospel of Mark*. Minneapolis: Fortress Press, 1991.

Frankmölle, H. "Amtskritik im Matthäus-Evangelium?" *Biblica* 54 (1973): 247–67.

Frend, W. H. C. *The Rise of Christianity*. Philadelphia: Fortress Press, 1984.

Freyne, Sean. *Galilee Jesus and the Gospels: Literary and Historical Approaches*. Philadelphia: Fortress Press, 1988.

Fuller, Reginald H., and Pheme Perkins. *Who Is This Christ? Gospel Christology and Contemporary Faith*. Philadelphia: Fortress Press, 1983.

Fung, Ronald Y. K. *The Epistle to the Galatians*. Grand Rapids: Wm. B. Eerdmans, 1988.

Gallagher, Eugene V. "Conversion and Salvation in the Apocryphal Acts of the Apostles." *Second Century* 8 (1991): 13–29.

Garrett, Susan. *The Demise of the Devil*. Minneapolis: Fortress Press, 1989.

Gee, D. H. "Why Did Peter Spring into the Sea (John 21:7)?" *Journal of Theological Studies*, n.s., 40 (1989): 481–89.

Gnilka, Joachim. *Das Evangelium nach Markus*. 2 vols. Evangelish-Katholischer Kommentar zum Neuen Testament 2. Neukirchen-Vluyn: Neukirchener, 1979.

————. *Das Matthäusevangelium. II Teil. Kommentar zu Kap. 14,1–28,20*. 2 vols. Herders theologischer Kommentar zum Neuen Testament 1. Freiburg: Herder, 1988.

Goodman, Marvin. *The Ruling Class of Judaea: The Origins of the Jewish Revolt Against Rome AD 66–70*. Cambridge: Cambridge University Press, 1987.

Goppelt, Leonhard. *Der Erste Petrusbrief*. Meyer Kom. XII/1. Göttingen: Vandenhoeck & Ruprecht, 1978.

Griffin, Miriam T. *Nero: The End of a Dynasty*. New Haven: Yale University Press, 1984.

Guelich, Robert. *Mark 1–8:26*. Word Biblical Commentary 34A. Dallas: Word Books, 1989.

Haenchen, Ernst. *The Acts of the Apostles*. Translated by B. Noble and G. Shinn. Philadelphia: Westminster Press, 1971.

Heil, John P. *The Gospel of Mark as a Model for Action: A Reader-Response Commentary*. New York: Paulist Press, 1992.

Held, H. J. "Matthew as Interpreter of the Miracle Stories." In *Tradition and Interpretation in Matthew*, edited by G. Bornkamm, G. Barth and H. P. Held, translated by P. Scott, 165–299. Philadelphia: Westminster Press, 1963.

Hennecke, Edgar. *New Testament Apocrypha*. 2 vols. Edited by Wilhelm Schneemelcher. Translated by R. McL. Wilson. Philadelphia: Westminster Press, 1963–1965.

Herron, Robert W. *Peter's Denial of Jesus: A History of Its Interpretation*. New York: University Press of America, 1991.

Hill, Craig C. *Hellenists and Hebrews: Reappraising Division within the Earliest Church*. Minneapolis: Fortress Press, 1992.

Himmelfarb, Martha. *Tours of Hell: An Apocalyptic Form in Jewish and Christian Literature*. Philadelphia: University of Pennsylvania Press, 1983.

Hippolytus [= *Ref.*]. *Refutatio Omnium Haeresium*. Patristische Texte und Studien 25; Ed. Miroslav Marcovich. Berlin: Walter de Gruyter, 1986.

Howard, George. *Crisis in Galatia*. Society for New Testament Studies Monograph Series 35. Cambridge: Cambridge University Press, 1979.

Ignatius of Antioch [= Ign. *Eph.*; Ign. *Rom.*; Ign. *Trall.*]. "Die Ignatius Briefe," *Die Apostolischen Väter*. Erster Teil. Ed. Karl Bihlmeyer. Tübingen: J. C. B. Mohr (Paul Siebeck), 1956, 82–120.

Irenaeus of Lyons [= *Adv. Haer.*]. *Contre les hérésies*. Ed. A. Rousseau et Louis Doutreleau, s.j. Paris: Éditions du Cerf. *Tome 1*, 2 vols. Sources chrétiennes 263, 1979; *Tome 2*, 2 vols. Sources chrétiennes 294, 1982; *Tome 3*, 2 vols. Sources chrétiennes 210, 1974; *Tome 4*, 2 vols. Sources chrétiennes 100, 1965; *Tome 5*, 2 vols. Sources chrétiennes 152, 1969.

Jeffers, James S. *Conflict at Rome: Social Order and Hierarchy in Early Christianity*. Minneapolis: Fortress Press, 1991.

Josephus. *Jewish Antiquities*. Loeb Classical Library. 6 vols. Trans. Louis H. Feldman. Cambridge: Harvard University Press, 1959.

Josephus. *The Jewish War*. Loeb Classical Library. Ed. H. St. J. Thackeray. 2 vols. London: William Heinemann Ltd., 1927.

Justin Martyr [= *1 Apol.*; *2 Apol.*; *Dial.*]. *Patres Apologistas Griegos*. Ed. Daniel Ruiz Bueno. Madrid: Biblioteca de Autores Cristianos, 1954. *San Justino Apología I*, 182–260; *Apología II*, 261–78; *Diálogo con Trifón*, 300–548.

Kaesemann, Ernst. "An Apologia for Primitive Christian Eschatology." *Essays on New Testament Themes*, SBT 41, trans. W. J. Montague. London: SCM, 1964, 169–95.

Kaestli, Jean-Daniel. "Les principales orientations de la recherche sur les Actes apocryphes des Apôtres." In *Les Actes apocryphes des Apôtres*, edited by F. Bovon et al., 57–67. Geneva: Labor et Fides, 1981.

Karrer, Martin. "Petrus im paulinischen Gemeindekreis." *Zeitschrift für die neutestamentliche Wissenschaft* 80 (1989): 210–31.

Karrer, Otto. *Peter and the Church: An Examination of Cullmann's Thesis*. Translated by Ronald Walls. Quaestiones Disputatae 8. New York: Herder and Herder, 1962.

Kingsbury, J. D. "The Figure of Peter in Matthew's Gospel as a Theological Problem." *Journal of Biblical Literature* 98 (1979): 67–87.

Knibb, M. A. "Martyrdom and Ascension of Isaiah." In *The Old Testament Pseudepigrapha*, edited by J. Charlesworth, 2:143–76. Garden City: Doubleday, 1985.

Koester, Helmut. *Ancient Christian Gospels*. Philadelphia: Trinity Press International, 1990.

Kraemer, Ross Shepard. *Her Share of the Blessings: Women's Religions Among Pagans, Jews and Christians in the Greco-Roman World*. New York: Oxford University Press, 1992.

Kümmel, Werner Georg. *The New Testament: The History of the Investigation of Its Problems*. Translated by S. MacLean Gilmour and H. C. Kee. Nashville: Abingdon Press, 1972.

Lee-Pollard, Dorothy A. "Powerlessness as Power: A Key Emphasis in the Gospel of Mark." *Scottish Journal of Theology* 40 (1987): 173–88.

Légasse, Simon. "La polémique antipaulinienne dans le judéo-christianisme hétérodoxe." *Bulletin de littérature ecclésiastique* 90 (1989): 85–93.

Lincoln, Andrew. "The Promise and the Failure—Mark 16:7, 8." *Journal of Biblical Literature* 108 (1989): 283–300.

Longenecker, Richard L. *Galatians*. Word Biblical Commentary 41. Dallas: Word Books, 1990.

Lohse, Eduard. "St. Peter's Apostleship in the Judgment of St. Paul, the Apostle to the Gentiles. An Exegetical Contribution to an Ecumenical Debate." *Gregorianum* 72 (1991): 419–35.

MacMullen, Ramsey. *Enemies of the Roman Order: Treason, Unrest and Alienation in the Empire*. Cambridge: Harvard University Press, 1966.

Malbon, Elizabeth S. "Fallible Followers: Women and Men in the Gospel of Mark." *Semeia* 28 (1983): 29–48.

Marshall, Christopher D. *Faith as a Theme in Mark's Gospel*. Society for New Testament Studies Monograph Series 64. Cambridge: Cambridge University Press, 1989.

Martin, Troy W. *Metaphor and Composition in 1 Peter*. Society of Biblical Literature Dissertation Series 131. Atlanta: Scholars Press, 1992.

Maurer, Ch., and H. Duensing. "Apocalypse of Peter." In *New Testament Apocrypha*, edited by Edgar Hennecke and Wilhelm Schneemelcher, translated by R. McL. Wilson, 2:653–83. Philadelphia: Westminster Press, 1965.

Meier, John P. *A Marginal Jew: Rethinking the Historical Jesus*. Garden City: Doubleday, 1991.

Michaels, J. Ramsey. *1 Peter*. Word Biblical Commentary 49. Waco, TX: Word Books, 1988.

Morris, Colin. *The Papal Monarchy: The Western Church from 1050 to 1250*. Oxford: Clarendon Press, 1989.

Mussner, Franz. *Petrus und Paulus—Pole der Einheit*. Questiones Disputatae 76. Freiburg: Herder, 1976.

Neyrey, Jerome. "The Form and Background of the Polemic in 2 Peter." *Journal of Biblical Literature* 99 (1980): 407–31.

Nielsen, Charles M. "Papias: Polemicist against Whom?" *Theological Studies* 35 (1974): 529–35.

O'Connor, Daniel William. *Peter in Rome: The Literary, Liturgical and Archaeological Evidence*. New York: Columbia University Press, 1969.

O'Connor, Jerome Murphy. *The Holy Land: An Archaeological Guide from Earliest Times to 1700*. 2d ed. New York: Oxford University Press, 1986.

Origen [= *c. Cels.*]. *Contre Celse*. Ed. Marcel Borret, s.j. Paris: Éditions du Cerf. *Tome 1*, Livres I et II. Sources chrétiennes 132, 1967; *Tome 2* Livres II, III et IV. Sources chrétiennes 136, 1968; *Tome 3* Livres V et VI. Sources chrétiennes 147, 1969; *Tome 4*. Livres VII et VIII. Sources chrétiennes 150, 1969; *Tome 5*. Introduction Generale, Tables et Index. Sources chrétiennes 227, 1976.

Origen [= *In Joh.*]. *Commentaire sur Saint Jean*. Ed. Cécile Blanc. Paris: Éditions du Cerf. *Tome 1*, Livres I-V. Sources chrétiennes 120, 1966; *Tome 2*, Livres VI et X. Sources chrétiennes 157, 1970; *Tome 3*, Livre X. Sources chrétiennes 222, 1975; *Tome 4*, Livres XIX et XX. Sources chrétiennes 290, 1982; *Tome 5*, Livres XXVIII et XXXII. Sources chrétiennes 385, 1992.

Origen [= *In Matt.*]. *Origenes Werke Zehnter Band Matthäuserklärung. I Die Griechisch Erhaltenen Tomoi*. Ed. Erich Klostermann. Griechischen Christlichen Schriftsteller 40. Leipzig: J.C.Hinrichs, 1935.

Overman, J. Andrew. "Who Were the First Urban Christians? Urbanization in Galilee in the First Century." In *Society of Biblical Literature Seminar Papers 1988*, edited by D. Lull, 160–68. Atlanta: Scholars Press, 1988,

———. *Matthew's Gospel and Formative Judaism: A Study of the Social World of the Matthean Community*. Philadelphia: Fortress Press, 1990.

Parrott, Douglas M. "Gnostic and Orthodox Disciples in the Second and Third Centuries." In *Nag Hammadi, Gnosticism and Early Christianity*, edited by C. Hedrick and R. Hodgson, 193–219. Peabody, MA: Hendrickson, 1986.

Pasquier, Anne. *L'Évangile selon Marie*. Bibliothèque Copte de Nag Hammadi 10. Québec: L'Université Laval, 1983.

Pelikan, Jaroslav. *The Emergence of the Catholic Tradition (100–600)*. Chicago: University of Chicago Press, 1971.

Perkins, Pheme. *The Gnostic Dialogue*. New York: Paulist Press, 1980.

———. "Irenaeus and the Gnostics." *Vigiliae Christianae* 30 (1976): 193–200.

Pesch, Rudolf. *Das Markusevangelium*. 2 vols. Herders theologischer Kommentar zum Neuen Testament 2. Freiburg: Herder, 1977.

Pesch, Rudolf. "Πετρος," *Exegetisches Wöterbuch zum Neuen Testa-*

ment. Bd. 3, ed. H. Balz & G. Schneider (Stuttgart: W. Kohlhammer, 1983) 194–202.

———. *Simon Petrus*. Geschichte und geschichtliche Bedeutung des ersten Jüngers Jesu Christi. Päpste und Papstum Bd. 15. Stuttgart: Anton Hiersemann, 1980.

Pilhofer, P. "Justin und das Petrusevangelium." *Zeitschrift für neutestamentliche Wissenschaft* 81 (1990): 60–78.

Pliny, the elder [= *Nat. Hist*.]. *Histoire Naturelle*. Livres I-XXXVII. 38 vols. Trans J. Beaujeu et al. Paris: Société d'Édition "Les Belles Lettres," 1950–1972.

Räisänen, Heikki. *The Messianic Secret in Mark*. Translated by C. Tuckett. Edinburgh: T. and T. Clark, 1990.

Robinson, James M., ed. *The Nag Hammadi Library in English*. 2d ed. San Francisco: Harper and Row, 1988.

Roloff, J. "Der johanneische 'Lieblingsjünger' und der Lehrer der Gerechtigkeit." *New Testament Studies* 15 (1968–1969): 129–51.

Rouleau, Donald. *L'Épître de Jacques (NH I,2)*. Bibliothèque Copte de Nag Hammadi 18. Québec: L'Université Laval, 1987.

Rudolph, Kurt. *Gnosis*. Translated by R. McL. Wilson. San Francisco: Harper and Row, 1983.

Sage, Michael M. *Cyprian*. Cambridge, MA: Philadelphia Patristic Foundation, 1975.

Sanders, E. P. "Jewish Associations with Gentiles and Galatians 2:11–14." In *The Conversation Continues: Studies in Paul and John*, edited by R. T. Fortna and B. Gaventa, 170–88. Nashville: Abingdon Press, 1990.

Satgé, John de. *Peter and the Single Church*. London: SPCK, 1981.

Schaffer, Susan E. "The Guard at the Tomb (*Gos. Pet*. 8:28–11:49 and Matt. 27:62–66; 28:2–4, 11–16): A Case of Intertextuality?" In *Society of Biblical Literature. 1991 Seminar Papers*, 499–507. Atlanta: Scholars Press, 1991.

Schillebeeckx, Edward. *Jesus: An Experiment in Christology*. Translated by H. Hoskins. New York: Crossroad, 1979.

Schnackenburg, Rudolf. *Commentary on Chapters 13–21*. Vol. 3 of *The Gospel According to St. John*. Translated by David Smith and G. A. Kon. New York: Crossroad, 1982.

Schneemelcher, Wilhelm. "Gospel of Peter." In *New Testament Apocrypha*, 2d ed., edited by Wilhelm Schneemelcher, translated by R. McL. Wilson, 1:216–22. Louisville: Westminster/John Knox Press, 1991.

————. "Acts of Peter." In *New Testament Apocrypha*, edited by Edgar Hennecke and Wilhelm Schneemelcher, translated by R. McL. Wilson, 2:259–322. Philadelphia: Westminster Press, 1965.

Schoedel, William. *Ignatius of Antioch*. Philadelphia: Fortress Press, 1985.

Smith, T. V. *Petrine Controversies in Early Christianity: Attitudes Towards Peter in Christian Writings of the First Two Centuries*. Wissenschaftliche Untersuchungen zum Neuen Testament 2 Reihe 5. Tübingen: J. C. B. Mohr (Paul Siebeck), 1985.

Stoops, Robert F., Jr. "Patronage in the *Acts of Peter*." *Semeia* 38 (1986): 91–100.

Strecker, G. "The Kerygmata Petrou." In *New Testament Apocrypha*, edited by Edgar Hennecke and Wilhelm Schneemelcher, translated by R. McL. Wilson, 2:102–27. Philadelphia: Westminster Press, 1965.

Suetonius, *Vies des douze Césars*. Ed. Henri Ailloud. 2 vols. Paris: Société d'Édition "Les Belles Lettres," 1932.

Tacitus [= *Ann.*]. *Annales*. Ed. Henricus Heubner. Stuttgart: B. G. Teubner, 1983.

Tannehill, Robert. "The Disciples in Mark: The Function of a Narrative Role." *Journal of Religion* 57 (1977): 386–405.

————. "The Functions of Peter's Mission Speeches in the Narrative of Acts." *New Testament Studies* 37 (1991): 400–414.

————. "The Gospel of Mark as a Narrative Christology." *Semeia* 16 (1979): 57–95.

————. *The Gospel According to Luke*. Vol. 1 of *The Narrative Unity of Luke-Acts: A Literary Interpretation*. Philadelphia: Fortress Press, 1986.

————. *The Acts of the Apostles*. Vol. 2 of *The Narrative Unity of Luke-Acts: A Literary Interpretation*. Minneapolis: Fortress Press, 1990.

Tertullian [= *Adv. Marc.*]. *Adversus Marcionem*. Ed. Ernest Evans. 2 vols. Oxford Early Christian Texts. Oxford: Clarendon Press, 1972.

Tertullian [= *Praescrip.*]. Bindley, T. H. *Tertulliani De praescriptione haereticorum, Ad martyras, Ad scapulam*. Oxford: Oxford University Press, 1893.

Tertullian [= *Praescrip.*]. *Traité de la prescription contre les hérétiques*. Ed. R. F. Refoulé. Sources chrétiennes 46. Paris: Éditions du Cerf, 1957.

Tertullian [= *Pud.*; *Scorp.*]. *Tertulliani Opera Pars II*. Corpus Christi-

anorum Series Latina 2. Turnholt. Typographi Breols Editores Pon-
tificii 1954. *Scorpiace* ed. A. Reifferscheid et G. Wissowa 1068–97;
De Pudicitia Ed. E. Dekkers; 1280–1336.

Tillich, Paul. *Systematic Theology*. New York: Harper & Row, 1951.

Tolbert, Mary Ann. *Sowing the Gospel: Mark's World in Literary-
Historical Perspective*. Minneapolis: Fortress Press, 1989.

Watson, Duane Frederick. *Invention, Arrangement, and Style: Rhetorical Criticism of Jude and 2 Peter*. Society of Biblical Literature
Dissertation Series 104. Atlanta: Scholars Press, 1988.

White, John L. *Light from Ancient Letters*. Philadelphia: Fortress
Press, 1986.

Wilkins, Michael J. *The Concept of Disciple in Matthew's Gospel*.
Supplements to Novum Testamentum 59. Leiden: E. J. Brill, 1988.

Williams, Michael. *The Immovable Race: A Gnostic Designation and
the Theme of Stability in Late Antiquity*. Nag Hammadi Studies 24.
Leiden: E. J. Brill, 1985.

Wire, Antoinette Clark. *The Corinthian Women Prophets: A Reconstruction through Paul's Rhetoric*. Minneapolis: Fortress Press,
1990.

Index of Subjects and Modern Authors

Achtemeier, Paul J., 128n.36
Acts
   imprisonment of apostles in, 88–
      90, 95
   persecution of Christians, 105n.33,
      105n.37, 119. *See also* Stephen,
      martyr
   speeches in, 33–35, 48n.30, 88–89
acts, apocryphal, 140–41
Acts of Peter, 140–44, 146, 149n.36,
   166n.31, 171
*Acts of Peter and the Twelve
   Apostles*, 144–46, 166n.31
Allison, Dale C., 78n.68, 79nn.81–82
Apocalypse of Peter, 132–34, 136,
   138, 146, 147n.4, 148n.9,
   167n.33, 177
Apocalypse of Peter (gnostic), 162–
   63, 167n.33
Apocryphon of James, 160, 166n.31,
   172
apostolic tradition, 160–61, 170–73,
   184
Attridge, Harold, 129n.59
Augustine, 163

Barrett, Charles K., 107n.57
Bauckham, Richard J., 130n.63,
   130n.69
Bauer, Ferdinand Christian, 4, 15n.9,
   156

Beasley-Murray, George, 15n.5,
   49n.33, 104n.5
Best, Ernest, 55, 74n.9, 76n.24
Betz, Hans Dieter, 126n.2
Bigane, John, 186n.2
Black, Clifton, 74n.3, n.9
Brown, Raymond E., 9, 46n.1,
   49n.32, 75n.16, 83, 107n.58,
   107n.60
Buchholz, Dennis D., 167n.33
Buckley, J. J., 166n.20
Bultmann, Rudolf, 8

Campenhausen, Hans von, 4
canon, 151, 155–57, 160–61, 165n.13
Caragounis, Chrys C., 41, 50n.49,
   78n.71
Catchpole, David R., 128n.31
Christology, 74n.7, 75n.21, 76n.25,
   79n.82
Claudel, Gérard, 50n.49
1 Clement, 159, 165n.13, 179n.3
conflict
   at Antioch, 9–11, 20, 33, 36,
      48n.26, 68, 93, 101, 110, 114,
      116–17, 128n.31, 128n.36, 154,
      169, 186n.5
   in early Christianity, 1, 4, 11–13,
      15n.9, 78n.65, 109, 114, 128n.31,
      165n.13, 174–75
   social, in Palestine, 27, 32–33,
      51n.56, 79n.77

Cosgrove, Charles H., 128n.31
Crossan, John D., 14n.2, 46n.1
Cullmann, Oscar, 5, 10, 15n.11,
    104n.17
Cyprian, 175–77

Davies, W. D., 78n.78, 79nn.81–82
Dietrich, Wolfgang, 104n.9, 106n.41,
    128n.35
Dialogue of the Savior, 157
disciples of Jesus, 1, 3, 15n.5, 18, 61,
    82–83, 87, 104n.5
    commission to preach, 78n.69, 85,
        87–88, 120, 145, 158–61, 164
    Gospel of John, treatment of, 96–
        100, 107n.58, 107n.65
    Gospel of Luke, treatment of, 85
    Gospel of Mark, treatment of, 57,
        59–62, 64–65, 74n.9, 75n.11,
        75n.23, 76nn.24–25, 76nn.29–30,
        76n.36, 77nn.39–40, 77n.42
    Twelve, the, 60, 95, 101–103, 112,
        165n.13
    weakness of, 64–66, 78n.61, 84–
        85, 96–97, 137, 156, 158–59
Donfried, Karl, 46n.1
Dowd, Sharyn E., 74n.7
Dunn, James D. G., 5

ecclesiastical authority
    development of, 41, 70, 79n.82,
        100–103, 122, 127n.5, 129n.44,
        162, 165n.13, 168–69, 171, 178–
        79
    Jesus' authority exercised in, 92
    Paul's understanding of, 4, 10, 41,
        83
    resurrection of Jesus as basis of,
        7–8, 31, 46n.1, 66, 111–12,
        127n.9
    Spirit as basis of, 4, 162, 166n.18
ecumenism, 4–6, 11–14, 15n.11, 183–
    86, 186n.2
Epistle of Peter to Philip, 161
Fee, Gordon, 127n.17

Fenn, Richard, 26, 51n.56
Fitzmyer, Joseph A., 47n.10, 47n.12,
    48n.23, 76n.27, 103n.2
form criticism, 107n.69
Fowler, Robert M., 75nn.19–20

Gallagher, Eugene V., 149n.36
Garrett, Susan, 91, 106n.41
Gee, D. H., 99
Gnilka, Joachim, 77n.42
Gnosticism, 4, 126, 129n.57, 132,
    145, 152–54, 156–63, 166n.18,
    172
Goppelt, Leonhard, 129n.44
Gospel of Mary, 158–59
Gospel of Peter, 136–38, 148n.13,
    148n.16, 148n.18
Gospel of Philip, 157
Gospel of Thomas, 157–58, 166n.20
Great Seth, Second Treatise of, 159
Guelich, Robert, 76nn.29–32

Haenchen, Ernst, 102, 105n.31
Heil, John P., 74n.5, 77n.39
Herron, Robert W., 47n.20, 48n.25
Hill, Craig C., 15n.9, 49nn.30–31,
    105n.33, 106n.47, 186n.5
historical criticism, 2, 6, 16n.16. 21–
    26, 33, 47n.4. 52–53
Howard, George, 128n.31

Ignatius of Antioch, 168, 179n.1

James, brother of the Lord, 1, 5, 9–
    10, 20, 41, 43, 94, 101, 112, 124,
    160
James, son of Zebedee, 36, 90, 102
    and John, 40, 60
Jeffers, James S., 179n.3.
Jerusalem
    council of, 1, 20, 33–36, 48n.26,
        94, 116–120, 128n.36
    Paul's visits to, 3, 11, 20, 48n.26,
        115

Jesus
   Ascension of, 134
   death of, 120. *See also* passion
      narrative
   family of, 60–61, 76n.36. *See also*
      James, brother of the Lord
   founder of the church, 16n.19, 26–
      29, 46n.1
   Gethsemane, agony in, 64–65,
      78n.61, 87
   preaches in Hades, 132–35
   tomb of, 83, 87, 137
   Transfiguration of, 18, 62–63, 84–
      85, 123–24, 131, 134, 177
Jewish Christianity, 4, 9–12, 15n.9.
   67, 93, 130n.69, 141, 151
John the Baptist
   death of, 62
   disciples of, 2, 18, 26
   mission of, 25–27
John, evangelist, 128n.42

Kaesemann, Ernst, 129n.56
Kerygmata Petrou, 173
Koester, Helmut, 148n.16, 165n.17
Kraemer, Ross, 166n.18

Leo the Great, 179
Lohse, Eduard, 10
Longenecker, Richard, 48n.26,
   126n.4
Lumen Gentium (Vatican II), 16n.17,
   185
Luz, Ulrich, 185

MacMullen, Ramsey, 165n.5
Marcion, 155, 169, 172
Mark, evangelist, 42, 53, 132, 155–56,
   170
Marshall, Christopher D., 63, 74
martyrs, 133–34, 139–40, 170

Mary Magdalene, 157–59, 165n.17,
   166n.22
Meier, John P., 9, 14n.2, 148n.16
messianic secret, 30–31, 47n.14, 62,
   77n.40
missionary activity, 28, 34–36, 63,
   106n.47
Montanism, 174
Morris, Colin, 14n.1
Murdoch, Iris, 2, 14n.3
Mussner, Franz, 17n.31

narrative criticism, 54–55, 58,
   74nn.4–5, 75n.11, 76n.24,
   77nn.39–40, 107n.58, 107n.69
Nero, 42, 139–40, 149n.22
Nielsen, Charles M., 165n.13

O'Connor, Daniel W., 181n.37
Origen, 177, 183
Overman, Andrew, 79nn.76–79

Pagels, Elaine, 165n.17
Papias, 132
Parable of the Sower, 77n.47
passion narrative, 64–65, 73, 85, 87,
   96–97, 99, 106n.53, 106n.56,
   136–37, 148n.16, 149n.24, 161–
   62
Pastor Aeternus (Vatican I), 3
Paul
   apostolic authority of, 10, 114–15,
      127n.17, 165n.13
   calling of, 9, 83, 92, 112
   martyrdom of, 49n.32, 169–70
   represented as Simon Magus, 151–
      56
Pentecost, 34, 82, 88–90, 161
Pesch, Rudolf, 50n.47, 78n.61
Peter
   bishop of Rome, 1, 41–43, 121,
      168–79, 183–84
   burial of, 144

Peter (*continued*)
  calling of, 2–3, 18, 25–29, 47n.10,
    50n.48, 58, 81, 84, 104n.9
  church founder, 8, 29, 42, 68–71,
    78n.71, 83, 86–87, 104n.4, 125–
    26, 162, 170, 176–78, 183–84
  confesses Jesus to be "messiah,"
    29–31, 52, 61–62, 67, 77n.42,
    78n.68, 84, 107n.57, 157, 176
  daughter of, 166n.31, 171
  denies Jesus, 18, 21–22, 31–33,
    47n.20, 48n.23, 48n.25, 55, 64,
    86–87, 95, 137
  family of, 2–3, 18, 27–29, 50n.56,
    60, 95, 144, 183
  Feast of Sts. Peter and Paul, 170,
    179, 183
  house at Capernaum, 27–29, 38–
    39, 70
  interpreter of Jesus' teaching, 66–
    72, 79n.76, 79n.81, 89, 100, 124,
    127n.5, 163, 185
  leadership among the disciples, 5–
    6, 16n.11, 18–21, 29, 32–33, 34–
    36, 60, 62, 65–67, 70–72, 80n.84.
    81–83, 85, 88, 94–95, 100, 113,
    116, 118, 120, 131–32, 160–64,
    177
  martyrdom, 20, 36–37, 41–43,
    49n.33, 96–97, 99–100, 120–21,
    131, 134–35, 138–43, 146, 162,
    168–69, 179, 181n.37
  miracles worked by, 89, 92, 95,
    143, 145, 149n.36, 161, 166n.31
  missionary activity, 5, 20, 35–36,
    42, 49n.37, 89–90, 92–94, 99–
    100, 105n.33, 113, 120, 134, 184
  mother-in-law, healing of, 47n.12
  name, 8, 29, 39–41, 50n.47, 60,
    76nn.32–33, 78n.71, 95, 103n.1,
    124, 177–78, 184, 186n.2
  orthodoxy, defender of, 91, 122–
    24, 126, 129n.56. 132, 135–36,
    141, 151–52, 157–59, 164

  papal authority, basis of, 3, 6, 10,
    14n.1, 15n.6, 79n.82, 101, 172–
    79, 185–86
  rebuked by Jesus, 31, 53, 62, 71,
    77n.39, 77n.42, 134
  relationship to Paul, 1–14, 17n.31,
    42, 68, 109–119, 154–55, 169–70
  Rome, activity in, 10–11, 37, 41–
    43, 170–73
  as shepherd, 83, 96–100, 121,
    129n.44, 131, 168–73, 176, 184
  tomb monument in Rome, 38, 42,
    49n.38, 165n.2, 168, 170, 174
  wife as martyr, 42, 144
  witness to risen Jesus, 3, 8, 33
Pharisees, 79nn.77–78
Pilhofer, P., 148n.13
Pistis Sophia, 159
Polycarp, 165n.13
Porphyry, 163
prayer, 64, 78n.61
*Pseudo-Clementine Homilies &
  Recognitions*, 154–55, 173

Räisänen, Heikki, 30, 47n.14
redaction criticism, 53–55, 74n.3,
  74n.5, 76n.24
resurrection, 135
Resurrection of Jesus
  appears to disciples, 18–20, 55–56,
    74, 82, 87, 99, 103n.3, 137, 161
  calling of apostles and, 9, 16n.23,
    19–21, 46n.1, 81–83, 103n.1
  Christology, basis of, 29–30
Reumann, John, 46n.1
rhetorical criticism, 110, 115–18,
  126nn.3–4
Roloff, J., 104n.5
Rome
  origins of Christianity at, 41,
    130n.69
  development of Christianity at,
    145, 179n.3. 184
  foreign cults in, 165n.5

Rouleau, Donald, 160
Rudolph, Kurt, 164n.1

Satgé, John de, 15n.6, n.11, 16n.16
Schillebeeckx, Edward, 7–8, 13–14,
    16nn.19–23, 19, 104n.4
Schnackenburg, Rudolf, 99, 103n.1,
    104n.5, 107n.69
Schoedel, William, 179n.1.
Shepherd of Hermas, 145, 179n.3
Simon Magus, 41–42, 91–92,
    106n.41, 141–43, 151–56, 163,
    166n.18 169
Smith, T. V., 129n.57
social conditions
    reflected in apocryphal acts, 143,
        145–47, 150n.39
    Graeco-Roman cities, 113
    Palestine, 26, 30–31, 39, 47n.5,
        50n.44, 79n.77
    Roman Christianity, 170, 179n.3,
        183

source criticism, 104n.7, 104n.10,
    107n.57, 128n.35
Stephen, martyr, 48n.30, 49n.31, 90,
    95, 105n.33
Stoops, Robert F., 150n.39

Tannehill, Robert, 93
Tertullian, 173–74, 178, 183
Tillich, Paul, 2, 14
Tolbert, Mary Ann, 57, 65, 76n.37,
    77n.47, 78n.62

unity of the church, 12, 170, 176–77,
    179

Walsh, John E., 49n.38
Watson, Duane F., 129n.60
White, John L., 126n.4
Williams, Michael, 149n.35
women, 166n.18, 166n.20. *See also*
    Mary Magdalene

Index of Scripture References

GENESIS
17:1–8   69
32:22–32   69

DEUTERONOMY
29:17–19   92

1 SAMUEL
16:1–13   58

1 KINGS
17:8–24   59
17:8–16   39
19:19–21   28, 58

SONG OF SONGS
6:9   176

ISAIAH
22:22   69
28:15–19   69
58:6   92

JEREMIAH
16:16   58
17:15   129n.56

AMOS
4:2   58

HABBAKKUK
1:14–15   58

ZEPHANIAH
13:7   32

MALACHI
2:17   129n.56

1 MACCABEES
2:65   124

MATTHEW
3:9   69
4:18–22   2, 18
4:18–20   27
4:18   66, 76n.33
4:19   28
5:25   70, 79n.77
5:40   70, 79n.77
6:14   77n.55
6:15   69
7:15–22   71, 78n.65
7:24–27   68
8:14–15   18, 27
9:8   69
10:2   66, 71, 102
10:17–23   37
10:21   51n.56
10:26–27   68
10:34–36   51n.56
10:37   24
11:25   68
13:16–17   68
13:51   66
13:52   12
14:22–32   53, 66
14:28–33   19, 71
14:28   68
15:3   71
15:7–9   71
15:10–17   67
15:15   66
16:5–12   71
16:13–23   52
16:13–20   18
16:15–20   3

16:16–19   31, 68, 71
16:16   40
16:17–20   16n.11,
            105n.17
16:17–19   29, 67,
            78n.68, 86,
            174, 176–
            78
16:17   72, 157
16:18–19   19, 33, 102
16:18   40, 184
16:19   20, 69–70
16:21–23   31, 72
16:23   184
17:1   18
17:4   134
17:20   77n.55
17:24–28   67, 70
17:26–27   66
18:10–14   121
18:15–18   70
18:18   20, 69
18:21–22   70
18:21   66
19:28   102
23:2–28   71
23:2–3   78n.65
23:3–4   147
24:4   133
24:32–33   133
26:33–35   18, 31, 72
26:37   18
26:51–54   96
26:56   18
26:57–58   31
26:58   18
26:60–61   48n.30
26:63   49n.30

205

MATTHEW (*continued*)
26:65   49n.30
26:69–75   18, 72
28:9–10   56, 74
28:16–20   19, 55–56,
                66, 74

MARK
1:10   58
1:11   62
1:14–15   58
1:15   27
1:16–20   18, 57, 63
1:16–18   27
1:17   28, 58
1:20   39
1:28   58
1:29–31   18, 27, 58–59
1:29   27
1:32–34   59
1:35   59
1:36   59
1:38–39   59
1:44   77n.40
2:1   29
2:12   70
2:13–17   60
2:19–20   55
3:5   59
3:6   55
3:13–19   60
3:16–17   64
3:16   40, 68
3:17   40
3:20–35   60
3:21   112
3:31–35   65, 112
3:34   61
3:35   61
4:6   57
4:10–12   61
4:11–12   59
4:13   61
4:15   62
4:17   57
4:34   61
4:39–41   61
5:21–43   58
5:37   18, 61
6:1–6   51n.56
6:14–16   62
6:45–52   53, 59
7:1–23   67
7:17   29

8:14–21   76n.29
8:21   61
8:22–26   55, 61,
                77n.55
8:27–33   12, 52, 62
8:27–30   18, 61
8:31–33   30–31, 57,
                97, 134,
                184
8:33   107n.57
8:34–38   33, 62
9:2–8   84
9:2   18
9:5   63
9:6   63
9:7   62
9:9   56
9:14–29   58
9:33   29
10:22   65
10:27   64
10:28–31   63
11:21   63, 133
11:22–25   63
13   64
13:3–4   135
13:3   133, 147
13:9–13   37, 56
13:9–10   58
13:33–37   78n.61
14:26–31   85
14:27–31   12, 55, 64
14:27–28   65
14:29–31   18, 31
14:29   57, 72
14:33   18
14:34   64
14:35   59
14:36–42   64
14:37   87
14:38–42   65
14:39   59
14:40–41   87
14:40   63
14:47   96
14:50   18, 32, 57, 65
14:53–54   31
14:54   18, 21, 64
14:56–57   48n.30
14:58   48n.30
14:61   49n.30
14:64   49n.30

14:66–72   18, 21, 31,
                57, 64
14:70   72
14:71   86
15:39   57
16:7–8   55, 57, 65,
                112

LUKE
2:41–52   47n.7
3:3   88
3:5–6   88
3:11   91
4:16–39   2
4:16   84
4:18–19   88
4:18   34
4:31–41   27
4:36   84
4:38–39   18, 27
4:43–44   88
5:1–11   2, 18–19, 21,
                23, 81, 84,
                96, 99
5:5   22
5:8   40, 50n.48,
                76n.33
5:10   28
5:17   84
6:12–16   87
6:13   102
8:1–3   47n.12
8:13   87
9:1–2   88
9:7–9   104n.7
9:10–17   104n.7
9:18–22   18, 53, 84,
                104n.7
9:22   31
9:23–27   84
9:28–36   84
9:28   18
9:29–32   84
9:34–35   85
10:17–20   85
10:21   68
10:23–24   78n.70
12:2–3   68
14:26   25
17:3–4   79n.80
17:6   77n.55
21:12–19   37
22:3   149n.24

22:24–27	95	10:15	100, 105n.53	21:18	186
22:30	102	10:16	107n.60	21:20–24	96, 98
22:31–34	18, 31, 81–82, 85–86	13:3–20	97	21:23	136
		13:6	40	21:24	3
22:31–32	149n.24	13:9	40		
22:31	62	13:23–25	82	ACTS	
22:32	184	13:24	40	1:4–5	91
22:33	90, 105n.56	13:27	62	1:4	82
22:35–38	106n.53	13:36–38	18, 31, 95, 97, 100	1:6	88
22:45	87			1:8	105n.33
22:46–47	87	13:36	32, 40, 98	1:15–26	20, 89, 101
22:49–51	96	13:37	184	1:15	86
22:54–62	18, 31, 86	16:32	83	2:14–36	20, 33–34
23:49	47n.12	18:10–11	40, 96, 98	2:38	88
23:55	47n.12	18:15–27	18, 31, 95	2:39	90
24	82	18:15	40	2:40	88
24:11	87	18:18	99	2:46	142
24:12	81, 87, 96	18:25	40	3:1–10	20, 88
24:21	88	18:26	98, 106n.53	3:1	89
24:24	81, 87	18:36	99	3:6	89, 92
24:26	84	19:25–27	83	3:11–26	20, 33–34
24:28–30	96	19:33–35	83	3:11	89
24:33–34	18	20:2–10	81, 96	3:12	92
24:34	33, 81, 86–87, 112	20:2	40	3:13–15	90
		20:4–5	83, 107n.65	3:16	92
24:36–49	87	20:8	83	3:17–18	90
24:36–43	19	20:19–23	19	3:21	88
24:44–46	88	20:21–22	176–77	4:2–7	89
24:46–48	34	20:30–31	75n.16	4:3–22	36, 90
24:47	88	21	75n.16, 82, 100	4:8–12	20, 33
				4:32–37	144
JOHN		21:1–14	19, 23, 50n.48, 81, 96, 99, 137	5:1–11	20, 89
1:19–23	77n.44			5:3	92
1:35–40	2	21:2	40	5:15–16	20, 88
1:40–44	40	21:3	40	5:17–42	36, 90
1:40–42	18, 95–97	21:7	40, 98	5:27–40	89
1:40–41	25	21:9	107n.67	5:29–32	20, 33–34
1:41–42	2	21:11	40, 98, 107n.67	5:29	89
1:42	3, 40, 68, 76n.33, 103n.1			5:38–39	91
		21:15–19	96, 120–21, 169	6:1–8:4	15n.9
2:23–25	101			6:1–6	89
4:14	158	21:15–17	19, 23, 56, 81, 83, 86, 97, 102, 131, 176, 184	6:1	43
4:38	28			6:8–7:60	90
6:8	40			6:11	49n.30
6:42	51n.56			6:13–14	48n.30
6:66–71	18, 95, 97, 176	21:15–16	3, 37	7:1	49n.30
		21:15	40	7:48	49n.30
6:68	40, 101	21:18–23	135	8–10	94
6:70	30, 107n.57	21:18–19	21, 37, 97–98, 100–101, 131	8:1–4	90
7:3–8	112			8:1	105n.33
7:37–39	158			8:9–24	141, 152
10:1–21	83			8:9–11	91
				8:13	92

ACTS (*continued*)
8:14–17	91
8:18–23	41, 91
8:23–24	153
8:26–40	93
9–11	9
9:1–31	92
9:32–42	88, 92
10	34, 186
10:1–11:18	20, 89
10:4	93
10:14	92
10:26	92
10:28–29	93
10:34–43	33
10:34–38	157
10:36–38	88
10:36	34
10:38	34
10:44–48	157
10:44–46	93
10:45–47	106n.47
11:1–2	35
11:2–18	34, 102
11:12	93
11:15–17	93
11:16	91
11:17	91, 157
11:19–21	94
11:27–30	48n.26
12	37
12:1–19	36, 90
12:2	102
12:11	95
12:25	37
13:16–41	34
15:1–33	33, 48n.26, 89, 118, 128n.36
15:1–21	1
15:1–6	94
15:4	50n.47
15:6–29	117
15:7–11	34, 94
15:14	40, 94, 124
15:15–18	94
15:20–29	10
15:23	86
15:32	86
15:36–41	117
15:40	37
18:2	37
20:17–38	101, 121, 129n.45

20:28–30	122
20:28	100, 169
21:11–12	49n.32
21:18	20

ROMANS
1:3–4	29
3:30	128n.27
4:9	128n.27
4:12	128n.27
11:13–16	10
14:1–15:13	10
15:8	128n.27

1 CORINTHIANS
1:12	11, 35, 40, 113, 127
1:13	37
1:18–2:16	113
3:4–9	113
3:10–11	11, 78n.71
3:21	114
3:22	40, 113
3:23	127
4:6	114
4:9–13	121
4:15	184
4:16	121
4:17	114
5:1–5	114
5:5	139
6:1–8	79n.79
7:29	144
7:35	144
8	118
9:1–6	114, 126
9:1–3	112
9:2	184
9:4	113
9:5	10–11, 20, 28, 40
9:14	11
9:19–23	113
10:4	177
11:11	21
15:1–11	155
15:3–11	11, 111
15:3–5	3, 33
15:5–8	112, 114
15:5	18, 40, 102, 113
15:7	9, 102

15:9	36
16:12	113

2 CORINTHIANS
1:19	37
5:16	111
10–13	11
11:22	15n.9
11:23–25	36
11:31	48n.26

GALATIANS
1:6–10	115
1:6	110
1:8	40
1:10	116
1:11–24	9, 110
1:11–17	115
1:13	36, 116
1:15–17	83, 131
1:17	82
1:12–2:14	117
1:18–2:14	112, 184
1:18–20	115
1:18	3, 10, 101, 114, 169
1:19	20, 101
1:22	49n.31
1:23	116
2:1–14	1, 33, 117
2:1–10	48n.26, 109–10, 115, 118
2:2	36
2:4–5	116
2:6–10	20, 94
2:6	111
2:7–9	10, 40, 116
2:7	114
2:9	35, 101
2:11–14	9, 11, 35, 68, 93–94, 109–110, 116, 118, 126, 128n.36, 154, 169
2:11	114, 116
2:12	101, 114
2:14	183
2:15–21	36, 118
6:14	121
6:17	121

EPHESIANS
4:4–6   176
4:8–10   134

PHILIPPIANS
3:5   15n.9

1 THESSALONIANS
1:1   37
2:14   36

2 THESSALONIANS
2:14   111

1 TIMOTHY
6:13   66

2 TIMOTHY
3:1–9   122
3:7   166n.19
4:9–18   121
4:11   37
4:21   172

HEBREWS
10:19–11:3

JAMES
1:19–21   159

1 PETER
1:1   120
2:4–5   12, 37
2:9–10   120
2:12   120
2:20   120
2:25   100, 129n.44
3:13–22   120
3:14–17   120
3:16   37
3:19–20   134
3:19   132
4:4   120
4:6   134
4:10–11   37
4:12–16   120
5:1–4   121–22, 169
5:1   37, 120
5:2   37, 100
5:10   37, 120
5:12   37, 120, 122
5:13   21, 41–42,
             120, 122,
             132, 138,
             155
5:14   37

2 PETER
1:1   40, 124
1:2–6   124
1:3–15   123
1:12   124
1:16–18   123, 131
1:16   135
1:19–21   124
2:17   163
2:20–21   124
3:1   124
3:2   122
3:3–4   122
3:8   124
3:15–16   111, 122,
             124, 132,
             156
3:16   12
3:18   124

JUDE
17–18   122

REVELATION
3:7   69
13   139
13:14   140
21:14   102